Bought from Saeed Book Bank

# A Comparative Analysis of
# Media & Media Laws in
# Pakistan

*by*

Yasmeen Aftab Ali

**SANG-E-MEEL PUBLICATIONS**
**25, SHAHRAH-E-PAKISTAN (LOWER MALL) LAHORE.**

371.32 Yasmeen Aftab Ali
A Comparative Analysis of Media & Media Laws in Pakistan/ Yasmeen Aftab Ali.-Lahore: Sang-e-Meel Publications, 2012.
312pp.
1. Pakistan - Communication - Media.
I. Title.

**2012**
Published by:
**Niaz Ahmad**
Sang-e-Meel Publications,
Lahore.

*ISBN-10: 969-35-2570-1*
*ISBN-13: 978-969-35-2570-0*

**Sang-e-Meel Publications**
25 Shahrah-e-Pakistan (Lower Mall), Lahore-54000 PAKISTAN
Phones: 92-423-722-0100 / 92-423-722-8143 Fax: 92-423-724-5101
http://www.sang-e-meel.com e-mail: smp@sang-e-meel.com

**PRINTED AT: HAJI HANIF & SONS PRINTERS, LAHORE.**

*This book is dedicated to the loving memory of my father Syed Aftab Ali, who gave me the wings to fly.*

## *Note By The Author*

In my years of teaching Media Laws, in the university, I did not come across any contemporary book on the subject which would help a student of Mass Communication understand the laws –who was not a law student and apply the concepts well to the field of communications, thus preparing them for their coming profession. This book is meant mainly as a handbook for them. It explains concepts, sharing benchmark cases and relating laws to current situation for better understanding. It also makes an effort to address the problems we see, particularly with relation to the social responsibility of media in Pakistan. It offers a set of steps the media should look into in order to overcome the problems faced.

The book does not aim to put down any one, or any institution. It is an objective analysis of issues discussed.

**Yasmeen A. Ali**

# *Foreword*

The history of the press in the sub-continent goes back to more than 230 years. The first printed newspaper approved in the colonial era of Calcutta was in 1780 in English language under the administrative control of the British East India Company. The next 42 years saw the flourishing of the institution of the English language Press in Bombay, Madras and Calcuutta. All the newspapers were owned by the English citizens–most of them ex-employees of the British East India Company. Because of the fact that all these newspapers were in English the Company Administration for those towns was not worried about the impact of these newspapers on the public opinion of the Indian population, as they were not included in English –speaking people.

The emergence of first local language newspaper, owned by an Indian, in Urdu; Jam-e-Jahan Numa, forced the Company Administration to go for a regular Press Law to regulate the printing industry and the institution of the Press. Thus, there appeared the first Press Law in 1823. Since then the Indian sub-continent, in which there are three countries now–Pakistan, India and Bangladesh, are continuing with this colonial legacy of Press Laws, including law for the installation of Printing Press.

After independence, Pakistan inherited the legacy of all the British Colonial Laws, including arrangements for controlling and monitoring the institution of Press, which had developed till then into an important vehicle of public opinion and information. Territories forming Pakistan and the rest of the Indian sub-continent had never been without proper Press Laws, though the former colonial masters have changed their system of monitoring and regulating the mass media, which in the present 21$^{st}$ century includes television, film, video broadcasting, face book, You Tube and other social media. The present age can rightly be called the age of Communication Revolution. Because of the boom in the field of communication, the culture of Iron Curtain exists no more. Therefore, the right to know of citizens, which is a part of Rights of Expression, enshrined in Article 19 of U.N Charter Declaration for Human Rights, has acquired immense importance. In Pakistan, access to information is a new idea and it was included in the 18th Amendment as late as 2011. After the permission from the government to have private television channels, the freedom available to media persons has created many controversies. The most controversial is the ignoring of Law of Defamation by the private TV channels in the name of media activism. Situation has created not only political uncertainty and social chaos in Pakistani Society but has also involved the judiciary into controversy. In these circumstances, this analytical volume by Ms Yasmeen Aftab Ali will be beneficial for not only students of Mass Communications and the general public but for working journalists as well.

***Dr Mehdi Hasan***

Acknowledgement

Dr Mehdi Hasan introduced me to the profession of teaching. He gave me the opportunity not only to teach in Beaconhouse National University–a name to be reckoned with in the field of education, but also showed great confidence by entrusting me to teach Media Laws as well–a subject of great importance in today's world of communication. Without his support and confidence, this book would not have been possible. Dr Mehdi: Thank you!

I would also like to thank my family; my husband Naveed Tajammal, who has always supported me in exploring my talents and has been instrumental in having this book published; my mother, Shamsa Aftab Ali, for her moral support, my daughter Sherbano, for proof reading the book, my son Nausherwan without whose technical help, compilation of the book would have been much tougher.

Last but not the least my profound gratitude to Mr Ikhlaq Ali Khan for supporting my endeavor.

# *About the Author*

The author has a Master's degree in Mass Communications and a second degree in Law–both from the Punjab University. She has diversified experience, having worked in both fields since 1984 to date. She has been teaching in The Beaconhouse National University, Lahore since 2004. She also taught Advertising in Kinnaird College, Lahore for two years as visiting faculty. The author is an established political writer having written for many local newspapers and foreign ones. She blogs at: http://pakpotpourri2.wordpress.com/ and

http://pakpotpourri.wordpress.com/

She can be reached on her mail account yasmeen.a.ali@hotmail.com
Twitter ID: @yasmeen_9

Photo credit: Salman : 0321-3244448

# *Contents*

**Introduction**: 15
A Brief Review of the History of Press in Pakistan

**Chapter 1** 19
Concept of Freedom of Expression:
(a) Concept
(b) Universal Declaration of Human Rights(Part 1)
(c) Limitations of Freedom of Expression
(d) Universal Declaration of Human Rights(Part II)
(e) Theories of Freedom of Speech
(f) Relation of Theories of Freedom of Speech with Democracy
(g) Concluding Comments

**Chapter II** 50
**Freedom of Expression in Pakistan (Part I)**
(a) Text of Article 19 & 19A Constitution of Pakistan
(b) Explanation of terms within Article 19
(c) Exceptions under Article 19
(d) Explanation of Article 19A
(f) A Brief Comparative with Parallel Laws of Other Nations
(g) A Comparative with Limitations in Other Nations
(h) Concluding Comments

**Chapter III** 81
**Freedom of Expression & Speech in Pakistan (Part II)**
**(Contempt of Court)**

(a) Text of Article 204 of Constitution of Pakistan with Explanation
(b) Issues sub-judice : Press & Contempt of Court
(c) Contempt of Court Ordinance 2003
(d) Why Amendment Bill of Contempt of Court 2012?
(e) Text of Amendment Bill of Contempt of Court 2012
(f) Explanation of Bill of Contempt of Court 2012
(g) Exceptions to Bill of Contempt of Court 2012
(h) Amendment Bill of Contempt of Court 2012 struck down
(i) Brief Comparison with Contempt of Court Act 1971 of India
(j) Cases of Contempt of Court from Around the World
(k) Concluding Comments

**Chapter IV** 125
**Defamation**
(a) Concept
(b) Factors that aggravate & mitigate damages
(d) Accidental Defamation
(c) Some questions relating to libel
(d) Defenses to a case of libel
(e) Text of Defamation Ordinance 2002 of Pakistan
(f) Explanation of Defamation Ordinance 2002 Pakistan
(g) Defamation cases from Around the World
(h) Concluding Comments

**Chapter V** 153
**Cyber Law**
(a) What is cyber- crime?
(b) Prevention of Electronic Crimes Ordinance, 2008(Pakistan)
(c) Reported cases of cyber- crime in Pakistan
(d) Cyber-crime cases from Around the World
(e) Concluding Comments

**Chapter VI** 170
**Psychological Warfare and Propaganda**
(a) What is psywar?
(b) Characteristics of Propaganda
(c) Tactics of Propaganda
(d) Angles of Propaganda
(e) Mediums of Propaganda
(f) Limitations of Propaganda
(g) Counter Propaganda
(h) What is a Spin?
(i) Concluding Comments

**Chapter VII** 197
**Electronic Media**
(a) Defining the electronic media
(b) TEXT OF PAKISTAN ELECTRONIC MEDIA REGULATORY AUTHORITY ORDINANCE 2002 Amended 2007
(c) Explaining the salient points of PEMRA Ordinance
(d) Some relevant clauses from PEMRA Ordinance(Amend)2007
(e) Code of Conduct for Media Broadcasters/Cable TV Operators (with discussion)
(f) Current problems in electronic media
(g) 11 Suggestions for PEMRA
(h) A Comparative with BBC News
(i) BBC's Editorial Values
(j) An Explanation of BBC's Editorial Values
(k) BBC's ground laying operative Principles
(l) Coverage of Issues by BBC
(m) Concluding Comments

**Chapter VIII** 270
**Social Media**
(a) Defining Social Media
(b) Problems with Social Media
(c) Increasing power of the Social Media

(d) Can Social Media be held Accountable?
(e) Concluding Comments

**Chapter IX** 279
**Social Responsibility of Media**
(a) Social Responsibility and the many "Gates of Communication"
(b) Authoritarian Theory of Communication
(c) Libertarian Theory of Communication
(d) Soviet Media Theory of Communication
(e) Social Responsibility Theory of Communication
(f) Report by Commission headed by Robert Hutchinson 1947
(g) Code of Ethics by the Society of Professional Journalists
(h) Code of Conduct by PFUJ
(i) A Modest Proposal by Sir Stephan Sedley to make media more Accountable
(j) Concluding Comments

**Annexure 'A':** 309
**Text of PEMRA(Amend)Ordinance 2007**

# Introduction

## *A Brief Review of the History of Press in Pakistan*

Laws evolve over time. They are a result of the on-going political situation faced by any country. The press in Pakistan has never been unfettered. No institution has had to struggle as much in Pakistan as the media, to attain the degree of independence they enjoy today. In so doing, it has passed through many tribulations, tests, sacrifices. The history of press in Pakistan has been well documented by senior journalists and many books are available to the effect. Here, I share the briefest outline for the readers–as the present is always connected to the past, and what is the present, if not the past of the future?

This is 1822.The first Urdu Newspaper makes its debut in the Indian sub-continent. Till then, all newspapers were in English–the Master's language. We slip into year 1823. The East India Company introduces the first Press Act.. The first, of the many restrictions, on media, to follow. It requires those wanting to take out a newspaper to file a "Declaration." Interestingly, the meaning of "Declaration" was to be that as taken as in the dictionary. Thereby, once a declaration is filed, the District Magistrate does not have the authority to turn down the request of the person filing. This law stayed in place till 1947.

This is 1957. "Abdus Salam Achakzai filed a writ petition in the West Pakistan High Court against the decision that refused him permission to take out two weekly papers from Quetta. The court ruled in accordance with the 1823 Press Act, that once a declaration has been filed, the District Magistrate may not refuse permission."[1]

---

[1] Dr Mehdi Hasan, discussion on the subject 1st August 2012. Dr Mehdi Hasan wears many hats. Only one hat is mentioned in the later pages.

This is 1950. Senior journalists of Pakistan, under the banner of Pakistan Federal Union of Journalists(PFUJ), lay down the country's first Code of Conduct for the journalists to follow. The struggle by PFUJ over years against anti-freedom press laws must be appreciated with a salute!

This is 1959; PPL, a premier news agency of Pakistan is taken over by the State.

This is 1961; APP, another premier news agency of Pakistan is also taken over by the State. Further, foreign news agencies are now directed not to release the news directly, but through the local news agencies. Enter "filtration" of news by a free medium of communication.

This is 1961 once again. We see the promulgation of the PPO(Press and Publications Ordinance), rightly dubbed as the "Blackest of the Black Laws" in Pakistan. On the face of it, the law aimed to bring together under one umbrella, different provisions; preventive detention of persons and control of persons and publications connected with maintenance of public order. But the truth of the matter is; to fine tune methods that lead to more repression and more suppression. A number of heavy handed laws were introduced via the PPO to keep the press in chains. The law was made much harsher through amendments in 1963. It remained in force for the next 25 years.

Year 1988. The caretaker government promulgates the Registration of Printing Presses and Publicatons Ordinance (RPPO). This is the law that awarded freedom of expression to the press. However, the struggle of PFUJ, must be acknowledged that led to the promulgation of this law. Without its struggle, the RPPO and its provisions may not have been possible.

Let us step back in time to 1964. We see the birth of the NPT or the National Press Trust. It placed a number of magazines and newspapers under its flagship. The reason given was, "to raise the standards of journalism and editorial policy."[2] It was PFUJ to the fore, who reacted first. The publications taken over by the NPT, were reduced to little more than the mouthpiece of the government.

The struggle of press under the auspices of the PFUJ has been arduous and long. PFUJ grew up facing odds–never once giving up!

[2] Press in Chains by Zameer Niazi

Whether it was the hunger strike led by the PPL (Pakistan Times and Imroze) workers union and joined by the PUJ for the reinstatement of the four lower grade employees in January 1977, the historic 10-days countrywide strike for the implementation of the interim award by the Second Wage Board in April 1970, and over 45-days long hunger strike movement in 1974 for the reinstatement of arbitrarily sacked journalists and other employees of the daily "Musawaat" Lahore, or it was fighting against draconian laws like the PPO–PFUJ has stood fast for freedom of expression in Pakistan.

Under different governments over time, journalists have faced public lashings, detentions, threats. They have suffered and stood up again –to fight back! Each of them deserves a glowing tribute. In a Pakistan when political parties were in a fledgling state, PFUJ took over the task and duties of the political parties.

As we look at the existing laws today, in Pakistan, we must bear in mind the long road of sacrifice the press has taken to get here. A price has been paid.

# Chapter 1

## Concept of Freedom of Expression

John Swinton, the doyen of the New York press corps, upon his retirement, made the following speech(Excerpt):

"There is no such thing, at this stage of the world's history in America, as an independent press. You know it and I know it. There is not one of you who dare write your honest opinions, and if you did, you know beforehand that it would never appear in print. I am paid weekly for keeping my honest opinions out of the paper I am connected with. Others of you are paid similar salaries for similar things, and any of you who would be foolish as to write honest opinions would be out on the streets looking for another job. If I allowed my honest opinions to appear in one issue of my papers, before twenty four hours, my occupation would be gone. The business of the journalist is to destroy the truth, to lie outright, to pervert, to vilify, fawn at the feet of Mammon, and to sell his country and his race for his daily bread. You know it and I know it, and what folly is this toasting of an independent press?...."[3]

Freedom of expression, is often confused with freedom of speech. Freedom of speech, is a part of freedom of expression. The latter is an umbrella term that covers many a form of expression that includes the freedom of speech, but only as a part thereof. It is deemed to be a basic human right, that includes; freedom of thought, freedom of press, freedom to express oneself in arts, poetry, architecture, crafts, lifestyles, dressing, eating, culture, music, sculptures so on and so forth.

---

[3] Titled, "Gaddafi, the Man who Came to Dinner" published 9th December,2011 in *The Nation Newspaper*

"Freedom of speech may be defined as the right to express one's ideas and opinions freely through speech, writing and other forms of communication but without deliberately causing harm to others' character and/or reputation by false or misleading statements. Freedom of press is part of freedom of expression."[4]

Freedom of expression is as a basic ingredient or a cornerstone to a functioning democracy. Freedom of expression is a term giving an umbrella to many types of freedoms including most importantly, freedom of speech; of the press, of association, of assembly and petition – all protected by the First Amendment of the US Constitution. The relevant portion of the First Amendment of the United States Constitution written in 1791 reads: *"Congress shall make no law respecting an establishment of religion, or prohibiting the free exercise thereof; or abridging the freedom of speech, or of the press; or the right of the people peaceably to assemble, and to petition the government for a redress of grievances."*

A well- known quote, largely attributed to Voltaire, is originally of Evelyn Beatrice Hall, who wrote under the pen name of S.G Tallentyre, known for her biography of Voltaire titled, "The Friends of Voltaire", Hall, wrote in that biography, "I disapprove of what you say, but I will defend to the death your right to say it" is the tenet on which the very principle of right to freedom of expression rests. This quote is often misattributed by some to be from Voltaire himself. ***Noam Chomsky***, correctly stated, "If we don't believe in freedom of expression for people we despise, we don't believe in it at all."

An interesting study here, in the case of freedom of expression has been the ban on niqab recently in France. From 11th April 2011, Muslim women were banned from wearing the niqab in any public place. Face veils were outlawed everywhere barring within the four walls of the home. Any third party, whether the father, husband or anyone having pressurized the woman to wear a niqab publically is to be fined €30,000 and may face one year in prison.

But the immigration historian Patrick Weil has warned that the law is open to challenge from the European court of human rights. He said the battle to stop women wearing niqab did not justify that "a woman who believes that her God orders her to wear it should be stopped from going

[4] Definition by BusinessDictionary. Com LINK: http://www.businessdictionary.com/definition/freedom-of-expression.html

out to buy food to feed herself, or from going to see a doctor"[5].Under the law, anyone refusing to lift a veil for an identity check can be persuaded to remove the garment at a police station. A woman who is defiant and insists on appearing veiled in public can be fined 150 Euros ($216) and will be ordered to attend re-education classes.[6] The question here is, is this in conformity with the international law? Can a certain section of the society be refrained from exercising their right to freedom of expression through their dressing by another section of the society?

***Daily Voice of Reason,*** a stimulating online SITE, put up an interesting viewpoint, "Although a ban of the Niqab, France is famous for its extreme interpretation of secularism. For example, state teachers are not allowed to wear a cross pin on their clothing, and Jewish men aren't allowed to wear the yammukah. .....Quite possibly the worst argument, but most used on to destroy the rights of others, is that of safety: The Niqab poses a direct threat to public safety. Opponents argue that terrorists can use the Niqab to hide bombs, and convicts use it to mask their faces while they steal or kill, but how many instances have there been? Terrorists: Never. They more often choose backpacks. Robbery: Once. Clearly not a threat to society or anyone's safety."[7]

Interestingly, somehow the western philosophy is never to see the desire to cover oneself up seen as empowerment. And why not? If a woman is comfortable in a clothing, be it skirt, pants, a dress or a niqab– so be it. Imposition of will of one section of the society, in terms of dressing on another section of the society may be deemed as a clear violation of freedom of expression.

Discriminating against any group of people and branding them with an adjective is racism.

I would define racism as prejudice or discrimination directed against someone of a different race based on a belief. It is just like stating all women not wearing a niqab are tramps, all Muslims are terrorists, the blacks in US have lesser rights than the whites or something equally sweeping and discriminatory.

---

[5] The Guardian story," Full faced veils outlawed in France spells out controversial niqab ban" by *Angelique Christafis* dated 3rd March 2011

[6] Arab News.com story titled," Mixed reactions to French niqzb ban", by *Marium Nihal* published on 12th April 2011

[7] Titled, "France's Niqab Ban" posted on 11th April 2011 LINK: http://dailyvoiceofreason.blogspot.com/2011/04/frances-niqab-ban.html

Freedom of expression is the corner stone in any democratic dispensation. A free exchange of ideas is generally viewed as a constraint to tyranny but is a basic element in a democratic set up. However, like any other liberty, the right to freedom of expression is not absolute. This is true for any country of the world. There are laws against hate speech, sedition, defamation, contempt of court, blasphemy etc. One may not indulge in these wrongful acts in the cover of exercising the right of freedom of expression.

***Freedom of speech*** includes not just the verbal word but also the non-verbal communication . An example is burning a nation's flag in USA which is viewed as a "symbolic communication."

Showing contempt for the national flag in any way, by trampling on it, or burning it, was prohibited under the first US Supreme Court Ruling in ***Halter v. Nebraska(1907).***In a Tribunal Ruling of 8-1, the Supreme Court upheld Halter's conviction, giving a judgment that state governments have every right to ban the desecration of the American flag.

This was the first ruling by the Supreme Court in USA regulating use of the national flag, that sought greater governmental regulation as opposed to greater individual liberty. Freedom of expression is supposed to be free from fear of punishment. Yet, each individual and institution must enjoy the same right. By virtue of this fact, there must be a point where the right of freedom of expression of one ends and that of the other begins. Failing which, we revert to the law of the jungle where each man has a right to express himself in any manner possible while trampling on the right of the other. Boundaries must therefore be established so that all individuals and groups enjoy this liberty equally, and fairly. The oft heard quote, "The right to swing my fist ends where the other man's nose begins", largely attributed to ***Judge Oliver Wendell Holmes*** can be aptly quoted here.

***Justice Corey*** of Supreme Court of Canada wrote, "It is difficult to imagine a guaranteed right more important to a democratic society than*freedom of expression.* Indeed a democracy cannot exist without that freedom to express new ideas and to put forward opinions about the functioning of public institutions. The concept of free and uninhibited speech permeates all truly democratic societies and institutions. The vital importance of the concept cannot be over-emphasized." [8]

However, *Justice Wendell Holmes* in the famous case ***Schenck v. United States(1919)*** clearly expressed his opinion that a restriction is legitimate only if it poses a real and clear present danger that relates to public interests or threat to safety. When America entered the World War I in 1917, Congress passed the Espionage Act . This law clearly enunciated that any individual working to cause disloyalty or disobedience among the soldiers will be deemed as a war crime. Charles Schenck was against the war. He mailed thousands of pamphlets to men who had been drafted into the armed forces. The government accused Schenck of violating the Espionage Act. The contention of the government was that the pamphlets were aimed to weaken the loyalty of the soldiers and create a clear obstruction in the recruitment procedure. Argument put forth by Schenck was that the Espionage Act was in violation of the First Amendment that clearly states, "Congress shall make no law...abridging the freedom of speech." The case was eventually decided by the Supreme Court in 1919. ***Justice Oliver Wendell Holmes*** wrote the decision for a Supreme Court that was unanimous in its decision. "When a nation is at war," he said, "many things that might be said in time of peace are such a hindrance to its effort that their utterance will not be endured so long as men fight and that no Court could regard them as protected by any constitutional right."[9]

The judgment delivered in ***Schenck v. United States*** clearly points towards limitations that must be exercised in certain circumstances and may not be deemed as absolute.

These limitations must be understood and respected by individuals and societies at large. Rights may be different in times of peace and different in terms of war. This reality needs to be understood.

In Pakistan, fraught with ethnic divisions within, involvement in War on Terror, divided more sharply into the liberals and rightists, with pockets of moderates, there is a need to exchange views and thoughts that can form a bridge between the two schools of thought. A balance needs to be struck so that the divergent views do not spark off violence due to use of "fighting words" or/and incitement to an offence.

---

[8] *Edmonton Journal V Alberta (1969)2 SCR 1326*

[9] Case Citation: *Schenck* v. *United States*, 249 U.S. 47 (1919)

On December 10th, 1948, the General Assembly of the United Nations adopted and proclaimed the **Universal Declaration of Human Rights** . Article 19 of Declaration states, " Everyone has the right to freedom of opinion and expression; this right includes freedom to hold opinions without interference and to seek, receive and impart information and ideas through any media and regardless of frontiers."

The Article 19 above clearly divides the right to freedom of expression in two parts. The first deals with the right to hold an opinion without another's right to interfere in that formation of opinion, may it be another individual, group or institution. The other part deals with the right to get and share any information or ideas from another individual, group or institution. Article 19 of the UN Declaration of Human Rights, removes any restriction of geographical barriers to this right held inviolate.

The UN General Assembly in 1946, before the adoption of any law on freedom of expression, adopted a resolution, 59(I) stating, "Freedom of information is a fundamental human right and ... the touchstone of all the freedoms to which the United Nations is consecrated."

However, is this right truly inviolate? Does this allow hate speech? Racism? Breach against the security of a country? Contempt of Court? Defamation? The list is long and the question demands a hard look at the question itself. A balance must be struck here. A line must be drawn .

Every nation has the right to constitute laws to deal with new challenges. Laws are for societies. As societies change, so must the laws to meet the ongoing challenges of time. Interestingly, USA has passed The Trespass Bill, in August 2011. The Bill creates a "bubble" zone around certain government officials, dignitaries and areas , using a broad meaning, giving room to interpretation by the prosecutor. ***John Glaser*** states, "Starting with making it illegal to trespass on the grounds of the White House, the grounds or buildings included as off-limits even cover those that the President – or whatever other official protected by the Secret Service – is residing temporarily. It would even include a peaceful protest outside a presidential candidate's concession speech, for example."[10] He goes on to say, in the same article, "The government

---

[10] "Trespass Bill Would Violate Peaceful Assembly Rights" : by John Glaser published 28th February 2012 in AntiWar.COM LINK: http://news.antiwar.com/2012/02/28/trespass-bill-would-violate-peaceful-assembly-rights/

already has inordinate ability to crush free speech, silence protesters, and arrest civilians peacefully assembling, but this legislation would mark the beginning of the end of the First Amendment."[11] Obama signed the Bill in March 2012 that essentially makes it a federal offence to create disturbance at certain political events.

***Limitations on Freedom of Expression***

Let us see some of these limitations that should and do create a bar against the right of unbridled exercise of the right to freedom of expression.

I would first like to discuss ***Hate Speech*** here as a justified bar on the right to freedom of expression. "Hate speech is a communication that carries no meaning other than the expression of hatred for some group, especially in circumstances in which the communication is likely to provoke violence. It is an incitement to hatred primarily against a group of persons defined in terms of race, ethnicity, national origin, gender, religion, sexual orientation, and the like. Hate speech can be any form of expression regarded as offensive to racial, ethnic and religious groups and other discrete minorities or to women."[12]

Use of derogatory expressions that incite negativism fall within the ambit of hate speech. Words like *nigger, faggot, homo, queer* are all terms used to provoke members of a society against others. Such terms degrade those for whom they are used. In the world that we live in today, with geographical barriers down, a world fraught with wars, hatred and conflicts, can the world, and media in specific, afford to vent more hatred, more conflicts by ignoring the legitimate and valid limitation that must be taken into consideration while exercising the right to freedom of expression? Media plays a powerful role today, in terms of forming opinions and attitudes and the impact of media cannot be undermined. Above all, choice of words by media practitioners must be carefully weighed before delivering.

In a piece carried by Defence Blog of Pakistan, by David Ben Gurion in 1948 during Israel's Independence Speech, "The world Zionist movement should not be neglectful of the dangers of Pakistan to it. And

---

[11] Ibid.

[12] Legal definition by USLEGAL.COM LINK: http://definitions.uslegal.com/h/hate-speech/

Pakistan now should be its first target, for this ideological State is a threat to our existence."[13]

Such a speech, words tipped with piercing poison, can only strike– and damage. The comments by politicians, opinion leaders, media all are part of creating opinions and affecting those who follow. This in turn can have a cascading effect on the actions of the members of society. How a news is projected, what angle is given, the choice of words therein, can and does, create hatred. Since 9/11 , attitudes worldwide in non -Muslim countries towards Islam are more negative than positive. Though, Islam explicitly prohibits taking the life of another human being, sometimes perceptions become more real than the reality itself. According to a 2010 Time magazine poll, 28 percent of voters do not believe Muslims should be eligible to sit on the U.S. Supreme Court, and nearly one-third think they should be barred from running for president.[14]

Media can play a huge function in playing a positive role in correcting these perceptions, and developing harmony between different religious groups inter countries and within a country. Unfortunately, media too, on many occasions, is hostage to vested interests . When hatred is fanned by media, of which social media has come up as a powerful means of communication, hate speech translates itself into actions that horrify.

***Geert Wilders,*** a popular Dutch MP, in 2008, released a 17 minutes film against Islam. Titled ***Fitna,*** the film demonstrates how the Koran encourages acts of terrorism, anti-Semitism, violence against women, homosexuals and infidels. "I don't hate Muslims. I hate Islam."[15] He had shown his film in the House of Lords in UK, sparking angry scenes of violence.[16]

---

13-. 1948 Speech by David Ben Gurion . LINK: http://www.defence.pk/forums/world-affairs/157035-hate-speech-israel-against-muslim-world.html

14-.TIME POLL:ARTICLE TITLED:" Majority Oppose Mosque, Many Distrust Muslims" by Alex Altmani published Thursday19th August 2010

[15] Article carried by The Guardian(The Observer) UK, by Ian Traynor, Sunday 17th , February 2008.

[16] BBC News: "Dutch MP Geert Wilder's Anti-Islam Film sparks protests. Published Friday, 5th March, 2010.

If those watching films like these commit an act of crime against those portrayed, who will be responsible? Movies are a powerful means of communication.

Irresponsible use of freedom of expression is an abuse of the right. Those exposed to hate speech are all kinds of people, educated, uneducated, frustrated, maybe having faced injustices. It is the frame of mind, it is that one moment that may accept the full impact of hate speech in any form and commit an act, later repented, but cannot be undone. An example of hate crime is the murder of ***Shaima Alawadi*** in California.[17]

An Iraqi- born mother of five, a note was found next to her body, saying, "Go back to your own country. You're a terrorist." Police said her 17 year old daughter found Shaima unconscious in the family room in El Cajon. Shaima died soon after being taken off the hospital lifesaving machine. What inspired the murderer to commit this hate act? A hate speech? Perceptions created by over influx of media reports? Questions to which answers may never be there. Except for that loaded note next to Shaima!

Another limitation to the exercise of the right of freedom of expression is ***defamation***. Generally described as a false statement against the reputation of another in verbal(slander) or recorded form(libel). It is vilification, aimed to damage the reputation about whom made.

***Slander*** is verbal communication, which by virtue of being verbal is transitory in nature. ***Libel*** on the other hand has a permanent form. It can be in writing, broadcast or in any from where it may be referred back.

A Saudi Arabian lawyer has threatened to use British courts to overturn a Danish free speech ruling by bringing a defamation case over cartoons of the Prophet Mohammed that depicted Islam's founder as a terrorist. Cartoon caricatures of the Prophet Mohammed were published in Danish newspapers in 2006 triggering violent protests across the Muslim world and riots which claimed the lives of over 50 people. Lars Barfoed, the Danish justice minister, has complained to the European

---

[17] Article in The Guardian UK by Dominic Rushe from New York published Sunday 25th March 2012. Titled, 'Savage Killing of Iraqi Woman in California investigated as hate crime'.

Commission that EU rules forcing Denmark to enact British court rulings would damage freedom of expression.[18]

***Christopher Warren,*** President IFJ states, "A free press must be held accountable for its conduct but criminal defamation laws threaten the liberty of journalists and the fearless nature of a truly free press. Meanwhile, outrageous civil defamation damages suits threaten the economic viability of media organizations."[19]

Nonetheless, this must not mean that anything goes. Without some degree of check and balance , a right can be abused. However, there is merit to the argument put forth by Christopher Warren, in certain cases. In a recent case of defamation ruling against Johnny Alberto Salazar, head of community radio station *Vida FM* and the online newspaper ***vidadominicana.com*** in Nagua, was sentenced to prison for six months and fined $25,600 on 18th January 2012. His crime? He libeled the lawyer Pedro Baldera, Chairman of the Human Rights Commission in the northern province of María Trinidad Sánchez.[20]

Slander can be more difficult to prove as compared to libel. Witnesses to a verbal communication can be coerced, pressurized, threatened and bought. This however, does not mean that slander cases are not filed or not settled. During my research I came across a particularly interesting one that I would like to share. Las Vegas surgeon ***Mark Kabins*** was convicted of a felony in federal court, agreed to pay $800,000 to settle a slander lawsuit filed against him by an anesthesiologist. The allegations in both the civil and criminal cases stem from the treatment of Melodie Simon, who became a paraplegic after Kabins and Thalgott performed spine surgery on her in August 2000. The lawsuit accuses the defendants of making "false and defamatory statements concerning Burkhead's ability to competently practice medicine." The malpractice case settled for $2.3 million, but prosecutors argued it was worth much more. After attorney fees and costs were deducted, Simon received $1.3 million. Kabins' plea agreement, which

---

[18] Article titled: " Defamation Case over Prophet Mohammad cartoons 'to be held' in Britain by Bruno Waterfield in Brussels", published by Daily Telegraph UK on 16th March 2010.

[19] Report on "Decriminalizing Defamation" by IFJ.(A campaign resource for defeating criminal defamation). SOURCE:IFJ SITE

[20] News Title: Journalist receives six months sentence and harsh fine in Defamation case . Published on 24th January, Tuesday, 2012 on site: REPORTERS WITHOUT BORDERS (For Freedom of Information). LINK: http://en.rsf.org/dominican-republic-journalist-receives-six-month-24-01-2012,41757.html

allowed him to avoid prison time, requires him to pay her another $3.5 million."[21]

***Incitement to offence*** cannot be allowed in exercise of the right to freedom of expression. Incitement to offence is a real encouragement to commit a crime. It can be through persuasion, threat, advice, direct help of any kind. The intention must be for the crime to be committed. A plea that the person encouraging the other to commit an offence, did not know the act was an offence will not stand. Ignorance of law is no excuse. Anger words spoken by politicians on electronic media, which has a huge impact in a country like Pakistan, irresponsible journalism by anchor persons whose words carry weight with the public at large, can have a cascading effect. It can result in acts akin to incitement, even if the desire to result in that act was not there, on face of it.

Incitement can be public ie encouraging a group of people to take a particular action and private incitement, encouraging an individual to do a particular act. Incitement to genocide was an unknown term, when Streitcher and Hans Fritzsche were charged and judgment against them passed in 1946, the grounds were crimes against humanity. But were they to be charged today for the same offence, it will fall within the ambit of incitement to genocide. Incitement to genocide became a crime under International Law with passing of this epic judgment against both by the International Military Tribunal.

***Julius Streitcher*** , founder, editor, of anti-Semetic weekly Magazine Der Strurmer, was found guilty of spreading hate propaganda. In many letters and articles that he wrote himself, Jewish people were portrayed as, "a parasite, an enemy, an evil doer, a disseminator of diseases", and "swarms of locusts that must be exterminated completely." [22] The Tribunal found Streitcher guilty of incitement to genocide. The Tribunal judged that he, "incited the German people to active persecution."[23] He was awarded death by hanging.[24]

Hans Fitzsche was a senior official from the Ministry headed by Goebbel for Proper Enlightenment and Propaganda. He also headed the Radio Division from 1942. He was accused of having , "incited and encouraged the commission of War Crimes by deliberately falsifying news

---

[21] Article published in Las Vegas Review-Journal by Carri Geer Thevenot published 7th March 2010.

[22] (1946)22 Trial of Major German War Criminals p. 501.

[23] Ibid.

[24] Ibid ,p. 529.

to arouse the German people those passions that led them to the commission of those atrocities."[25] Fitzsche was acquitted, the Tribunal having judged that , ".....his position and official duties were not sufficiently important......to infer that he took part in originating or formulating propaganda campaigns."[26]

Freedom of expression, like any other liberty, brings with itself a very heavy responsibility, on the shoulders of all of us exercising that right and in particular upon those who are placed in positions to influence policies, impact and form public opinion. At no stage, can we encourage criminal acts and then feign innocence or shrug off the responsibility that goes with freedom.

Whether incitement is against an individual person or a group which may be based on ethnic, racial or any other ground, it stands as limitation against the right to freedom of expression.

***Obscenity*** generally may be described as disgusting and in violation of standards acceptable in a given society of decency or morality. Obscenity differs from culture to culture, even in the same culture, it is different from one geographical area to the other. Or, different during different times in the same country, province, area. This is especially true of developing nations like Pakistan, where norms, life styles, dressing, etc are completely different in rural areas as compared to urban areas. One may not be obscene in garb of freedom of expression. In any liberal society we must determine the boundaries to a right. If all limitations from freedom of speech are removed, as clamored for by certain sections of societies, does this mean, we endorse pornography? Does this then endorse, a lifestyle, dressing et al in complete contempt of the value structure on which our society is built? Does this mean obscenity in behavior becomes acceptable?

***Yasmin AliBhai-Brown*** writes in her article, " Libertarians and free expression campaigners were jubilant last week. An obscenity case was due to be heard against Darryn Walker, a 35-year-old civil servant who had posted an essay on a website, titled Girls (scream) Aloud, imagining the sexual torture and mutilation of the each of the women who make up the pop group. In his fantasy, they are slashed and dismembered and, according to Don Grubin a consultant psychiatrist, the singers "are

[25] (1946)22 Trials of Major German War Criminals. P. 526.
[26] Ibid.

sexually aroused in spite of and, indeed, because of the humiliation, pain and domination". This is apparently modern erotica known as "pop slash." Cool, man.

"The case was dropped and is celebrated as another important knock-back for censorship. Sadly I felt unable to join in with the good cheer. Something is deeply troubling about the validation given to Walker and those who think they have the right to say whatever they wish and excitedly share with others the thrills of extreme violence against women."[27] She goes on to say "..... it is never an absolute entitlement, not unless you believe it is worth the resulting social discord and terrible individual wreckage."[28]

In any society, we must look towards the greater good of the society, that promotes greater harmony between individuals, groups, institutions. Even if each one of us do not know exactly where to draw the line, we know the lines exist and are very much there. It has a lot to do with the rare commodity known as common sense! In the most liberal of countries too, obscenity as a limitation on freedom of expression very much exists. It will be wrong to claim there is none. The Supreme Court of United States has made many a rulings against misuse of this right where obscenity was involved. In ***Butler v. State of Michigan*** court made it a misdemeanor to sell or make available to the general reading public any book containing obscene language "tending to the corruption of the morals of youth" violated the Due Process Clause of the Fourteenth Amendment.[29]

The political and moral climate of a country changes with time. What may be deemed an obscenity today may not be deemed an obscenity tomorrow. In a country like Pakistan, sharply divided between rightists and the liberals, with a good number of moderates thrown in, there must be a balance struck between the different shades of opinion. Laws made must take into consideration, the cultural, social, and on occasions, the religious values of its people along with the internationally accepted moral code of behavior–in most parts of the world.

Fundamental to protect human rights is the underlying principle of awarding dignity and equality to all. Being sensitive to the religious

---

[27] Article Titled: "Freedom of Speech cannot be unlimited" by Yasmin AliBhai- Brown published in The Independent UK, Monday 6th July 2009

[28] Ibid

[29] 352. U.S 380(1957)

feelings of others. ***Dr. Agnes Callamard*** states in his article, " States may, but are not required to introduce legislation on ***blasphemy***. Several established democracies still have blasphemy provisions on the books, although most of these are rarely, if ever, used. In the United Kingdom, for example, there have been only two prosecutions for blasphemy since 1923. Norway saw its last case in 1936 and Denmark in 1938."[30]

The universe is full of people with diverse beliefs. Religions are many, followers of each religion believes they follow the "best" one. Irrespective of whether someone is a Muslim, a Christian, an Atheist, so on and so forth, the best course of action to maintain peace and harmony is to be respectful towards the other's beliefs. As we would want respect to be shown to ours. Why hurt feelings and create a chain reaction that may gather speed and erupt like a volcano? And like a volcano, destroy everything that comes its way.

Chapter 272 (36) of the Massachusetts code (concerned with "crimes against chastity, morality, decency and good order") thus provides that: "Whoever willfully blasphemes the holy name of God by denying, cursing or contumeliously reproaching God, his creation, government or final judging of the world, or by cursing or contumeliously reproaching Jesus Christ or the Holy Ghost, or by cursing or contumeliously reproaching or exposing to contempt and ridicule, the holy word of God contained in the holy scriptures shall be punished by imprisonment in jail for not more than one year or by a fine of not more than three hundred dollars, and may also be bound to good behavior."[31]

Section 298 of the Indian Penal Code 1860 prohibits intentional wounding of religious feelings by word or gesture, supplementing Section 295A regarding "intentional and malicious" outraging of religious feelings of any class of citizens by the spoken or written word."[32] Pakistan's blasphemy law has often been the source of severe criticism. "Religious parties had condemned passage of Resolution by the US House of Representatives calling for change in the Blasphemy Laws in Pakistan, saying it hurt the sentiments of Muslims across the world. They have

---

[30] Article published in Equal Voices , magazine for European Monitoring Centre on Racism and Xenophobia (EUMC),Issue, 18th June 2006

[31] Caslon Analytics Blasphemy ,pg. 1 LINK: http://www.caslon.com.au/blasphemyprofile10.htm

[32] Ibid, pg.2

demanded of the UN to take notice of the violation of the religious freedom of Muslims."[33]

In October 2008 twelve world experts met from around the world and participated in a ground- breaking seminar intended to clarify the links between articles 19 and 20 of the International Covenant on Civil and Political Rights on freedom of expression and advocacy of religious hatred that constitutes incitement to discrimination, hostility or violence.[34]

One of the clear messages that came out of the two-day discussion was that governments already have at their disposal various tools and capacities which should be used to build a tolerant society, such as education, interfaith dialogue and intercultural exchanges. Martin Uhomoibhi, President of the Human Rights Council, told the participants in the seminar "It is obvious that one of the most critical challenges facing all governments the world over today is how best to ensure the full enjoyment of freedom of expression and combating incitement to religious hatred..."[35]

The list of limitations is by no means exhausted and includes ***copyrights and patents***. Any logo, product name, patent product by a company, may not be used by another in exercise of right of freedom of expression. Copyright laws are governed by legal doctrines for example Anti-Trust Law in US ( 1995) and Competition Laws in the European Union. Each country has its own set of copyright laws.

Accountability is difficult in societies that generally lack respect for the law. The two intrinsic elements for a person to be guilty of ***perjury*** are that he/she must have deliberately lied to mislead and this must have been done under legal oath.

"I still think President Clinton may have some real problems because he testified under oath. There is a real question of perjury and obstruction of justice."[36] This came from ***Don Nickles*** , an American businessman

---

[33] The News(Pakistan): Tuesday, 15th March, 2011

[34] United Nations Human Rights site posted under title, 'World experts meet to discuss Freedom of Expression and Advocacy of Religious Hatred LINK: http://www.ohchr.org/EN/NEWSEVENTS/Pages/WorldexpertsdiscussFreedomExpression.aspx

[35] Ibid

[36] Great-Quotes.com (Perjury Quotes). LINK: http://www.great-quotes.com/quotes/category/Perjury#action=like&id=1255231&type=document&data=like&increment=0

and politician who was a Republican United States Senator from Oklahoma from 1981 till 2005 on Clinton-Lewinsky case on the testimony by Clinton in court. Bill Clinton was impeached and the House approved Articles that alleged perjury and obstruction of justice for lying under oath and obstructing justice for cover up with an intern in the Oval Office.

Perjury is yet another limitation to the right to freedom of self - expression. On no account can it be condoned as it leads to obstruction of justice.

How can we, while discussing limitations on freedom of expression, overlook ***profanity***?

The vulgar, irreverent word or action that we hear so commonly in the course of conversation, even by the educated, what to speak of the rickshaw drivers, that one is likely to forget that this too, is a bar on as we exercise freedom of expression. And profanity is not just restricted to one-to-one exchanges but is gaining greater acceptance in form of crude comedy and sitcoms. Do we allow society and media as a powerful instrument of opinion formation, to exercise this right with no limitations and governed only by good sense? If in spite of the limitations, we see so many violations, how can we allow an unrestricted profane choice to the people? It will be akin to giving a loaded gun to a two year old and expect him not to shoot himself in the foot- or shoot off his mouth, in this case!

In the well- known case ***Cohen v. California,*** the United States Supreme Court overturned a " disturbing peace conviction" of a man wearing a jacket decorated with profanity.[37] On 26th April 1968, Paul Robert Cohen was arrested for wearing a jacket with profanity written on it. He was convicted of violating California Penal Code sentencing him to 30 days in jail. The conviction was upheld by California Court of Appeal, and the California Supreme Court denied review of the case.

In November 2011, Pakistan Government, banned text messages with obscenity and use of word, "Jesus."[38] A list of 1500 words were sent to the three largest mobile carriers by The Pakistan Telecommunication Authority(PTA). "The list includes many crude and sexual terms that the government is attempting to root out as part of a 1996 ban on transmitting information through telephone systems that is "indecent or

---

[37] 403 U. S 15(1971)

[38] Times News Feed titled Purity in Pakistan: Government Bans Text Messages With Obscenity –Or the Word "Jesus" by Nick Carbone published 19th November 2011

obscene."[39] PTA banned pornographic websites in Pakistan in January 2012. According to SITE ***News Pakistan*** , " PTA has provided a list to the ISP's in Pakistan to block the frequently accessed adult sites. It is believed that more web pages will be added to the initial banned list of 1,000 websites and as many as 170,000 websites may be banned in the near future." [40] Yet another limitation on freedom of expression is ***treason***. Treason may generally be defined as (a)The offence to overthrow one's government or to harm or kill it's sovereign, or (b)a violation of allegiance to one's sovereign or to one's state. However, different constitutions of the world are very specific in laying out the legal meaning of treason in their laws.

As an example, the Constitution of Pakistan defines High Treason in Article 6. Any action may not be taken with the excuse to express the right of freedom of expression while committing High Treason.

***Invasion of privacy*** by media, governments, or institutions, are a part of privacy laws of many countries. A good example of privacy is reflected in the *Fourth Amendment* of the American Constitution, " The right of the people to be secure in their persons, houses, papers, and effects, against unreasonable searches and seizures, shall not be violated, and no warrants shall issue, but upon probable cause, supported by Oath or affirmation, and particularly describing the place to be searched, and the persons or things to be seized."

***The second part of the right to freedom of expression as enunciated in the United Nations Declaration of Human Rights Article 19*** is, "....... freedom to hold opinions without interference and to seek, receive and impart information and ideas through any media and regardless of frontiers." An individual or/and a media person has the right to seek information, the right to access to information is the second important and cardinal principle of freedom of expression. The geographical boundaries are no bar on this right.

Freedom of information allows the seeker of information to request for government for any information. Often, a nominal cost needs to be incurred for information sought as cost of copies of documents made. There is a huge debate between the right to know

---

[39] Ibid.

[40] Titled "PTA banned pornographic websites in Pakistan" published on *News Pakistan* by 23rd January 2012 by Ahmed Babar

and the right to privacy regarding disclosure of sensitive information. Yes, there may be certain instances where sharing sensitive information may not be possible, this information, in wrong hands can cause damage to a nation's security and sovereignity, generally speaking though access to information is deemed to be vital and basic to curb on corruption, nepotism and encourage good governance and transparency in dealings. Governance does not only imply political governance but also includes economic governance.

An example worth sharing, "The World Bank, makes it very easy for public to seek information regarding projects under progress, analytic and advisory activities, and Board proceedings."[41]

***Raniya Khan,*** in her article states, "The media also feels that it is being barred from access to information, which in turn, limits its role as a government 'watchdog.' The media is a tool through which the people are able to monitor the acts of the government, and a free media acts as a voice for the people in democratic countries."[42]

I would briefly like to state here, that the role of media as a watchdog, is being eroded to a certain degree, owing to untrained entrants in the field, more particularly in the electronic media, as one of the causes of irresponsible journalism. This is discussed at length in later chapters.

### *Theories of Freedom of Speech*

The subject of freedom of expression will not be complete without discussing the ***theories of freedom of speech*** and the concept of democracy as the freedom of expression is closely tied in to operating in a democratic dispensation.

Social Scientists have expounded many theories in favor of freedom of speech. These must be viewed with a pinch of salt. There is no existence of a "pure democracy" in which operation of these theories are envisaged.

---

[41] The World Bank Online Site "Access to Information". LINK: http://web.worldbank.org/WBSITE/EXTERNAL/PROJECTANDOPERATIONS/EXTINFODISCLOSURE/0,,menuPK:64864911~pagePK:4749265~piPK:4749256~theSitePK:5033734,00.html

[42] Article titled "Strengthening Democracy through access to information" published by Jinnah Institute. LINK: http://jinnah-institute.org/programs/governance/345-strengthening-democracy-through-access-to-information

In western democracies, the concept may apply better than in under developed countries , with dictatorships and dynastic politics at play. Even in developed democracies, we see perceptions being built by media, a one sided view of issues, a media trial in which the hapless reader/viewer is trapped like a fly in the cobweb. These "angles" are guided by policies of the owner of that medium of communication.

Media is increasingly being used for psychological warfare, invasion of alien culture, projection of vested interest viewpoints, all over the world.

***Dr Mehdi Hasan,*** renowned intellectual, winner of Sitara-e-Imtiaz[43] in year 2012, currently Dean of Department of Journalism and School of Mass Communication in Beaconhouse National University, Lahore, stated, "As part of psychological warfare, concepts are imparted, subtly and sometimes not so subtly, it invades and occupies the mind. Once the mind has been won, there is no need for a physical invasion."[44] Aptly said! Even more relevant today than it was in 1984–when he said this.

"Freedom of speech is the liberty to express views without fear of punishment and government restraint. Freedom of speech is firmly embedded in the American political fabric. This is reflected in the First Amendment to the US Constitution, 'Congress shall make no law....abridging (limiting) the freedom of speech, or of the press..."

Let us take a look at the theories that are put forward in favor of freedom of speech by the social scientists.

The propagators of freedom of expression put forth a strong argument for the theory of freedom of speech. They argue, that on a broad based level, freedom of speech helps in ***Self Governance***. Self-governance may be defined as a philosophy that helps govern a nation by popular representation, having autonomy and political independence. With competing ideas and policies, it is argued, the public has a clear understanding of the choices various candidates for election have to offer and thus the public is in the best position to make a choice out of the options available, thereby reaching a level of self -governance with

---

[43] The Sitara-e-Imtiaz is "Star of Excellence", the third highest civilian award in the State of Pakistan

[44] Dr Mehdi Hasan, in a lecture on "Psychological Warfare", to the class of Mass Communication, Department of Journalism 1984 in Punjab University, Lahore

complete knowledge and confidence. ***John Milton,*** the author of the treatise ***Areopagatica***, which became the base for the liberal view regarding freedom of expression had a huge impact in the liberal thought processes of UK, United States and throughout the British Empire, gave the lofty ideas on freedom of expression that nations today continue aspire to achieve. ***John Milton*** says, "Give me the liberty to know, to utter, and to argue freely according to conscience, above all liberties."[45]

The questions that are raised in my mind are many. I would like to explore these thoughts with you, dear readers, as I go along. First, does the right to freedom of speech, by politicians, opinion leaders and others, truly expose their inner thoughts? Or, would they, in their exercise of this right be guided by their party policies or other vested interests, more prominent; the desire to get elected, project views contrary to their inner thoughts? Two, does a promise made owing to a desire for popular vote, actually translate itself into action, once duly elected ? If it does not, can the propagators of this theory still lay a claim to its veracity? If this is the case, does the theory then, not become just a cover to advance vested interests' viewpoint– and not instrumental in self-governance as claimed?

Nixon resigned (the only American President to do so) once the impeachment became imminent. The scandal unfolded with burglary in the National Democratic Headquarters on 17$^{th}$ June 1972. The burglars turned out to be employees of Committee for Re-Election of the President. Political investigations began in early 1973,when the Senate established a committee to look into the affair. During investigations, the committee uncovered secret White House tape recordings, erupting into a major legal battle between the President and the Congress.

He resigned in early August 1974 after the Judiciary Committee appointed by the House of Representative voted to accept three Articles of Impeachment. Supreme Court too, had directed Nixon to release more White House tapes.

The question is, at the time of election, candidates then too, had an opportunity to exercise the right to freedom of speech, share their thought processes regarding governance with the public. The public in turn, listened to all the candidates and made a considered decision in making a choice of candidate. Or, was it a considered choice? Like the candidates themselves, were the voters too, divided, based on predetermined mindset

---

[45] Milton's Aeropagatica 1644

into Democrats and Republicans casting their votes based on this criteria alone, irrespective of the quality of the candidate? It may be validly argued, that he was after all, made to impeach owing to the steps taken. My question though, pre-dates the action. The fact that the choice was made through electoral ballot of a person who thought nothing of taking these steps. Did this freedom of speech ultimately help in self-governance by popular representatives? The popular having become unpopular sooner than the mandatory period of governance casts a shadow of doubt on the bottom line advantage promised by the theory.

In a country like Pakistan, with low rate of literacy, majority of the population living in rural areas, dependent on the landlords of their region in all matters in their lives, whether it is pertaining to a water dispute, land dispute, recovery of an abducted woman from the tribe etc , how can that poor man with no support but of that landlord , deny him his vote where that landlord wants it cast?

Like anywhere else in the world, Pakistan too, is divided in support of the multi parties having their niches i.e. PPP(Pakistan Peoples Party), PML-N(Pakistan Muslim League-Nawaz Faction), PML-Q(Pakistan Muslim League-Quaid League), MQM(Muttahida Quami Movement), PTI(Pakistan Tehreek-i-Insaaf), Jamait-e-Islami so on and so forth. Their voting decisions may not be based on the individual caliber of the candidate but the party ticket he/she holds. Or, the "landlords" or tribal heads of a tribe have their own vote bank–irrespective from which forum they contest from.

How do we then correlate the theory of self -governance in the above stated scenarios? Or should the public make the determination based on party basis only? In the latter case, individual merit loses out to party platform. If individual will gives way to collective platform of a political party, does that diminish the individual? "A representative government [is] a government in which the will of the people will be an effective ingredient." [46] But is the will of the people indeed a part of the representative government if the choice is based on a different set of reasons as opposed to the set of reasons it should be based on?

> "Every man, and every body of men on earth, possesses the right of self-government... This, like all other natural rights, may be abridged or modified in its exercise by their own consent, or by the

[46] Thomas Jefferson to Benjamin Austin, 1816. ME 14:388

law of those who depute them, if they meet in the right of others." [47]***(Thomas Jefferson)***

Another theory expounded for freedom of speech is ***Discovering the Truth.*** The theory is closely associated with ***John Stuart Mill,*** the British philosopher. Mill felt that with a broad base to exchange thoughts, views, issues, one finally reaches the truth. One is able to separate flak from the real and determine the truth of an issue.

Quoting from Mill's book ***On Liberty,*** he summarizes his argument on freedom of expression, "We can never be sure that the opinion we are endeavoring to stifle is a false opinion; and if we were sure, stifling it would be an evil still."[48]

Mill felt truth is found only if individuals are free to exchange views and a free and open discussion is allowed to take place.

Only after knowing the truth an individual can utilize it for the betterment of the society itself. For him, in a free society, individuals must be allowed complete freedom of speech especially in issues pertaining to public matters. Freedom of speech is intrinsic to raise the intellectual level or ordinary mortals to a level better than the one they will otherwise achieve. "Free thought and discussion are accepted as the sole way in which truth can be acquired by rational being, however, someone might go on to object that it is only necessary for some instructed elite, rather than mankind in general, to go through the process."[49]

Mill strongly believed in the possibility of social progress through an absolute right of freedom of expression.

In the known case law, ***Abrams v. United States,***[50]Justice Oliver Wendell Holmes, introduced the powerful thought of ***"marketplace of ideas"***. He felt that when all ideas, on a topic are awarded opportunity to present themselves, it is easier for a rational choice to be made as to which one should be chosen over others.

This approach raises a lot of questions.

---

[47] Thomas Jefferson: Opinion on Residence Bill, 1790.ME.3:60

[48] Mill : *On Liberty* published by Clarendon Press 1980. Pg 79

[49] Mill *On Liberty* Pg. 62

[50]Citation. 549 U.S. 1145; 127 S. Ct. 1012;166 L. Ed. 2d 763; 2007 U.S.

First, it is assumed that all ideas will reach the marketplace. In a population of millions, a country does not have a forum whereby every individual idea on issues reach the marketplace. This just does not happen. Second, it is assumed that truth will win over an idea not based on truth. This too, is a fallacy. Not all, to whom an idea may be presented have the knowledge and depth of understanding regarding the question under deliberation and to make a wise distinction between truth and falsity and choose the truth. Third, it is assumed, that those determining upon the question, will make a choice based on rationality. The decision may not necessarily be made on thought process alone. People are swayed by emotions. They are swayed by pressure. They are swayed by vested interests. The theory also overlooks the strong impact by psychological warfare.

I would like to share here an interesting quotation by ***Herman Goering*** [51]at the ***Nuremberg Trials,*** "Of course the people don't want war. But after all, it's the leaders of the country who determine the policy, and it's always a simple matter to drag the people along whether it's a democracy, a fascist dictatorship, or a parliament, or a communist dictatorship. Voice or no voice, the people can always be brought to the bidding of the leaders. That is easy. All you have to do is tell them they are being attacked, and denounce the pacifists for lack of patriotism, and exposing the country to greater danger."[52]

However, supporters of the theory say that this theory of freedom of speech has lesser pitfalls than the absence of it, thereby placing all rights to censor with the government. "First Amendment freedoms are most in danger when the government seeks to control thought or to justify its laws for that impermissible end. The right to think is the beginning of freedom, and speech must be protected from the government because speech is the beginning of thought."–***Supreme Court Justice Anthony M. Kennedy.***[53]

Another advantage of freedom of speech is propagated in the theory of ***Promoting Tolerance.*** Associated with ***Professor Lee***

---

[51] German politician, military leader, leader member of Nazi Party. Veteran of World War1 , ace fighter pilot decorated with *Pour le Mente.* Appointed Commander-in-Chief of Air Force in 1935.
[52]*ALA(American Library Association)* Online Data. LINK: http://www.ala.org/offices/oif/ifissues/issuesrelatedlinks/quotations
[53]Ashcroft V. Free Speech Coalition (00-795) 198 F.3d 1083, affirmed.

***Bollinger***[54] , it embraces diversity. The theory puts forward the view that exchange of different viewpoints helps develop tolerance for opposing views, even if it is intolerant. By so doing, it helps develop better homogeneity between society members. This theory states that to have tolerance is an admirable quality, both individually and collectively. To tolerate an intolerant view itself is a great act of tolerance. Tolerance pertains to standards of morality, ethics, different religious beliefs, political approach, so on and so forth. Interestingly, in a society based on tolerance, as envisaged by Professor Bollinger, the government may not be able to legislate against the contents of speech. This act will be deemed as a violation of freedom of speech as it will be a prime example of intolerance. However, allowing all kinds of speech may lead to bias, bigotry, stereotyping and more intolerance. Hate speech can spiral into hate filled actions. For example, stating that "All Muslims are terrorists" is a manifestation of hatred towards a huge group of multicultural people on the basis of religion.

"Just as the right to speak and the right to refrain from speaking are complementary components of a broader concept of individual freedom of mind, so also the individual's freedom to choose his own creed is the counterpart of his right to refrain from accepting the creed established by the majority. At one time, it was thought that this right merely proscribed the preference of one Christian sect over another, but would not require equal respect for the conscience of the infidel, the atheist, or the adherent of a non-Christian faith such as Islam or Judaism. But when the underlying principle has been examined in the crucible of litigation, the court has unambiguously concluded that the individual freedom of conscience protected by the First Amendment embraces the right to select any religious faith or none at all. This conclusion derives support not only from the interest in respecting the individual's freedom of conscience, but also from the conviction that religious beliefs worthy of respect are the product of free and voluntary choice by the faithful and from recognition of the fact that the political interest in forestalling intolerance extends beyond intolerance among Christian sects — or even intolerance among religions — to encompass intolerance of the disbeliever and the uncertain."[55]

---

[54] Professor Lee C. Bollinger is a lawyer serving as 19th President of the Columbia University USA. Author of four books including *The Tolerant Society: Freedom of Speech and Extremist Speech in America(Oxford University Press, 1986)*

[55] Supreme Court Justice John Paul Stevens in Wallace V. Jaffree 1985

The important question that arises here with reference to this theory is that, is tolerance of diverse ideas more important than the negative cascading effect it can have on the society itself? To share an example, the Ku Klux Klan, an anti-Semitic, racist group which believes in white supremacy, and implementation of violence to achieve its objectives. Should members of this group be allowed to influence minds openly in pursuance of this theory? There are people out there who have predetermined mind sets. These mind sets create disenchantment in the society, by spreading hatred and violence.

On March 27th 2012, a news report, recounts how a JetBlue pilot stormed through his plane screaming, "They're going to take us down." Further, "Josh Redick, who was sitting near the middle of the plane, said the captain seemed 'irate' and was 'spouting off about Afghanistan and souls and al-Qaida.' The outburst came weeks after an American Airlines flight attendant was taken off a plane for rambling about 9/11 and her fears the plane would crash."[56]

Although one cannot overrule the thought that a close encounter with terrorism may be the cause, with the pilot of JetBlue, likely chances are, this breakdown may be due to the impact of an avalanche of negative reports by media and personal free exchange of views. Reports, opinions, that can have such disastrous effect on society members cannot be supported. Different people have different levels of breakdown thresholds.

Irresponsible reporting and creating stereotypes, has nothing to do with creating tolerance in society, conversely it creates fear, wariness of each other and intolerance.

In a world brought increasingly closer owing to multicultural and multiethnic fabric of societies as a result of immigration, it can become an increasingly volatile situation if certain vested interest groups are allowed to spew hatred against others which will be detrimental to the larger interest of the society.

This theory assumes good will, lack of use of propaganda, and a conscious avoidance of hate filled words in dialogue. ***Albert Einstein*** was bull's eye when he opined, "Laws alone cannot secure freedom of

---

[56] News Report by Associated Press published on 27th March 2012 in The Washington Post titled "Passenger: JetBlue Captain yells, "They're going to take us down" during Las-Vegas Bound flight

expression. In order that every man present his views without penalty there must be spirit of tolerance in the entire population."

Last but not the least, the theory that supports freedom of speech on basis that it ***Advances Autonomy.*** This theory propagates that by having freedom of speech and expression, this right manifests itself in many ways. Taking out a protest rally may not have the desired impact but it may be defined as self-definition. Not only in politics, but individual talents develop and bloom in an unbridled environment. This may be in art, drama, sculpture, poetry, prose and any other form of expression.

However, what we need to keep in mind here is that every country has its own culture and sub-culture. In a completely unchecked environment, things may get written, created, that may hurt the sensitivity of certain segments of the society. Example quoted may be Satanic Verses by ***Salman Rushdie*** that was banned in Pakistan.

***Christopher Coleman,*** says, " It is not intended to review the book in this article. Nevertheless, it must be said that it is a thoroughly vile book. There are sequences in the book, clearly referring to the Prophet Mohammed, which are calculated to be deeply offensive to believers of Islam."[57] He goes on to state, " Firstly, it is surely not right to insult people's religious beliefs in this way. The world is made of believers and non-believers, and while all democratic people would oppose the use of religion by various ruling circles to mislead and oppress the people, it is accepted that personal religious belief must be respected. This is only civilized behavior.......Freedom of expression must certainly be defended, but this cannot mean the right to publish anything. It must be in the context to what is or what is not in the interests of the masses of the people. It surely cannot be extended to the group insult and the incitement of millions, as with this book."[58]

As for the right to take out protest processions, the biggest objection I have to this is that when people are grouped together for political reasons and made to come out in a procession, reactions can quickly spiral out of control, even if the initial intention is peaceful. It can lead to

---

[57] Article originally published by The *New Weekly Magazine, 1st March , 1989,Volume 3, Number 8,by Chris Coleman,* member of National Union of Journalists, was the magazine's correspondent for Britain and Europe. Re published at SITE "Shunpiking". LINK: http://www.shunpiking.com/ol0105/05ControversyoverSatanic.htm

[58] Ibid

people getting hurt, even causing death, public and private property being destroyed.

In a Dissertation presented to the Faculty of the Graduate School of Cornell University, by Cheoljoon Chang [59] in 2008, he states, "Traditionally, autonomy has been understood in terms of pursuing an individual's self-interest by denying the government's paternalistic intervention from the perspective of anti-perfectionist liberalism. In the arena of free speech, autonomy has been the prevalent justification, by theorists, for the protection of individual speech with minimum governmental interference so as to increase an individual's self-fulfillment. However, collectivist approaches lay a persuasive foundation for governmental intervention in speech in order to reinforce people's autonomous deliberation through the democratic decision making process by restraining the side-effects of large media's monopolization of deliberation. This justified paternalism does not harm autonomy ,which is the foremost concern of individualist theorists of free speech."

In western dispensations, individuals, according to this theory, have to determine their own place in social and political structures. This is very much the creation of the Enlightenment Humanism . To be autonomous is to explore oneself–one's abilities, strengths and to translate these into forms of expression. To be guided in this process of exploration by external forces is a cruelty beyond imagination. However, the clash of values can come when the form of expression by the individual is at confrontation with the norms of the society. What it accepts and what it rejects. These challenges lead us to look at the relationship of individuals and societies and changing cultures. What is accepted and not accepted can be different for the same society in different areas and different times.

All the theories discussed above have their merits. As I had stated earlier, these theories make certain assumptions in terms of presence of individual and societal qualities. The foremost amongst it is the existence of democracy. The chapter will not be complete without a ***brief discussion on democracy***.

---

[59]Cheoljoon Chang was born in Gwang-ju, South Korea in 1975. He graduated from Yonsei University majoring law in 1998. After obtaining master's degree in the same University in 2000, he served in the military. He went to America in fall 2004 in order to study at Cornell Law School. His LL.M. degree allowed him to study further J.S.D. course at Cornell. His academic concern is constitutional law, law governing lawyers, and jurisprudence.

### *Relation of Theories of Freedom of Speech with Democracy*

U.S President Abraham Lincoln described democracy as, "Government of the people, by the people and for the people."[60] On a more legal level, it is defined in ***Black's Law Dictionary*** as "That form of government in which the sovereign power resides in and is exercised by the whole body of free citizens, directly or indirectly through a system of representation , as distinguished from a monarchy, aristocracy or oligarchy."[61]

This definition pre supposes some basic ingredients. First, the right to be exercised by "free citizens." Citizens to be free, must be free from pressures of any kind, may that be economic, emotional, coercive or of any other nature. A society where people are free and truly empowered to take a decision on the choice of their candidates.

Second, it presupposes a direct or indirect exercise of this right through a system of representation. The system of representation is divided at two levels. Representation process within the party and representation process to be elected for Parliament. Both the levels complete the circle of representation. The choice of candidate can either be direct or indirect. USA is a country which bases its elections on an indirect system. Many countries with parliamentary systems elect their presidents indirectly, like Italy, Germany, Hungary, Czech Republic and many others.

A democracy allows citizens equal rights to be elected. But do countries in the world follow the same "degrees" of democracy? I would say, no. The "degrees" or "levels" of democracy followed by different countries is different depending upon their economic conditions, social development, levels of education, and placement in comparison to international comity of nations.

In a perceptive article by ***Anup Shah,*** titled ***Democracy,*** he writes, " However, even in established democracies, there are pressures that threaten various democratic foundations. A democratic system's openness also allows it to attract those with vested interests to use the

---

[60] Abraham Lincoln(1809-1865)

[61] Black's Law Dictionary, Sixth Edition ,Pg. 432(*Centennial Edition 1891-1991)*

democratic process as a means to attain power and influence, even if they do not hold democratic principles dear."[62]

In a brilliant article, ***Tom Engelhardt,***[63] writes, " Support for democracy is the province of ideologists and propagandists. In the real world, elite dislike of democracy is the norm. The evidence is overwhelming that democracy is supported insofar as it contributes to social and economic objectives, a conclusion reluctantly conceded by the more serious scholarship.[64]

"Elite contempt for democracy was revealed dramatically in the reaction to the WikiLeaks exposures. Those that received most attention, with euphoric commentary, were cables reporting that Arabs support the U.S. stand on Iran. The reference was to the ruling dictators. The attitudes of the public were unmentioned. The guiding principle was articulated clearly by Carnegie Endowment Middle East specialist Marwan Muasher, formerly a high official of the Jordanian government: "There is nothing wrong, everything is under control." In short, if the dictators support us, what else could matter?"[65]

***Che Guevara,*** states," Democracy cannot consist solely of elections that are nearly always fictitious and managed by rich landowners and professional politicians."[66]

In an extremely interesting paper by ***Brian Martin***[67] titled "Democracy without elections" he says, "At the simplest level, voting simply doesn't work very well to promote serious challenges to prevailing power systems. The basic problem is quite simple. An elected representative is not tied in any substantial way to particular policies, whatever the preferences of the electorate. Influence on the politician is greatest at the time of election. Once elected, the representative is released from popular control (recall is virtually impossible before the

---

[62] Article by Anup Shah published on SITE: *Global Issues*. LINK: http://www.globalissues.org/article/761/democracy

[63] Engelhardt is the creator of Nation Institute's *tomdispatch.com* , an online blog. He is also the co-founder of the American Empire Project

[64] Article titled " Noam Chomsky, who owns the world?" Published 21st April 2011 by OpEdNews.com LINK: http://www.opednews.com/articles/Noam-Chomsky-Who-Owns-the-by-Tom-Engelhardt-110421-825.html

[65] Ibid

[66] Speech on August 8th 1961 Source: Our America –Kennedy and the Alliance for Progress ,Ocean Press, @2005

[67] Published in *Social Anarchism*, Number 21, 1995-96, pp. 18-51

next election) but continues to be exposed to powerful pressure groups, especially corporations, state bureaucracies and political party power brokers.... Usually the sell-outs are attributed to failures of personalities, but this is both unfair and misleading. Politicians are morally little different from anyone else. The expectations and pressures on them are much greater. Positions of great power both attract the most ambitious and ruthless people and bring out the worst features oı those who obtain them." He gives two alternatives to elections ie referendums and elections.

However, the point here is, to reinforce that unless and until there is democracy(and no, it is a process and not interchangeable with the term elections which at best is part of the process only), application of these theories in any nation not having "democracy" will be self-defeating-as democracy is a means to an end, not an end in itself.

In my article published in the ***Pakistan Observer***, titled, "Democracy or Dictatorship", I wrote, and share an excerpt here, "Even though there is no specific, universally accepted definition of 'democracy', there are two principles that any definition of democracy includes: equality and freedom. These principles are reflected in all citizens being equal before the law and having equal access to power, and the freedom of its citizens is secured by legitimized rights and liberties which are generally protected by a constitution. This explanation raises many questions: Do our political parties within their cadre, allow its workers equal access to power? Can a worker within a party structure have the opportunity to rise to the status of the Chairperson of that party, in due course of time? Lady Warsi's appointment as Conservative Party Chairperson and a full cabinet minister reflects on the progress the UK has made in terms of maturity in their political sphere. ...The second part of the definition deals with the right of citizens that is protected by the Constitution. These rights are determined from Articles 8 to Article 28 in the Constitution and deal with various rights of the citizens of Pakistan, for example, Article 25 professes that all citizens are equal before law and have a right to equal protection of law. Article 14 deals with inviolability of dignity of man and subject to law, in privacy of his home is inviolable, so on and so forth. However, words on a piece of paper without implementation loses any standing whatsoever, of any kind. Many think "elections" is synonymous with "democracy". I am often told that once the system is "allowed to continue" it will lead to a "better democracy". Those advocating this thought process fail to appreciate, that elections are a step only in the process of democracy, it is not democracy itself."[68]

I cannot but be reminded here of the masterly words of ***Aristotle,*** "If liberty and equality, as is thought by some are chiefly to be found in democracy, they will be best attained when all persons alike share in the government to the utmost."[69]

### *Concluding Comments*

The world has become a global village. Any incident happening in one part of the world is reported in another part of the world within seconds owing to electronic media, social media and forums like Twitter and Face Book. A very, very responsible approach is needed by the players involved to avoid trampling on this right of others while exercising their own.

This may be a tough call owing to multifaceted ethic and sub ethic groups, different hues of culture and religious beliefs.

Freedom of expression is a desired trait for any nation. We must all aspire to achieve this. However, with every freedom comes responsibility. Limitations that are reasonable and in the larger benefit of the society must be respected and followed. Not because they are forced, but because of the understanding that this leads to harmony. Similarly, the theories that propagate freedom of speech are to be admired for their forceful support. Each is valid. However, it carries an assumption that all nations follow a "pure" form of democracy. This is what nations must aspire to. Though they might not be at equal levels of democracy today. Democracy and freedom of expression are two sides to a coin. One cannot exist without the other.

Even today nations around the world are struggling to decide where to draw a line. What should be the balanced boundaries drawn in exercise of the right to the freedom of expression.

---

[68] LINK: http://pakobserver.net/detailnews.asp?id=40743

[69] Aristotle in his treatise *Politics.* Quoted in The Telegraph UK titled, "Famous quotes about Democracy" 12th July 2007.

# Chapter II

## Freedom of Expression in Pakistan (Part I)

The concept of freedom of expression in Pakistan was dealt by Article 19(Freedom of Speech etc) and Article 204(Contempt of Court) and these are to be read together for understanding; dealt in two parts for lucidity. However, as I had written these chapters and moved on, a new Contempt of Court Bill 2012 was approved, repealing Article 204. The said law was struck down by the Supreme Court in August 2012 and the Ordinance of Contempt of Court 2003 stands revived in its stead.

### *Text of Article 19 in Constitution of Pakistan 1973*

***Article 19:"Freedom of Speech etc:-*** Every citizen shall have the right of freedom of speech and expression, and there shall be freedom of the Press, subject to any reasonable restriction imposed by law in the interest of the glory of Islam, or the integrity, security or defence of Pakistan or any part thereof, friendly relations with foreign states, public order, decency or morality, or in relation to contempt of court[commission] of or incitement to an offence."[70]

The Constitution did not originally include the right to citizens of Pakistan to allow access to information, as stated in Article 19 of the United Nations Bill of Human Rights. Article 19A was inserted to cover the right of access to information, much later.

[70] Constitution of the Islamic Republic of Pakistan by Justice Muhammad Munir, Formerly Chief Justice of Pakistan Vol. I published in 1996 by PLD Publishers, Pg 345

***Article 19A: "Right to Information:-*** Every citizen shall have the right to have access to information in all matters of public importance subject to regulation and reasonable restrictions imposed by law."[71]

Certain terms used in Article 19 must be understood for better grasp of the law.

## *Explanation of Terms used within the Article 19*

The first is the term "citizen". ***Merriam-Webster***[72]defines citizen as, "an inhabitant of city or a town; especially one entitled to certain privileges and rights of a freeman."[73] Another definition is, "Member of a State."[74]

"Citizens are members of a political community , who in their associated capacity, have established or submitted themselves, to the dominion of a government, for the promotion of their general welfare and the protection of their individual as well as collective rights."*Herriot v. City of Seattle, 81 Walsh . 2d 48, 500 P. 2d 101,109*[75] A citizen of a country in a layman's language, is a citizen of a country either by birth, or by acquiring citizenship of the given country. It does not award right of freedom of speech and expression to one group of people, whether based on gender, religion, political affiliation, ethnicity ,education or any other ground and deny it to the other.

Pakistan Constitution by virtue of Article 19 awards the right of freedom of expression and speech to all its citizens.

Being a **citizen of Pakistan**, the Constitution of Pakistan stipulates equal freedom to people from different walks of life ie professions, education levels, sects, political affiliations, cultural backgrounds, to exercise the right of freedom of expression and speech. Interestingly, the right is awarded to every citizen of Pakistan. Briefly, I would like to touch upon the issue of dual nationality. This issue was highlighted recently by the media recently when the Supreme Court declared null and void the

---

[71] The Constitution of Pakistan on Pakistani. Org Part II Fundamental Rights and Principles of Policy. LINK: http://www.pakistani.org/pakistan/constitution/part2.ch1.html

[72] An Encyclopedia Brittanica Company

[73] Merriam-Webster Online Page: m.w.com LINK: http://www.merriam-webster.com/dictionary/citizen

[74] Ibid

[75] Black's Law Dictionary Sixth Edition, Centennial Edition(1891-1991) Pg 244

seat in the Parliament of many members owing to the reason of being dual nationals. Article 5 of the Constitution of Pakistan makes it impossible for a person holding a Pakistani nationality to owe allegiance to another country. It clearly states:

**5. Loyalty to State and obedience to Constitution and law.**

(1) Loyalty to the State is the basic duty of every citizen.

(2) Obedience to the Constitution and law is the [inviolable] obligation of every citizen wherever he may be and of every other person for the time being within Pakistan.

Many political pundits and intellectuals claim dual citizenship may lead to conflict of interest in certain cases. Freedom of expression, yes, but not at the cost of compromising national interests. To quote one example only, I share here the *Oath of Allegiance* taken for citizenship in USA:

*'"I hereby declare, on oath, that I absolutely and entirely renounce and abjure all allegiance and fidelity to any foreign prince, potentate, state or sovereignty, of whom or which I have heretofore been a subject or citizen; that I will support and defend the Constitution and laws of the United States of America against all enemies, foreign and domestic; that I will bear true faith and allegiance to the same; that I will bear arms on behalf of the United States when required by the law; that I will perform noncombatant service in the armed forces of the United States when required by the law; that I will perform work of national importance under civilian direction when required by the law; and that I take this obligation freely without any mental reservation or purpose of evasion; so help me God."*

How can Article 5 and the Oath of Allegiance to USA be reconciled?

It was in the Constitution of 1973 when **Freedom of the Press** came as an explicit right. By press, today, it would be understood as all means of mass communication, including the print media, being the oldest form of modern communication. In today's world of modern technology, the definition shall also apply to the electronic media.

Freedom of the press is the main ingredient in a nation aspiring to good governance. A press free to comment on the efficiency of government and works as a "watchdog" to the greater national interests.

It is also called the fourth pillar of the state because of the role it plays in informing the public on issues of public interest.

More, and more, it is being debated to what "levels" and "degrees" freedom of expression and speech may be awarded to press. Should the right be absolute? As we studied the concept of freedom of expression and speech in Chapter 1, we are wise to the fact that, no right is absolute. For the greater good of society, the right is curtailed by certain given limitations.

The following paragraph expresses the importance of a free press:

"It needs no emphasis that a free press, which is neither directed by the executive, nor subjected to censorship, is a vital element in a free State, in particular, a free, regularly published Political Press is essential in a modern democracy. The citizen called upon to make political decisions, must be comprehensively informed, know the opinion of others, and be able to weigh them against each other. The Press keeps these dialogues alive, it provides the information, adopts its own point of view, and thus works as a directive giving force to the public debate. It stands as a permanent means of communication and control between the people and their elected representatives, in the Parliament and Government." (*Journal of the International Commission of Jurists Vol VIII, p. 132)*[76]

However, what the paragraph above assumes, is that press not directed by the executive is free from all direction and all pressures. It assumes complete impartiality by all players, whether it is the owner, or the worker, to be free from biases, political affiliations and prejudices. It assumes that even if the biases , prejudices and political affiliations exist, it will not come in play while putting forth opinions and discussing issues of public interests for the citizens to form their opinion. This is not the ground reality. Even in USA where media is far more developed than in Pakistan and the principles of democracy deeply etched in the fabric of the society as compared to an evolving democratic country like Pakistan, media is not free from prejudices.

---

[76] Constitution of the Islamic Republic of Pakistan by Justice Munir, Formerly Chief Justice of Pakistan, published by PLD Publishers 1996, Pg 349

In an article titled , "Who rules America?"[77] biases projected by various media groups in USA owing to ownership affiliations are discussed in considerable detail–the biases involved and the resulting "angle" of news.

In an interesting ***Express News Blogpost***[78] commenting on a biased press , the writer says and I quote:

"A blog on the *TIME* magazine website rejected the concept of a proper border between Pakistan and Afghanistan. The post states that: "there is no well-defined difference between the Pakistani military and anti-American insurgents crowded along (the) rugged frontier."[79] The writer goes on to state," The report by Mark Thompson concludes that the American forces mistook Pakistani forces as Taliban militants by accident and were confused about the border demarcation between Pakistan and Afghanistan.

"Perhaps Thompson does not know that the attacks were conducted through gunship helicopters and jets which are fully equipped with GPS and can easily distinguish between the borders of two countries. The author also conveniently forgot to mention what would have happened if a similar "mistake" was made by Pakistani forces on NATO troops."[80]

The writer of the above piece gives extracts on NATO attacks coverage by leading newspapers like the Washington Post, New York Times, USA Today, ABC News and others to support his point of view as to how media is used to propagate the perspective of vested interest groups while completely ignoring the other side of the argument. *The Other View* as I would describe it.

Pakistan media , especially the print media, has been under restrictions of all sorts, and the journalists have suffered all kinds of punishments and threats for being vocal against policies by the various governments. The non-state owned electronic media came into existence in early 2000s and is in the fledgling stages needing direction, training and guidance for better coverage of issues, expression of views and how coverage should be done. This was missing till the PEMRA Amendment

---

[77] Published by "The National Alliance" in November 2004

[78] Express Tribune Blogs , Article titled, "The US Media(biased)version of the NATO Attack by *Gulfam Mustufa* dated 28th November 2011

[79] Ibid

[80] Ibid

2007, to a limited degree. However, a fast developing electronic media makes it unavoidable to revisit policies. This is discussed in great detail in a later chapter.

There has been no consistency to press freedom in Pakistan. There has been a proliferation of newspapers and channels often ignoring the quality of contents(more often than not related to electronic media), leading to a reprimand or clamp down by the concerned institutions, of TV channels, thereby leading to the accusation that freedom of expression is being violated.

This problem is not restrictived to Pakistan alone. ***Kuldip Nayar***[81] in an article titled, "***Freedom of Press***" [82]states, "How free is the media or, for that matter, how free is the right to express one-self? This is the question which has arisen in India after the three speeches, one by Vice-President Hamid Ansari, another by Prime Minister Manmohan Singh and yet another by Justice Markandey Katju, Chief of Press Council.

"The right to say has assumed all the more importance after Salman Rushdie's non-participation at the Jaipur Literary Festival because of threats. In Pune, screening of a documentary on Kashmir was stopped following protests by the students' wing of the BJP. Talking of the first two speeches, both Vice-President and the Prime Minister have asked the media to introspect their role because of sensationalism that has crept into their dissemination. There was not even a hint of direct or indirect control of the media in their speeches. However, Justice Katju has warned the media that some regulation may have to be imposed as self-regulation is no regulation."[83]

Freedom of press means many things. It includes that the advertising cuts will not be made on a house of media which directly affects the income . Government releases many advertisements, that are a source of income for the newspapers/channels. If government curtails their advertisement, it will be considered akin to curtailment of freedom of expression. Freedom of press also means that the press has the right to publish not only its own views but also those designated correspondents. "Any restrictions to the right to publish, to disseminate information, or to

---

[81] Veteran Indian journalist, syndicated columnist, human right activist and author, left-wing political commentator, also Member of Upper House Parliament in 1997

[82] Published by "Pakistan Today" on Sunday 5th February 2012

[83] Ibid

circulate would be considered an attack on freedom of press. When we say freedom of the press, it implies right to circulate, to include within its ambit, the matter to be circulated as well as the volume of circulation."[84]

I would like to reiterate here, for emphasis, with vested interests involved, this open cheque can lead to serving vested interests at the cost of national interests. Freedom of publication is a huge responsibility. To whom are we entrusting the responsibility to? In a race to sell more than the competitor, media panders to sensationalism, indulging in speculations that can ultimately harm the national interests. This tendency must be curbed.

The Constitution of USA, forbids any statutes that impose **pre-censorship** . ***Pre-censorship*** means censoring before something is presented ie films, advertisements, print media and other mediums of mass communication. Pre-censorship may rightly be deemed as a restriction on the exercise of right of freedom of speech on the press in light of boundaries already laid down in form of exceptions contained within Article 19.

In certain cases however, it may be justified. Owing to a proliferation of TV channels showing Indian Movies 24/7, some may be controversial and not in line with the cultural norms and the message content, inappropriate for Pakistani viewership. One example is the film, ***Delhi Belly,*** that was axed by pre–censorship. According to a news report, "Delhi Belly, the latest Indian comedy film has been banned in Pakistan due to its abusive language and bold scenes..... the dialogues of film are offensive and also the songs are controversial. Although a private screening was done in Lahore but after watching the movie some influential Pakistani film personalities called its ban."[85]

More recently, the Indian film ***Agent Vinod*** faced a similar ban. According to a news report, "Pakistan banned the Indian film 'Agent Vinod' a few days before its scheduled release, likely because of its critical portrayal of the country's generals and spies. They are shown providing

---

[84] Constitution of The Islamic Republic of Pakistan by Justice Munir , Formerly the Chief Justice of Pakistan, published by PLD Publishers , 1996. Pg 349

[85] The Daily Mail Online Edition LINK: http://dailymailnews.com/0711/08/ShowBiz/index.php?id=2

support for the Taliban in Afghanistan and scheming to set off a nuclear suitcase bomb in India's capital."[86]

The latest example is the banning of 'Ek Tha Tiger' by PEMRA.[87] The grounds were that it tarnished the image of ISI. A letter was issued by PEMRA (Pakistan Electronic Media Authority) to all satellite TV channels and cable networks last week It said that *Ek Tha Tiger*, set for world release on August 15, is "reportedly based on the activities of ISI and RAW." It continues to state, "Besides, the basic theme of the story revolves around Inter-Services Intelligence (ISI) agency with the objective to tarnish the image of state owned institution." PEMRA directed the channels and cable networks to "refrain from airing promos/reviews" of the movie till it is issued a no-objection certificate by the Central Board of Film Censors.

"The matter should be given utmost preference and due care be ensured to uphold the country's image and any unintentional lapse in this regard be avoided," the letter added. The film sees Salman play a Research and Analysis Wing (RAW) agent who is sent to Pakistan to keep an eye on a college professor's activities, who is suspected of selling missile technology secrets to Pakistan.

That the big picture has tremendous impact on its viewers–of that there is no doubt. Take, for example, the recent viewing of the film "Batman" in Colorado in July 2012.The 250-seater cinema was packed with families and high school students. Holmes, who dropped out of a neuroscience Ph.D. at the University of Colorado School of Medicine last month, shot 71 people, including at least one person in an adjacent cinema who was hit as the bullets penetrated the walls.[88] When Holmes was arrested outside the cinema, he told the police: "I'm the Joker."

## For interpretation of Freedom of Expression and Freedom of Speech, please refer to Chapter 1

The latter part of Article 19 explains the boundaries, which are not to be crossed in exercise of this right by citizens and press of Pakistan. Let us explore these one by one.

---

[86] The Dawn Newspaper published 26th March 2012 titled," Agent Vinod banned from Pakistani cinemas"

[87] The Times of India 10th July 2012 titled ,'Pakistan restrains airing of Ek Tha Tiger.

[88] The Telegraph, 'Batman cinema shooting: killer said he was 'The Joker' published 20th July 2012 By Gordon Rayner, Mark Hughes in New York and Nick Allen in Denver.

## *Exceptions to Article 19 Constitution of Pakistan*

Exceptions denote the bar to the right of exercise of right to exercise freedom of speech both by citizens and press. We cannot violate the bar and then cry foul. Let us study the exceptions to the freedom of speech.

### *The first exception is stating, doing or acting in a way that opposes the glory of Islam:*

Many students over the years have asked me, why glory of Islam? Why not any act against the religions of the minorities of Pakistan? I would like to address this question in these pages.

Since Article 2 of the Constitution of Pakistan 1973 declares Islam as the state religion of Pakistan[89], any act said, done or viewed as against the glory of Islam will not be covered by the umbrella of Freedom of Expression and Speech. According to a research,[90] census data shows 96% of Pakistan's population is Muslim. It therefore stands to logic that the sensitivity of the major chunk of population's religion should be respected. In no way does this mean, or be taken to mean, that the feelings of the minorities should be ignored. The Chapter of Fundamental Rights in the Constitution from Article 7 to Article 40 fully applies to all citizens of Pakistan, inclusive of minorities whether a Christian, Hindu, Sikh, Parsee or belonging to any other religion.

In May 2010, Pakistan Authorities blocked access to Facebook, a popular social site, after it offered its users a competition page to make drawings of the Prophet Muhammad. According to a news report[91], "The court action was triggered by a Facebook page entitled Everybody Draw Mohammad Day – May 20 which contains over 200 images, many of them certain to offend Muslims, who consider all depictions of the prophet to be blasphemous.

"As of today, the site had 5,000 followers and listed links to the pages of prominent critics of Islam, such as the rightwing Dutch politician Geert Wilders and the Somali feminist Ayaan Hirsi Ali."

---

[89] The Constitution of The Islamic Republic of Pakistan 1973 published by Irfan Law Book House Lahore in 1993 with commentary by *Muhammad Daud Advocate*

[90] Census Data by New World Encyclopedia

[91] News Report by Declan Walsh for The Guardian UK published Wednesday 19th May 2010

The ban stayed for two weeks but as it was reported, "....... it would continue to block individual pages containing 'blasphemous' content."[92]

The same news of ban was carried by ABC News and I would like to share extract of the Report:

"The Facebook page threatens to trigger another round of outrage and possibly violence over cartoon versions of the prophet."[93] It goes on to state, " The sketch competition on Facebook has the potential to attract wrath and criticism from not only Pakistan but the entire Islamic world."[94]

I had supported the ban then. On Express 24/7(English Channel), I was asked to share my expert opinion on this subject when the ban took place, on the 9.00 pm Khabarnama,(News Time). My reasons for the support were simple. First, it was against the respect we award to the Holy Prophet(PBUH). Secondly, in a country where the proportion of educated people is low, had the government not banned the page, it could have been viewed as diminishing the issue. This in turn could have led to protests of destructive nature.

***The second exception is; no one can use freedom of expression or speech to damage or violate the security, defense and integrity of Pakistan:***

The government has an inherent right to protect the security of the motherland. It includes any *part* of Pakistan.

Therefore, any group of people, country or entity cannot threaten the security of Pakistan by claiming freedom of expression, either through *external threats* nor by *internal threats*. Security of the country will also mean an attempt to overthrow the government or create a public disorder of a serious nature that becomes a security hazard.

---

[92] News Report by Declan Walsh for The Guardian UK published Monday 31st May 2010
[93] Official website for abc NEWS LINK: http://abcnews.go.com/Technology/International/facebook-banned-pakistan-prophet-muhammad-sketch-competition/story?id=10688625#.T3lxXjGw8kg
[94] Ibid

According to ***Merriam-Webster***, defense will mean, "means or method of defending or protecting oneself, one's team, etc *also* a defensive structure."[95]

Integrity of a country would mean, "the state of being united as one complete thing ie the territorial integrity of a country."[96]

On 26th November 2011 NATO attack took place on two military check posts of Pakistan along the Afghanistan-Pakistan border. Two NATO *Apache helicopters*[97], an *AC -130 gunship*[98] and two *F-15E Eagle Fighter jets* entered our area of ***Salala.*** In the ensuing fire they opened on Pakistan check posts, up to 24 [99]Pakistani soldiers were killed and 13[100] others injured.

Drone attack in the territory of Pakistan will be deemed as an attack on the security of Pakistan. A series of drone attacks have been made in Pakistan on targeted areas of North West Pakistan. " Drones or the unmanned aerial vehicles are the new weapon of armed warfare. A large number of civilians including women, children, men were killed in these attacks. The first known attack by the U.S drone inside Pakistan killed two children ."[101]

"Bureau of Investigative Journalism estimates, that out of 312 drone strikes, of which an incredible 260 have been under Barack Obama, over 3000 people have been killed, including 175 children."[102] In a rare acknowledgement of the controversial strikes, Barack Obama, "confirmed" that unmanned drones have regularly struck Pakistan's tribal areas in his government's efforts to dismantle what it alleges are al-Qaeda

---

[95] Merriam-Webster an Encyclopedia Brittanica Company.(m.w.com) LINK: http://www.merriam-webster.com/dictionary/defense

[96] *Longman Dictionary of Contemporary English. LINK:* http://www.ldoceonline.com/dictionary/integrity

[97] Saeed Shah; Luke Harding (29 November 2011). "Taliban may have lured Nato forces to attack Pakistani outpost – US". *The Guardian* (London). Retrieved 29 November 2011

[98] Ibid

[99] Article by Nazar ul Islam "NATO 'regrets' Pakistan Strike" published by *Newsweek* November 27th 2011

[100] *BBC News Report "Pakistan buries 24 troops killed in NATO airstrike"* posted on 27th November 2011 LINK: http://www.bbc.co.uk/news/world-asia-15908760

[101] *Titled, "The Bush Years: Pakistan Strikes 2004-2009" by* The Bureau of Investigative Journalism posted 17th June 2004. LINK: http://www.thebureauinvestigates.com/2011/08/10/the-bush-years-2004-2009/

[102] *"The Case Against Drone Attacks"* by Asad Rahim Khan published by *Express Tribune, Pakistan,* dated 7th March 2012

sanctuaries in the region. Obama's rare public acknowledgement of the US drone programme in Pakistan came on Monday during an hour-long online video chat with users of the Google social network.....The controversial drone programme run by the CIA has often been met with protests in Pakistan amid concerns of civilian casualties. ..A spokesperson for Pakistan's foreign ministry reiterated the government's public protest in response to Obama's comments."[103]

"Amnesty International, the UK-based rights group, called for the US to pay closer attention to the Pakistani civilians being killed by drones."[104]

It was not till 12th March 2012 that news came from a British Law firm that " it was to sue Foreign Secretary William Hague, on behalf of a Pakistani man, over claims that British Intelligence was used to assist drone attacks."[105]

"Khan says his father, Malik Daud, was killed by a drone missile while at a council of elders meeting in northwest Pakistan. Drone attacks have become a key feature of US President Barack Obama's fight against terrorism in Pakistan, but many inhabitants are deeply unhappy about the civilian death toll incurred in the raids."[106]These are *external* threats to Pakistan.

In a later development, White House counter-terrorism adviser John Brennan offered a rare public defense of drone strikes on Monday and said the attacks were legal and ethical and were directed only at "legitimate military targets."[107]

"It justifies US use of drone strategy on grounds that the government of the country itself refuses to take appropriate action against militants, in an indirect reference to Pakistan. A two day seminar was held in Washington, peace activists had insisted and urged the US government to halt the drone strikes, thus eliciting the first ever detailed statement . Brennan rejected both arguments put forth in the Seminar (a) it was illegal and unethical and (b)it caused death of many innocent civilians."[108]

---

[103] *"Obama admits Pakistan drone strikes"* published by ALJAZEERA 31st Jan 2012
[104] Ibid
[105] *"Britain's Hague sued over Pakistan drone attacks: Legal Firm"* published by *Pakistan Today* dated 12th March 2012
[106] Ibid.
[107] Anwar Iqbal for Dawn News titled," *Drone strikes legal, ethical says US* "dated 1st May 2012
[108] Ibid.

In a speech that was delivered at the occasion of Bin Laden's death anniversary, he stated drones were only used in case of imminent threat.[109]

***Ejaz Haider***[110], commenting on Brennan's stance on behalf of the White House, in his piece states, "Domestic law cannot override accepted principles of international law or customary state practice, especially the principle of non-intervention. Doing so is an exercise of power, not law. Two, nothing in international law or the UNSC legal regime on terrorism allows State X to operate on the territory of State Y unless the latter expressly permits such action. Therefore, the issue of 'unable or unwilling' does not arise as grounds for unilateral determination and action. Nor can such be determined by another state through its own estimation because any action flowing from such unilateralism cannot be subjected to a limiting principle, i.e., there will be no limit to what a powerful state could do to weaker states."[111]

In the same piece he goes on to comment that "Brennan also defended the use of drones on the principles of necessity, distinction, proportionality and humanity and gave reasons for why such use is wise. The problem with his framework is that the operation of these 'principles' — and these factors are essentially operational, not foundational — becomes relevant *only* after it has been determined that it is indeed legal for a state to use drones (or force) in the manner that the US has done so far and which scores of experts deem to be illegal because it is unilateral and violates the basic principle of non-intervention. In other words, the necessity, distinction, proportionality and humanity of weapon system X as opposed to Y becomes a relevant defence or debate only after the legality of the conflict in which it is to be used and the manner of such usage has been accepted."[112]

***Center for Research & Security Studies*** share gruesome reports of five bloody incidents since the middle of December 2011 causing over 80 deaths, mostly personnel from security, rocking and disrupting the security and civilian apparatus. At least 25 para-military troops were executed in early January. Also in early January, 35 died in a car bomb "that ripped through a bus terminal in the town of Jamrud in

---

[109] Ibid.

[110] The writer is a senior journalist and has held several editorial positions including most recently at The Friday Times. He was a Ford Scholar at UIUC, a visiting fellow at the Brookings Institute

[111] Titled *Brennan's Realpolitik*! Published by Express Tribune on 1st May 2012

[112] Ibid.

the Khyber Agency."[113] In early January, 14 or so personnel of the Frontier Corps died as they were ambushed in Turbat District. On 14th June, three civilians, a policeman and four bombers were killed in a militant attack.[114]

Examples like these can be quoted by hundreds, and are a threat to the security of Pakistan *internally*. All those who indulge in such nefarious crimes are guilty of endangering the security of Pakistan and cannot be allowed to carry on such acts under the garb of freedom of expression.

A United States Congress Committee on Foreign Affairs in early February 2012 held a meeting for the exclusive discussion on issues in Balochistan. Republican Congressman Dana Rohrabacher, chaired the hearing. Rohrabacher, earlier, had showed support for an independent Balochistan, in his article. He wrote, "Perhaps we should even consider support for a Balochistan carved out of Pakistan to diminish radical power there (in Pakistan)."[115]

In another article, on the same subject, writer ***Eddie Walsh***[116]said a few congressmen are presenting an alternative policy to U S A for Southwest Asia. It supports remnants of Northern Alliance and Baloch insurgents, who seek to carve out an independent Balochistan, mostly from Pakistan area. To quote Walsh, "They have asserted that an independent Balochistan and autonomous Northern Alliance territories would provide Western companies with valuable new economic opportunities, which could help offset the costs of two failed wars in Afghanistan and Iraq and spur economic growth following the global economic downturn. They have also said that the West should do so to prevent potential strategic adversaries, including China, Iran, Pakistan, and Russia, from profiting off the natural resources of Central and Southwest Asia at their expense."[117]

It is interesting to note that the term used by ***Ishaal Zehra*** in his article on the same subject is "insurgents"; "A glimpse into Balochistan

---

[113] Center for Research and Security Studies Online Site. Titled, "Pakistan's security status under attack again!" posted 15th Jan 2012 LINK: http://crss.pk/beta/?p=2248

[114] Ibid

[115] Pakistan Today: *"Congressional Meeting Annoys Pakistan"* published 8th Feb 2012

[116] Foreign Correspondent for ALJAZEERA covering Africa and Asia-Pacific.

[117] "Should the US support an independent Baluchistan?" Published 3rd March 2012 in ALJAZEERA

region confirms the large number of militant, insurgent and sectarian attacks in 2010."[118]

***Merriam-Webster*** defines an insurgent as, "a person who revolts against civil authority or an established government..."[119]

Interestingly, Eddie shares extract from on-the-record interview with Dana Rohrabacher:

*"There is a natural extension from the Berlin meeting with the Northern Alliance to the Balochistan bill. I have always stood for self-determination, but there are certain things that activate me to start pushing more on that philosophy. Clearly, the whole issue of the Taliban being reintegrated in Afghanistan and Pakistan, providing safe haven to terrorists like Bin Laden, are major factors. There is also my support for immediately withdrawing troops from Afghanistan. To do so, we need to have a major policy dialogue on what our policy is in Southwest Asia, how we properly transition out of Afghanistan, and what will be our ongoing relationship with Pakistan. Balochistan is clearly part of that debate."*[120]

This hearing created an uproar in Pakistan. It was seen as an attack on the integrity and oneness of Pakistan. No country can join hands with insurgents with an aim to balkanize that country. Of course it annoyed Pakistan and put further strain on the relationship between both the countries. The following resolution was unanimously adopted by the Parliament of Pakistan:

**"RESOLUTION TO CONDEMN THE BLATANT INTERFERENCE IN PAKISTAN'S INTERNAL AFFAIRS EVIDENCED BY US CONGRESSIONAL FOREIGN RELATIONS SUB-COMMITTEE HEARING ON BALOCHISTAN ON 8TH FEBRUARY, 2012**

"This House strongly condemns the blatant interference in Pakistan's internal affairs evidenced by US Congressional Foreign Relations Sub-Committee hearing on Balochistan on 8th February, 2012.

---

[118] "America's lost sleep for Balochistan" on MARK THE TRUTH: http://www.markthetruth.com/current-affairs/2770-americas-lost-sleep-for-balochistan.html

[119] Merriam-Webster: An Encyclopedia Britannica Company LINK: http://www.merriam-webster.com/dictionary/insurgent

[120] "Should the US Support an Independent Baluchistan?" by Eddie Walsh, published 3rd March 2012 in ALJAZEERA

This House notes with great concern that at a time when Pakistan - US relations are already under severe stress, the holding of such a hearing by the US Congress cannot but jeopardize the healing process and further inflame public opinion against the US by adding to the prevailing sense of mistrust and suspicion regarding US intentions towards Pakistan.

This House, therefore, calls upon the Government of Pakistan to convey to the United States Administration, in no uncertain terms, that:-

a) such hearings relating to the internal affairs of Pakistan are totally unacceptable and the US Administration needs to play a more proactive role to discourage such ill-informed and motivated debate on sensitive issues relating to a sovereign country;
b) to re-build mutual trust and confidence, the US Administration should respect and comply with the will of the people of the Pakistan as expressed through various parliamentary resolutions and discontinue' drone attacks forthwith.

Sd/-

**Ch. Nisar Ali Khan**

Leader of the Opposition

National Assembly of Pakistan

**Resolution Date:** February 13, 2012"[121]

This is an unfortunate plan of proceeding by U S . Completely misguided. It has created more bad feeling and strengthened the anti - American feeling in the common man on the street rather than achieve any pressure scoring brownies. Leaving political expediencies aside, it has had an unhealthy cascading effect of an independent Balochistan being discussed by every Tom, Dick and Harry and every person, country, institution having an axe to grind or vested interests in supporting the handful of insurgents.

When we talk of exception under freedom of expression , we need to understand that no nation should violate the security and integrity of

[121] SITE National Assembly of Pakistan LINK: http://www.na.gov.pk/en/resolution_detail.php?id=57

Pakistan–and no Pakistani may be party with any one that does so. Hence the description of both internal and external threats to the security and integrity of Pakistan with modern day examples.

***Exercise of the right of freedom of expression and speech so to negatively effect the friendly relations Pakistan has with another country is also an abuse of this right:***

This ideally means, no one will commit an act that will endanger the relations of Pakistan with other states. In 2009, a coordinated attack was made on visiting ***Sri Lankan Cricket Team*** in Lahore. Eight died. "The police said the gunmen — using assault rifles, grenades and even antitank missiles — assaulted the bus with the Sri Lankan team at a grassy traffic circle near the city's main Qaddafi Stadium during a five day-match. Six police officers in an escort van were killed, and six cricketers were injured, the police said. Two bystanders were also killed."[122]

Incident like these can be a recipe for disaster between relations of Pakistan with the other country involved. Also, it projects a poor opinion of our country in the international comity of nations.

Wall Street Journal reporter ***Daniel Pearl,*** 38, was killed in 2002. He was kidnapped on his way to interview a Muslim fundamental leader in Pakistan. Later, FBI and Pakistani authorities received a videotape containing indisputable confirmation that he was dead. [123] The international reaction was swift and harsh. **The Wall Street Journal,** in a posting by a Staff Reporter, released a statement on the murder, stating, "His murder is an act of barbarism that makes a mockery of everything Danny's kidnappers claimed to believe in."[124] ***David Cohen,*** for ***London Evening Standard*** writes about the pain of Professor Judea Pearl, Daniel Pearl's father. " When Professor Judea Pearl says that he 'wants revenge' and that 'it's a natural, primitive feeling', you can understand why."[125]

Such incidents lead to having an impact, negative of course between Pakistan and the country in question and leave a scar. It has a far reaching

---

[122] *Jane Parlez* for New York Times titled, "For Pakistan, Attack Exposes Security Flaws", published 3rd March 2009.

[123] CNNWorld, posted February 21st 2002, titled, "Sources: U.S Journalist Daniel Pearl Dead".

[124] WSJ Online "Reporter Daniel Pearl is Dead, Killed by his Captors in Pakistan", posted 24th Feb 2002.LINK: http://online.wsj.com/public/resources/documents/pearl-022102.htm

[125] By Daniel Cohen, Senior Feature Reporter for *London Evening Standard* & carried by Daniel Pearl Foundation 1st Nov 2006

effect on the relationship between Pakistan and other states with which Pakistan has friendly relations, establishing Pakistan as an insecure state.

The murder of a Chinese woman, Jiang Hua and a Pakistani associate Mohammad Suliman Shams, who were targeted in a busy marketplace, in Peshawar , is suspicious. Jiang was on a tour of the region. The incident took place on 28th February 2012. ***The Express Tribune*** writes in its Editorial, " The murder of a Chinese woman and a Pakistani man in Peshawar on February 28, should remind Pakistan that even the strongest ties between nations must be tended to with great attention. Pakistan's relationship with China has kept the country afloat in many a difficult time, but this does not mean that China turns a blind eye to Pakistan's internal turmoil: the problem of militancy and the rise of religious extremism are issues that China takes very seriously. Pakistan must respect this concern if the country's vital link to its neighbor is to be maintained."[126]

As I had stated above, these incidents can have a negative impact on relationships that can and do have a rankling effect that lingers only to bloom in a major relationship issue at a later stage . They tend to pile up. Not disappear.

"Propaganda for a foreign State at war with a friendly country, or in favor of a claimant as against a person, who has been recognized as the sovereign of a foreign State , will fall within this exception."[127]

***Disturbing the public order is also an exception to the exercise of right of freedom of expression and speech:***

" Disturbing the public peace is punishable under Section 153-A Pakistan Penal Code. Making public utterances ,deliberately and maliciously intended to outrage the religious feelings of any class by insulting its religion.......will not receive any constitutional protection."[128]

Let us first see what exactly **public order** means. "The term public order has reference to the maintenance of conditions where under the orderly functioning of the government can be carried on. It is the duty of the government to ensure that the lives, properties, and liberties of the

---

[126] Editorial in *Express Tribune* titled, "Attack on Foreigner" published 1st March 2012

[127] Constitution of the Islamic Republic of Pakistan published by PLD Publishers, 1996, by *Justice Muhammad Munir,* Former Chief Justice of Pakistan, Pg 359

[128] Ibid.

citizens are not endangered. The term public order is wider than the term public safety and implies absence of internal order, rebellion, interference to the supply and distribution of essential commodities or services."[129]

Public order seeks to minimize crimes like arson, murders, rape, targeted violence, striking fear in the hearts of people in their free movement. Lack of public order can be strikingly destabilizing for economies creating fear, hatred between coexistence of ethnic groups and sub-groups and destroy the base of a peaceful society. Activities that are either politically motivated or criminally motivated, create a cascading effect of negativity, like kidnappings, misuse of power, illegal detentions, so on and so forth. In situations of breakdown of public order, people may be caught up in a rush, be trampled underfoot and in cases of shoot outs innocent bystanders may lose their lives.

***Hooligans in Khrushchev's Russia*** offers the first comprehensive study of how Soviet police, prosecutors, judges , and ordinary citizens during the Khrushchev's era (1953-64), understood, fought against, or embraced this catch-all kind of criminality. Swearing, drunkenness, promiscuity, playing loud music, brawling—in the Soviet Union these were not merely bad behavior, they were all forms of the crime of "hooliganism."

Defined as "rudely violating public order and expressing clear disrespect for society."[130]Our beautiful Karachi nicked the "City of Lights", is a victim of such breakdown of public order. World Report 2012 by Human Rights Watch, titled, "World Report 2012:Pakistan – Events of 2011"[131] taking Karachi as a case example states, "Karachi experienced an exceptionally high level of violence during the year, with some 800 persons killed."[132]

In another report by Islamabad ***Pulse,*** it states, " For the last two years, target killings have resulted in hundreds of casualties in Karachi. According to the HRCP statistics, a total of 1,138 people have been killed in the city during the first half of 2011, with 490 of them killed in targeted killings on different grounds including political, sectarian and ethnic basis. Almost 748 people lost their lives in Karachi targeted killings in

---

[129] Ibid Pg 360

[130] Hooligans in Khrushchev's Russia carried by University of Wisconsin Press, by Brian LaPierre, Assistant Professor of History at the University of Southern Mississippi

[131] LINK: http://www.hrw.org/world-report-2012/world-report-2012-pakistan

[132] Ibid

2010 alone. From the holy month of Ramadan to September 2011, more than 200 people lost their precious lives in Karachi. The situation is out of control because many political and ethnic groups are involved in this mass killing."[133]

***Also incitement to violence may not be committed while exercising the right to freedom of expression and speech:***

How do we determine what's incitement to violence and what is not? Any person, who, knowingly, urges another, by an act or by words to commit an offence under law, will be said to have incited that person to violence. Legally defined to incite will mean, "To arouse, urge, provoke, encourage, spur on, goad, stir up, instigate, set in motion, as to 'incite' a riot."[134]

Can media be used to incite violence?

Yes, it can.

The "angle" used in news and views, the choice of words, what is shown and how(special reference to electronic media), does create peace or incite people to violence. The huge impact of TV can no longer be ignored in our lives. Media has penetrated our bedrooms. It can create strong opinions. To a degree that perceptions become realities. Media trial of issues can result in making an innocent person the culprit and a culprit; innocent. Anchor persons hold sway over their followers. Not only in a developing country like Pakistan, but in USA as well. ***Oprah Winfrey*** is rated as possibly the most influential woman in the world, number 9 at a rating of 1-20 in the list of the most influential by ***The Telegraph.***[135] She is the undisputed "Queen of Talk" since the 1980's to date, forming opinions on issues that matter.

Likewise, Pakistan too, has its share of anchor persons both men and women having their own following. Depending on where an anchorperson, or media person stands on a particular issue, readers/viewers can be swayed to a particular point of view. The suicide of

---

[133] "Target Killing in Karachi: Possible way out" published 16th September 2011 by *Masood Ur Rehman Khattak* in Islamabad

[134] *Black's Law Dictionary, sixth edition. Centennial Edition (1891-1991) Pg 762*

[135] The Telegraph: 31st October 2007 LINK: http://www.telegraph.co.uk/news/worldnews/1435442/The-most-influential-US-liberals-1-20.html

Shamaila Faheem[136] is a case to the point. Taking one's own life is an act of violence. Shamaila was convinced the man who killed her husband will be freed without due process of law. In the media trial that ensued soon after the killing of her husband, instead of a balanced view point, discussions revolved around conspiracy theories and speculations.

In the final analysis, it is the negative and biased reporting, the conspiracy theories against the civilian government, the spontaneous and habitual anti Americanism that made Shumaila believe that justice would never be served in her case.

"I do not expect any justice from this government," said Shumaila Kanwal in a statement recorded by the doctor before she died. "That is why I want to kill myself."[137]

It goes on to state, "The media's sensationalism in their reporting and selective coverage of certain issues work to worsen problems in society and create unrest."[138]

Contempt of Court too, cannot be condoned as having constitutional cover. It falls within an exception of freedom of expression and speech. Dealt by Article 204 in the Constitution of Pakistan 1973, it is dealt with in detail in the next chapter as it is a subject by itself.

## *Explanation of Article 19A*

Before we discuss Article 19A , it will be pertinent to note that this was an amendment that came much after Article 19. The law of Freedom of Speech follows from Article 19 Universal Bill of Human Rights. The latter contained two sides. First the right to freedom of expression second, the right to access of information. The latter, did not form part of the Constitution of Pakistan till years later .

Focusing on Article 19-A, relates to the right of Access to Information. In order to share information, educate the public and bank discussions more on facts and less on speculations, access to information is mandatory. In an atmosphere of transparency, openness and sharing

---

[136] Wife of Faheem Shamshad, one of the two men killed by Raymond Davis in Lahore on 27th January 2011

[137] SITE: "Let's Build Pakistan", LINK: http://criticalppp.com/archives/39894

[138] Ibid

good information, propaganda and gossip dies a natural death. There are many examples to this effect.

The first Pakistani Prime Minister Liaqat Ali Khan was assassinated in Rawalpindi in broad daylight on 16th October 1951. To date, it has not been clarified as to who killed him and why. His murder irreparably damaged a fragile, newly hatched Pakistan. He was rushed to the hospital where he was attended by Dr Col. Mian and Dr Col. Sarwar, in spite of their best efforts the Prime Minister succumbed to his wounds.

Deaths remain mysterious and shrouded in more mystery. Gen. Zia-ul-Haq is another example. In a book, titled, "Shopping for Bombs," ***Gordon Correra***[139] disclosed the first link to Gen. Zia's death. He discloses that A.Q. Khan sold the first nuclear secrets to Iran in 1987. He feels in all likelihood, this was not with the approval of the General, who preferred the Arabs over Iran. Correra deals with many questions in the book. Was General Zia privy to the sale? Corerra feels it was unlikely. Or did he know about it? Was General Zia killed because he got too close to the information in August 1988?[140]

But there are conflicting versions, in absence of access to information, conspiracy theories flourish. In my opinion, the best report on the crash of the ill -fated flight was by ***Edward Jay Epstein***[141], for ***Vanity Fair*** , published September 1989.He discussed the various possibilities of who could have been the culprits. Soviets he felt were one. [142]

He writes, " Zia had offended Moscow to such a degree that it had declared publicly, only a week before the crash, that Zia's 'obstructionist policy cannot be tolerated.'[143]He further states, " In Delhi, Rajiv Gandhi, the prime minister of India, informed Pakistan on August 15 it would have cause 'to regret its behavior' in covertly supplying weapons to Sikh terrorists in India."[144]

---

[139] Gordon Correra was BBC Security Corrospondent

[140] *U. Mahesh.Prabhu* ,"Who Killed Zia-ul-Haq"?Review of book by Correra LINK:http://indiamahesh.wordpress.com/2007/12/23/who-killed-gen-zia-ul-haq/

[141] Born 1935, an American Investigative Journalist. Author of many books ,the first, *"Inquest: The Warren Commission and the Establishment of Truth"* published 1966

[142] "Who Killed Zia?" by Edward Jay Epstein published by Vanity Fair in September 1989

[143] Ibid

[144] Ibid

There is no conclusion to the reason leading to Gen Zia's death. Access to information needed to unearth the true culprits was not available for reasons best known to those in charge then.

Benazir Bhutto's death adds to the unfortunate chapter of killings of those at the helm of affairs and in limelight. On the ill- fated date of 27th December 2007 she was killed in Rawalpindi. Twice Prime Minister of Pakistan, on her way back from a political rally in Liaqat National Bagh, a suicide bomb was detonated immediately following the shooting. Seven people including five militants and two policemen were indicted by an antiterrorism court for her murder.[145] Once again, we face an impasse here to reach the bottom of the truth as to who, is behind the murder of Benazir Bhutto.

Lack of access to information cases extend not only to murders, but financial scams, corruption cases, kidnappings excetra. And before we think that this kind of thing happen in Pakistan only, re think quick on that one! It does not. Remember the gorgeous ***Princess Diana?*** Conspiracy theories surround her death even to this date. In a car accident with her friend Dodi Al Fayed, both he and his driver Henri Paul died on the spot as the car collided into a pillar in the Alma Tunnel of Central Paris. Diana was taken by ambulance to Pitié-Salpétrière Hospital, where she died a few hours later of cardiac arrest. First reports stated the driver was speeding to escape the paparazzi photographers. Later, it came to surface that the driver had an alcohol level in blood three times higher than the legally allowed limit. Though after two years of investigation, French courts gave a verdict, that it was owing to Henri-Paul being intoxicated and speeding to escape the paparazzi photographers that caused the accident,[146] the Scotland Yard investigators after 7 years of the accident returned to the site of the accident with laser technology which was not available at the time of the accident. It is reported that the tunnel was closed off for eight hours on 25th February 2005.[147] Many conspiracy theories abound on this tragic death.

***John F Kennedy,*** the 35th President of the United States of America, was assassinated on 22rd November 1963 in Dealy Plaza, Dallas, Texas. Evelyn Lincoln, former secretary to President Kennedy, made a list

---

[145] New York Times, news report by *Waqar Jillani,* published 5th November 2011 titled, "Pakistan indicts 7 in Bhutto Assassination"

[146] "British Police Investigate Diana Crash Site", By Buddy. T on About.com LINK:http://alcoholism.about.com/od/diana/a/diana020516.htm

[147] Ibid.

of possible suspects immediately after he was gunned down.[148] It was concluded by the 10-month Warren Commission set up to investigate the assassination concluded that Lee Harvey Oswald acted alone in assassinating the president.[149] In a story on ***CBSNews.com by Jarrett Murphy,***[150] he states that ,"the notion that Lee Harvey Oswald did not act alone in killing the president might be the ultimate 'conspiracy theory' because it is one that most Americans believe." [151] In absence of transparency, clarity, above the board facts, misguided theories flourish. Perceptions become stronger than reality itself!

In innumerable cases where lack of access to information has caused confusion, conspiracy theories, accusations and counter accusations, there will be an equal or more number of cases where this has not happened because access to information was available.

The Watergate Scandal is a glaring example. Named after the Watergate apartment complex, the effect of the scandal was resignation of American President Richard Nixon. It also led to the indictment and conviction of several administration officials of the then President. It all began with the break-in of a hotel, residential and official complex in Washington D.C, the mystery was solved by Bob Woodward and Carl Bernstein, both reporters for Washington Post. The most horrifying and dazzling part of the scandal came to light in July 1973 when White House Aide Butterfield gave the information to the Inquiry Committee that Nixon recorded his conversations at the Oval Office via a taping system.[152]

Cavlin Woodward and Nancy Benac, in an Op-Ed in ***The Huffington Post***[153]in an article titled, " Nixon Watergate Testimony to be Unveiled after Decades," says, "Offering a rare look into confidential grand jury proceedings, and the first ever to have a former president testifying, the National Archives and its Nixon Presidential Library

---

[148] "Who killed JFK? List of suspects made by secretary of assassinated President goes up for auction" .By Paul Thompson, published Mail Online LINK: http://www.dailymail.co.uk/news/article-1337999/Who-killed-JFK-List-suspects-assassinated-Presidents-secretary-goes-auction.html

[149] Ibid.

[150] "40 Years Later: Who killed JFK?" Jarrett Murphy for CBSNews.com posted 5th December 2007

[151] Ibid.

[152] Washington Post coverage of the story in Part 2 of 4 parts titled, "The Government Acts." Link: http://www.washingtonpost.com/wp-srv/politics/special/watergate/part2.html

[153] Internet Newspaper, widely read and owned by Arianna Huffington

released a transcript of the testimony after a judge ordered the government to do so."[154]

This is what access to information is about. It exposes the wrongs, making public officials accountable for their actions, setting standards for good governance and paving way for better leadership. To the contrary, its absence leads to gossip, speculations, ignoring of ground realities and erecting realities where there are none.

By January 2012, at least 90 countries in the world have established statutes to ensure access to information, establishing procedures whereby the common man may request and receive government held information.[155]

Sixteen countries in Asia and the Pacific have access to information laws: Australia, Bangladesh, Cook Islands, India, Indonesia, Japan, Kyrgyzstan, Mongolia, Nepal, New Zealand, Pakistan, South Korea, Taiwan, Tajikistan, Thailand, and Uzbekistan. In addition, China has actionable ATI regulations.[156]

Then we have the case of Ronald Reagan who apologized to the American nation for selling weapons to Iraq in mid 1980s. At that time, an embargo was in operation against Iraq for sale of weapons. Reagan's reason was that the monies received from sale of weapons to Iran was used in Latin America and in order to raise funds, weapons were sold to Iraq violating the embargo.

Many incidents exist in Pakistan as well where information is available that makes for better opinion formation.

The spot-fixing controversy that broke out in August 2010, involving Muhammad Amir, Salman Butt and Muhammad Hanif is an example.[157] The incident is well recorded by Afia Salam in September 2010 issue of the ***Newsline Magazine*** titled, "In a Fix Again: How did Pakistan Cricket Arrive in This Tight Spot?"

---

[154] Link: http://www.huffingtonpost.com/2011/11/10/nixon-watergate-testimony_n_1085924.html

[155] Good Law & Practice(Online SITE)."ACCESS TO INFORMATION: LAWS OVERVIEW AND STATUTORY GOALS. Link: http://right2info.org/access-to-information-laws

[156] Ibid.

[157] "Just how innocent is Muhammad Amir?" published The Dawn Newspaper dated 28th March 2012

In the famous case of Haris Steel Mill , public opinion was formed due to factual communication of knowledge by the media. According to news reports there is on ground, no entity called Haris Steel Industries.[158] Sheikh Afzal, owner of Haris Steel and his brother Seth Munir were sanctioned loans worth over Rs 8.6 billion by the Bank of Punjab in the name of Haris, Haider and Prime Steel Industries.[159]

Where information is available, public finds it easy to form clean judgments.

***Do constitutions of other countries have exceptions to Freedom of Expression and Speech too? A Brief Comparative:***

Do all the countries of the world enjoy unbridled freedom of speech and expression in their constitutions and in reality? Though it may not be possible to make a comparison to every constitution in the world, ***I will briefly touch upon the exceptions in the Constitution of India.*** I will also highlight some exceptions in other constitutions of nations so we get a better picture of the fairness or unfairness of the exceptions within Article 19 , Constitution of Pakistan. I am a great believer in seeing the "bigger picture" which is only possible if we open the door wide for light to pour in–make a comparative analysis. Also, every law must deal with the particular situations in a given country. A law that makes sense in Pakistan may not relate well in let's say USA or Australia. The laws may differ partially, or completely with those of other nations. Article 19 of the Constitution of India[160] lays down the provision for ***Freedom of Speech***. It allows freedom of speech and expression, to assemble peaceably and without arms, freedom to form associations or unions, to move freely within India, to reside in any part of India, and to practice any profession or trade.

However, it then clearly lays down the exceptions, in later sub clauses of Article 19. The State reserves the right to impose any existing law or create new ones, in the interest of the sovereignty and integrity of India, or public order, or morality, in relation to incitement to offence, contempt of court and affecting friendly relations with a foreign state and defamation.

---

[158] The Nation, 29th October 2008 titled, "Who is Who in Haris Steel?"

[159] Ibid.

[160] The Constitution of India LINK: http://lawmin.nic.in/olwing/coi/coi-english/coi-indexenglish.htm

Freedom of speech and expression cannot be used to violate the aforementioned points. The State may also impose restrictions relating to the professional and technical qualifications necessary for practicing any profession or carrying out any trade or business, or, carrying out by State or a corporation owned or controlled by the State, of any trade, business, industry or service whether to exclusion, complete or partial, of citizens or otherwise.

In ***Ranjit D. Udeshi v State of Maharashtra***[161]the issue of obscenity and the conflict with freedom of speech and expression has been discussed at length and the court was of the opinion that obscenity is offensive to modesty or decency, and decency and morality are reasonable grounds for restricting the right to freedom of speech and expression of the people as per Article 19(2) of Constitution of India. The country today may not have the same level and sense of morality and decency, which it had in fifties or sixties, as standards change in different time zones, but abhorrence to obscenity, vulgarity and pornography has remained unchanged.

In an article by ***Sumera B. Reshi,*** titled, "Restrictions on the Indian Press and the Freedom of Expression,"[162] she states," Surprisingly, the Constitution of India does not mention 'freedom of the Press' specifically in the Chapter on Fundamental Rights. Dr. Ambedkar however clarified later that it was not necessary to stipulate it specifically as it is implicit in the guarantees of Freedom of Speech and Expression in Article 19 (1) (a) of the Constitution. Despite the constitutional guarantee, press in India has been inhibited by barriers caused by religious, social, linguistic differences and government restrictions off and on throughout its 64 years of existence."

She further states, "From time to time governments have been harassing press through lawsuits, exploiting restrictive laws governing criminal defamation. To illustrate government's apathy, one of the best example is the treatment of a news weekly magazine Tehelka. In 2001, Tehelka exposed the political corruption behind India's defence contracts. Soon after the revelations, government started bullying Tehelka. The

---

[161] 1965(1) SCR 65 SC

[162] KashmirWatch Op-Ed published 25th September 2011 LINK: http://kashmirwatch.com/opinions.php/2011/09/25/restrictions-on-the-indian-press-and-the-freedom-of-expression.html

worst that came after this episode was that none of India's media rallied in support of Tehelka, fearing punishment from the government."[163]

### *A Comparative with Limitations in other Countries of the World*

In other countries of the world, too, there are various restrictions on freedom of expression and speech. It is not absolute anywhere in the world.

The American Constitution says, "Congress shall make no law respecting an establishment of religion, or prohibiting the free exercise thereof; or abridging the freedom of speech, or of the press; or the right of the people peaceably to assemble, and to petition the government, for a redress of grievances."

However, ***Harold L. Nelson and Dwight L. Teeter Jr,***[164] feel the term "freedom of speech and press" has not been defined and it was a much-debated concept in England and America at that time.[165]

As the states in USA adopted their own constitutions, each had a provision for protection of freedom of speech. To share two here, for elucidation and better understanding.

***Constitution of Massachusetts***, Part I, Art. XVI,[166] "The liberty of the press is essential to the security and freedom in a state; it ought not, therefore to be restrained, in this commonwealth. The right of free speech shall not be abridged."

***Constitution of New York,*** Article 1 and 8 state, "Every citizen may freely speak write & publish his sentiments on all subjects, being responsible for the abuse of that right; and no law shall be passed to restrain abridge the liberty of the press. In all criminal prosecutions or indictment for libels, the truth may be given in evidence to the jury, and if it shall appear to the jury, that the matter charged as libelous is true, and was published with good motives, and for justifiable ends, the party shall

---

[163] Ibid.

[164] Harold Nelson at time of publication of the book was Professor of Journalism University of Wisconsin-Madison and Dwight Teeter Jr Professor and Chairman, Dept. of Journalism University of Texas at Austin

[165] "Law Of Mass Communications: Freedom and Control of Print and Broadcast Media" Third Edition published by Foundation Press Inc. 1978, Pg. 5

[166] Ibid.

be acquitted, and the jury shall have the right to determine the law and the fact."[167]

In an interesting case ***Tinker v Des Moines Independent Community School District***[168](1969), the petitioners or complainants pleaded to the court that they were suspended from school for wearing black arm bands as a protest against the Vietnam War. They claimed it was a violation of the right of freedom of speech.

Note that it is not only the written and spoken word that may be construed as speech but symbolic gestures also fall within the ambit, much like desecration of the national flag. The court ruled in the favor of the students determining that it was indeed their right of freedom of speech.

**Anti- harassment law,** first adopted by California State in 1990, is a clear exception to the right of freedom of speech and expression. One must not over exercise the right to step onto the privacy of another. Actress Rebecca Shaeffer was shot dead by Robert De Bardo on 18th July 1989. He was stalking her for the past three years and eventually entered her apartment building and shot her. California Penal Code 646.9 defines a stalker as "someone who willfully, maliciously and repeatedly follows or harasses another (victim) and who makes a credible threat with the intent to place the victim or victim's immediate family in fear for their safety." [169] The victim does not need to prove that the stalker intends to carry out the threat.

The Fifth Amendment to the United States protects the right of a citizen to remain silent. It states, " No person shall be held to answer for a capital, or otherwise infamous crime, unless on a presentment or indictment of a Grand Jury, except in cases arising in the land or naval forces, or in the Militia, when in actual service in time of War or public danger; nor shall any person be subject for the same offense to be twice put in jeopardy of life or limb; nor shall be compelled in any criminal case to be a witness against himself, nor be deprived of life, liberty, or property,

---

[167] Ibid, Page 6

[168] eNotes LINK:http://www.enotes.com/freedom-speech-reference/freedom-speech-299523

[169] Oncle LINK: http://law.onecle.com/california/penal/646.9.html

without due process of law; nor shall private property be taken for public use, without just compensation."[170]

The right was won by "Freeborn John" Lilburn in 1641 in UK, whipped and pilloried because he refused to take oath before the Star Chamber on his refusal to answer questions truly about his alleged importing of seditious and heretical books. [171] On petitioning to Parliament, it declared the sentence, "illegal and against the liberty of the subject."[172]

Laws are never static. Or, they should not be static. They are made, they evolve and develop according to the needs of the people, as societies develop and evolve, to meet the challenges of changing times.. When we talked of the press, initially, it meant the print journalism, with time, the circle included the electronic media too. Times change, parameter of judging a value too can change and laws must change alongwith to serve vibrant, dynamic societies. In Pakistan in 2009, with increasing urban population, higher rate of female education and more women than before moving into the work arena to make a mark, the National Assembly unanimously passed a bill to punish sexual harassers. The draft, was presented earlier in the year by ***Sherry Rehman.*** [173] This bill acknowledges the needs of a huge section of the society to feel safe at their working place.

Pakistan is a society in evolution. It is a mix of the rightists, the moderates and the liberals–again sub divided into different classes on basis of income. Pakistan faces many problems. It is a cauldron of many issues. It becomes that much important to have laws that help provide justice to our multifaceted society. However, the presence of laws itself does not and will not ensure provision of rights to people. It requires implementation of the laws. We need to build a system that expedites cases and larger number of judges and short dates for hearing of cases are just two suggestions. But first and foremost, who will educate the common man about this fundamental right? Ludicrous it may sound, but most are not even aware of this right. I believe our media is well placed and has access to our homes to educate the masses.

---

[170] Cornell University Law School, "Bill of Rights from Cornell University Law School." Retrieved 2007-12-16

[171] Law of Mass Communications by Harold L. Nelson & Dwight L. Teeter, published by Foundation Press Inc. 1978 Pg 8

[172] Ibid.

[173] Presently serving Ambassador of Pakistan to the USA.

Like any right that will have boundaries, freedom of speech and expression too must have a limit where it stops to avoid encroaching on the same right of another society member, institution. There is a delicate balance between rights of press and rights to privacy. This has been discussed in the later chapter. This must be followed.

### *Concluding Comments*

Like in any other country in the world, Pakistan too places certain restrictions on freedom of expression for the greater good of the country. This must be understood and respected. The mark of a mature nation is not to belittle and humiliate the Constitution, but to respect and follow it.

The character of any nation is judged by their understanding and willingness to follow the laws of the land. Nations who fail to do so, lose their place in the annals of history.

# Chapter III

## Freedom of Expression & Speech in Pakistan (Part II)

## Contempt of Court

## Constitution of Pakistan

Article 204 is one of the exceptions within Article 19 dealing with the limitations on freedom of speech . It must be read together with Article 19 to see the bigger picture. This was later substituted with Contempt of Court Ordinance 2003 and more recently by Amendment Bill of Contempt of Court 2012. The last was struck down by the court as null and void on 3rd August 2012.

### *Contempt of Court Article 204*

The text of Article 204 states:[174]

> *(1) In this Article, "Court" means the Supreme Court or a High Court.*
> *(2) A Court shall have power to punish any person who;*
> (a)*abuses, interferes with or obstructs the process of the Court in any way or disobeys any order of the Court;*
> *(b) scandalizes the Court or otherwise does anything which tends to bring the Court or a Judge of the Court into hatred, ridicule or contempt;*
> *(c) does anything which tends to prejudice the determination of a matter pending before the Court; or*
> *(d) does any other thing which, by law, constitutes contempt of the Court.*

---

[174] Constitution of Pakistan 1973 by Justice Muhammad Munir Formerly Chief Justice Pakistan, published by PLD Publishers 1996, Pg 1190 Volume II.

*(3) The exercise of the power conferred on a Court by this Article may be regulated by law and, subject to law, by rules made by the Court.*

Each of the term above needs to be examined closely to understand the scope and implications of the law.

The Article awards the right to the Court to punish any individual, institution, corporation if it is guilty of committing contempt of court. It then goes on to outline the meaning of contempt of court in sub-clauses (a) (b) (c) and (d).

The object of the clause is not to hold the Courts sacrosanct or a super human being as stated by Justice Muhammad Munir,[175] the object here is to hold the confidence of the people in the justice of decision taken to guard against any vicious attack on the courts.

In an excellent paper by ***Justice Markanday Katju***, [176] former Judge Supreme Court of India, shares his views that in any society there must be a forum to settle issues. These forums are courts that provide relief to the common man. If these forums are not present, issues will be settled by murders, guns, kidnappings and complete lawlessness. He goes on to state, "Looking at it from this angle, one can immediately realize that in a democracy, the purpose of the Contempt of Court power can only be to enable the Court to function. The power is not to prevent the master (the people) from criticizing their servant (the Judges) if the latter do not function properly or commit misconduct."[177]He questions the applicability of the law, in today's world, as it is passed over from the days of the British Raj. Then it was an alien ruler ruling an alien nation. This is not the situation today. He states, "Much of our Contempt Law is a hangover from British rule. But under British rule India was not free and democratic, and the people were not supreme, rather it was the British rulers who were supreme."[178]

He further shares in the same piece, "As observed by Lord Denning in R vs. Commissioner of Police (1968) 2 QB 150:

---

[175] Ibid. Pg 1191

[176] He is currently Chairman Press Council of India

[177] Titled," Contempt of Court: Need for a Fresh Look" by Former Justice Katju LINK: http://districtcourtallahabad.up.nic.in/articles/contempt.pdf

[178] Ibid.

Let me say at once that we will never use this jurisdiction as a means to uphold our own dignity. That must rest on surer foundations. Nor will we use it to suppress those who speak against us. We do not fear criticism, nor do we resent it For there is something far more important at stake. It is no less than freedom of speech itself. It is the right of every man, in Parliament or out of it, in the press or over the broadcast, to make fair comment, even outspoken comment, on matters of public interest. Those who comment can deal faithfully with all that is done in a court of justice. They can say that we are mistaken, and our decisions erroneous, whether they are subject to appeal or not. All we would ask is that those who criticize us will remember that, from the nature of our office, we cannot reply to their criticisms. We cannot enter into public controversy. Still less into political controversy. We must rely on our conduct itself to be its own vindication."[179]

In the earlier chapter, I had pointed out the need for changing laws for a vibrant, evolving, dynamic society.

"To speak generally, contempt of Court may be said to be constituted by any conduct that tends to bring the authority and the administration of law into disrespect or disregard or to interfere with or to prejudice parties litigant or their witnesses during litigation."[180]

Contempt of Court can be either Judicial, Civil or Criminal Contempt. Let's briefly touch upon these types for better understanding.

**Judicial contempt** Section(2) (c) defines judicial contempt as," the scandalization of a court and includes personalized criticism of a judge while holding of office" ( Contempt of Court Ordinance 2003).

**Criminal contempt** will be committed if any individual stops a witness from giving evidence in a case, induces the witness by pressure tactics or attractive offers not to give the truth in any kind of legal proceedings.

The third category of contempt is **Civil contempt**. If any contempt is committed on "face of the Court" it will be construed as a civil contempt.

---

[179] Ibid.
[180] The State Vs Abdul Latif PLD 1961 Lah. 51

The first contempt described in clause(a) states abuse, interference with or obstruction in the process of the Court in any way or disobeying of any order of the Court. Abuse is generally described as , " Everything which is contrary to good order established by usage. Departure from reasonable use, immoderate or improper use."[181]

Therefore any individual or institution or organization that abuses the court, by act, word or writing, will be deemed to have committed contempt of Court. If anyone interferes with or obstructs the process of court will be said to commit contempt of Court.

Likewise, if an order passed by the Court is disobeyed. "Any violation of such order could attract provisions of contempt of Courts Act- Any wilful disobedience to an order of court by contumacious conduct, with a view to obstruct course of justice or to conspire and collude to frustrate order pass by any court will amount to contempt of Court–A person knowing about any order passed by Court on undertaking of party even if such party is not party to proceedings but assisted in contriving a device to frustrate order passed by the Court and by willful disobedience showed disrespect to this court and tried to pollute the foundations of justice and obstruct smooth running of administration of law is guilty of contempt of Court.[182]

In 2010, the incumbent Vice Chancellor of NED University Karachi was served with a contempt of court notice by former ***VC Professor Dr Muhammad Munir Hasan*** whose pension was not paid for the last 16 years."[183]

The news goes on to state: "In a contempt application filed in the Supreme Court (SC) by Prof. Hasan with Kalam as respondent it was stated that the SC took suo moto notice on Criminal Misc. Application No. 226 of 2006, made by Advocate Haji Muhammad Ismael Memon in the pension case of Prof. Ghazi Khan Jakhrani. In a vide order dated May 18, 2006, the SC directed all concerned for finalization of pension cases of retiring civil servants in accordance with the West Pakistan Servants Pension Rules, 1963. The case is quoted in PLD 2007 SC 35, and operating

---

[181] Black's Law Dictionary, Sixth Edition, Centennial Edition( 1891-1991) Pg 10

[182] *Naveed Nawazish Malik Vs Ghulam Rasool Bhatti: PLJ 1996*SC 1616=1997 SMAR 193= NLR 1996 Criminal 495(PLJ Digest 1996-97 Pg 575 Vol I)

[183] "Aggrieved Professor seeks contempt of court case against NED VC" posted 21st May 2010 www. Ilmkiduniya.com LINK: http://www.ilmkidunya.com/edunews/aggrieved-professor-seeks-contempt-of-court-case-against-ned-vc-4125.aspx

paras (8 and 11) of order dated May 18, 2006 are reflected as under: "We... direct that all the government departments, agencies and officers deployed to serve the general public within the limits by the Constitution as well as by the law shall not cause unnecessary hurdle or delay in finalizing the payments pensionary/retirement benefits cases in future and violation of these directions shall amount to criminal negligence and dereliction of the duty assigned to them...

"We direct all the chief secretaries of the provincial governments as well as the accountant generals and the Accountant General of Pakistan Revenues, Islamabad to ensure in future strict adherence of the pension rules reproduced herein above and clear such cases within a period not more than two weeks without fail.

"We also direct that in future if there is any delay in the finalization of pension benefits cases of the government servants, widows or orphan children and matter is brought to the notice of this court, the head of the concerned department shall also be held liable for the contempt of the court and shall be dealt with strictly in accordance with law."[184]

Clause (b) states it is also a contempt if it scandalizes the Court or otherwise does anything which tends to bring the Court or a Judge of the Court into hatred, ridicule or contempt.

The concept of "scandalizing the court" has its roots in English common law. Criticism of a court in a manner to cause a scandal ie scandalizing the court shall be deemed to fall within this preview. The key idea here is to act as a hindrance to those who are wishful of shaking the confidence of the public by acting as a deterrent. In a case law, ***R vs Almon***,[185] Wilmot J. stated, "[Criticism of judges] excites in the minds of the people a general dissatisfaction with all judicial determinations, and indisposes their minds to obey them; and whenever men's allegiances to the laws is so fundamentally shaken, it is the most fatal and most dangerous obstruction of justice, and, in my opinion, calls out for a more rapid and immediate redress than any other obstruction whatsoever..."[186] When a judge is scandalized with relation to the discharge of his duties, bringing into disrespect the office of the judge will be said to have scandalized the court. It can create hatred in the public, and form opinion about that judge or heap ridicule upon him.

---

[184] Ibid.

[185] (1765 )97 ER

[186] Ibid. Pg 100

But the very basis of the public confidence has been laid bare by ***David Pannick*** as he argues that "public confidence in the judiciary is not strengthened by the deterrence of criticism." After all, ***Lord Atkin*** in the Privy Council case of Ambard v. Attorney-General for Trinidad and Tobago, had ruled that "the path of criticism is a public way: the wrong-headed are permitted to err therein: provided that members of the public abstain from imputing improper motives to those taking part in the administration of justice, and are genuinely exercising a right of criticism, and not acting in malice or attempting to impair the administration of justice, they are immune. Justice is not a cloistered virtue: she must be allowed to suffer the scrutiny and respectful, even though outspoken, comments of ordinary men."[187]

Now this is an extremely interesting distinction, putting emphasis on the motive of criticism. Criticizing for the purpose of demeaning the judge will not be accepted and is contempt of court. However, criticizing without malice , even if the comments are outspoken would not amount to contempt of court.

To go back to his article, he further discusses the assumption that a judge is beyond pressures and unbiased. He says, "Courts are loath to admit that they may be susceptible to political, economic and moral prejudices that hold favor in a society."[188]

Clause (c) says that if anyone does anything which tends to prejudice the determination of a matter pending before the Court. This can be done in any way–trying to pressurize the judiciary in any manner, trying to withhold evidence or pressurize another to withhold evidence, disregarding court's stay proceedings, ignoring and not complying with the order issued by a court and creating a problem in the smooth administration of justice are all forms of contempt under sub clause(c).

This does not mean that a fair comment on the working of the court will be deemed as contempt of the court. Fair comments on merits of a case decided and judgment delivered may not be considered contempt of court. If a fairly accurate account of a judicial proceeding is published, this is not contempt of Court. Neither will be a comment made or published by someone who was not aware that the case was under trial in the court.

---

[187] *"Questions of Contempt"*, paper by Zafar F. Ibrahim , an Advocate of High Court in Pakistan, in *FRONTLINE,* from the publishers of *THE HINDU,* Vol 16-Issue 29,Seot 25th to Oct 8th 19999

[188] Ibid.

In divorce cases, for example, if a court issues a decree, any party to the case which fails to comply with the decision of the court will be said to be in contempt of the court. Should the court direct the father of the children to pay a certain amount for the education and expenses of the children whose custody is with the mother of the children and he willfully fails to do so, he will be considered to be in contempt of the court.

### *Issues Sub-judice to the Court: Press & contempt of Court*

There is an important aspect of the exception curtailing Freedom of Expression and Speech , that falls within the ambit of contempt of the court that is not only important but is also linked with the press. Therefore it is being commented upon separately. This relates to matters that are sub-judice to the court. The term "sub-judice" is Latin. It simply means "under judicial consideration." Thereby meaning to state any matter that is under judicial consideration must not be commented and debated upon, unless and until the Court delivers a verdict. This makes sense.

If a matter is pending before court, and the same is being discussed in all its speculative splendor in media, it will be fair to assume that it will create public perceptions. There are vested interests. Media persons, just like any other have their own biases and prejudices. Besides, media persons, not being lawyers may not grasp the elements within a case. The projection of news, may lead to running of a media trial and deliver a media judgment before a judgment from the court. Even if truth is spoken in the media , is it fair to prejudge a case before being presented in Court and before it may be judged by a court of competent jurisdiction? What if facts by the media are not what they are? There can be a genuine misunderstanding of legal points– after all, everyone is not a lawyer, notwithstanding the desire to act as one– is this not seriously compromising an issue by virtue of running a media trial?

"We must not allow *trial by newspaper* or *trial by television* or trial by any medium other than the courts of law."[189]

Is it not likely for a media trial to endanger and jeopardize the fair trial of a man? Can it not put in danger the life of a key witness? Or his/her family? Can it not sway a judge by a public trial? The newspaper and TV is read and viewed by people from across the board. Or other

---

[189] *Attorney General v Times Newspaper [1973] 1 Q.B 710*

officials involved in the investigation? Or pronounce a sentence on half truths where there should be none, on an innocent person?

"It was axiomatic that courts could not function properly, that the administration of justice would be harmed that the scales of justice would be jogged, if news media were freely allowed to publish criticisms of judges while cases were pending, or to attempt to influence judges, or participants in a pending case, or to publish grossly false or inaccurate reports of court trials."[190]

"When a case is finished," states Justice Oliver Wendell Holmes in a Federal decision of 1907, "courts are subject to the same criticism as other people, but the propriety and necessity of preventing interference with the course of justice by premature statement , argument or intimidation hardly can be denied."[191] The very suspicion of bias can overturn the judgment of a case. The famous case that formed a precedence for this emerged in UK, in ***R vs Sussex Justices.*** In a case of dangerous driving, McCarthy appeared before a Magistrates Court that had led to a road accident. He was convicted.

The solicitors and the defendant were both unaware that the Clerk to the Justices was member of the firm of solicitors acting in a civil claim against the defendant arising out of the accident, giving rise to prosecution. Once this came to light, the defendant went in an Appeal against the judgment. It was a Judicial Review heard by King's Bench headed by Lord Chief Justice Hewart. It was a landmark judgment and set a precedence .

Lord Hewart CJ stated:

"It is said, and, no doubt, truly, that when that gentleman retired in the usual way with the justices, taking with him the notes of the evidence in case the justices might desire to consult him, the justices came to a conclusion without consulting him, and that he scrupulously abstained from referring to the case in any way. But while that is so, a long line of cases shows that it is not merely of some importance but is of fundamental importance that justice should not only be done, but should manifestly and undoubtedly be seen to be done.

---

[190] Laws of Mass Communications by *Harold L Nelson & Dwight L Teeter Jr* published by The Foundations Press Inc 1978, Pg 344

[191] Ibid. Patterson Vs State of Colo. ex.rel Attorney General,205 U.S 454, 27 S. Ct 556(1907)

"The question therefore is not whether in this case the deputy clerk made any observation or offered any criticism which he might not properly have made or offered; the question is whether he was so related to the case in its civil aspect as to be unfit to act as clerk to the justices in the criminal matter. The answer to that question depends not upon what actually was done but upon what might appear to be done. Nothing is to be done which creates even a suspicion that there has been an improper interference with the course of justice. Speaking for myself, I accept the statements contained in the justices' affidavit, but they show very clearly that the deputy clerk was connected with the case in a capacity which made it right that he should scrupulously abstain from referring to the matter in any way, although he retired with the justices; in other words, his one position was such that he could not, if he had been required to do so, discharge the duties which his other position involved. His twofold position was a manifest contradiction.

"In those circumstances I am satisfied that this conviction must be quashed, unless it can be shown that the applicant or his solicitor was aware of the point that might be taken, refrained from taking it, and took his chance of an acquittal on the facts, and then, on a conviction being recorded, decided to take the point. On the facts I am satisfied that there has been no waiver of the irregularity, and, that being so, the rule must be made absolute and the conviction quashed."[192]

Yet another point to be taken into consideration is, if the decision by the court is different than a direction taken by the media, the popular perception can be, that justice has not been served. There is a known saying, *"Not only must Justice be done; it must also be seen to be done."* The courts are not to serve popular wishes of the masses ie play to the gallery, but to ensure that justice is served.

***Muhammad Ziauddin***[193] in a report published 5th February 2012, [194] states, "Media commentary on sub-judice matters were disrespectful to the judiciary.

"Mujeebur Rehman Shami, chief editor of Daily Pakistan, said the rising trend of open debate on pending cases hurt the judiciary's image

---

[192] Via: http://en.wikipedia.org/wiki/R_v_Sussex_Justices,_ex_parte_McCarthy

[193] Executive Editor of Express Tribune

[194] Titled" Courts and Press: Media must not comment on sub-judice matters". *Express Tribune* 5th Feb 2012

and should be curbed.[195] These views were discussed at a seminar organized by the Press Council of Pakistan and Lahore Bar Association."

The question of practical relevance that arises here is: in any case that arises and is in court, some may have great public interest. Now, this interest is heightened during the pendency of the case. The case may take a year or more to reach the decision by a court.

Does the media, then, stay mum till the conclusion of the proceedings?

To address the above question, the principle of "clear and present danger" was developed; whether the publication presented an immediate likelihood that justice would be thwarted, –whether there was a "clear and present danger that the publication would obstruct justice."[196] The famous rule, expressed first in 1919 by Justice Homes in Schenck v United States.[197] Over time, other tests developed and came to the fore, but this one freed the media from maintaining zero silence in the garb of contempt of court.

In a known case of ***Saadat Khialy***, an article was carried by some newspapers. The article made some comments on some pending cases in the court. The Supreme Court ruled it was contempt of the court. The ruling stated:

"If the Article, read reasonably and as a whole, was calculated or had the tendency to prejudice mankind against one or the other of the parties involved in the proceedings, it is enough to amount to an interference with the course of justice, for the question in the case is, not as to whether the publication has, in fact, interfered with it or not, or as to what was the intention of the author and/or publisher, but whether it has the tendency to produce such prejudicial effect. The principle on which this type of contempt is punished is to keep the stream of justice unsullied so that the parties against whom litigations are pending in courts of law should get a fair trial from the Courts and not be subjected in advance to a trial by newspapers."[198]

---

[195] Ibid

[196] Law of Mass Communications by *Harold L Nelson & Dwight L. Teeter Jr* published by The Foundation Press Inc. 1978, Pg 345

[197] Ibid. 249 U.S. 47,39 S.Ct. 247(1919)

[198] Saadat Khialy Vs The State PLD 1962 SC 457

There is some wisdom behind a policy of extreme caution when a lawyer or litigant seeks to speak to the media in their ongoing case. That wisdom was best expressed by Lord Denning in A.G. v Times Newspaper:

"It is undoubted law that, when litigation is pending and actively in suit before the court, no one shall comment on it in such a way that there is a real and substantial danger of prejudice to the trial of the action, as for instance by influencing the judge, the jurors, or the witnesses or even by prejudicing mankind in general against a party to the cause....

"Even if the person making the comment honestly believes it to be true, still it is a contempt of court if he prejudges the truth before it is ascertained in the proceedings. We must not allow trial by newspaper or trial by television or trial by any medium other than the courts of law.

"But in so stating the law, ... it applies only when litigation is pending and is actively in suit before the court.... There must appear to be a real and substantial danger of prejudice to the trial of the case or to the settlement of it. And when considering the question, it must always be remembered that besides the interest of the parties and a fair trial or a fair settlement of the case there is another important interest to be considered. It is the interest of the public in matters of national concern, and the freedom of the press to make their comment on such matters. The one interest must be balanced against the other....

"Our law of contempt does not prevent comment before the litigation is started nor after it has ended. Nor is it prevented when the litigation is dormant and is not being actively pursued.... No person can stop comment by serving a bit and let it lie idle.... it is active litigation which is protected by the law of content, not the absence of it."[199]

## *Contempt of Court Ordinance 2003*

In 2003 the then President General Pervez Musharraf initiated a Contempt of Court Ordinance .

It defines Contempt of Court as: "Whoever disobeys or disregards any order, direction or process of a court, which he is legally bound to

---

[199] 'Media and Litigation: Sub Judice in the New Millennium: dunhaime.org LINK: http://www.duhaime.org/LegalResources/CivilLitigation/LawArticle-1212/Media-and-Litigation-Sub-Judice-in-the-New-Millennium.aspx

obey; or commits a wilful breach of a valid undertaking given to a court; or does anything which is intended to or tends to bring the authority of a court or the administration of law into disrespect or disrepute, or to interfere with or obstruct or interrupt or prejudice the process of law or the due course of any judicial proceedings, or to lower the authority of a court or scandalize a judge in relation to his office, or to disturb the order or decorum of a court is said to commit "contempt of court". The contempt is of three types, namely: the "civil contempt", "criminal contempt" and "judicial contempt."

NOTE:(The concept of contempt remains the same as before, and has been discussed at length earlier, however the addition is the three *kinds* of distinct contempt ie civil contempt, criminal contempt and judicial contempt and need to be analyzed, though I had briefly touched upon them earlier in the chapter).

2. Definitions: In this Ordinance, unless there is anything repugnant in subject or context:

(a) "civil contempt" means the willful flouting or disregard of -

(i) an order, whether interim or final, a judgment or decree of a court;

(ii) A writ or order issued by a court in the exercise of its constitutional jurisdiction;

(iii) an undertaking given to, and recorded by, a court;

(iv) the process of a court;

(b) "criminal contempt" means the doing of any act with intent to, or having the effect of, obstructing the administration of justice;

(c) "judicial contempt" means the scandalization of a court and includes personalized criticism of a judge while holding of office;

(d) "notice" means a notice other than a show cause notice issued by a court;

(e) "pending proceedings" means proceedings which have been instituted in a court of law until finally decided after exhausting all appeals, revisions or reviews provided by law or until the period of limitation thereof has expired;

Provided that the pendency of an execution application shall not detract from the finality of the proceedings.

(f) "personalized criticism" means a criticism of a judge or a judgment in which improper motives are imputed; and

(g) "superior court" means the Supreme Court or a High Court.

3. Contempt of Court(Stated at the opening of the Ordinance of Contempt of Court 2003).

4. Jurisdiction: (1) Every superior court shall have the power to punish a contempt committed in relation to it.

(2) Subject to sub-section (3), every High Court shall have the power to punish a contempt committed in relation to any court subordinate to it.

(3) No High Court shall proceed in cases in which an alleged contempt is punishable by a subordinate court under the Pakistan Penal Code (Act No.XLV of 1860).

5. Punishment:

(1) Subject to sub-section (92) any person who commits contempt of court shall be punished with imprisonment which may extend to six months simple imprisonment, or with fine which may extend to Rs100,000, or with both.

(2) A person accused of having committed contempt of court may, at any stage, submit an apology and the court, if satisfied that it is bona fide, may discharge him or remit his sentence.

Explanation: The fact that an accused person genuinely believes that he has not committed contempt and enters a defence shall not detract from the bona fides of an apology.

(3) In case of a contempt having been committed, or alleged to have been committed, by a company, the responsibility therefore shall extend to the persons in the company, directly or indirectly, responsible for the same, who shall also be liable to be punished accordingly.

(4) Notwithstanding anything contained in any judgment, no court shall have the power to pass any order of punishment for or in relation to any act of contempt save and except in accordance with sub-section (1).

***Criminal Contempt*** is described as following:

6. Criminal contempt when committed:

(1) A criminal contempt shall be deemed to have been committed if a person

(a) attempts to influence a witness, or proposed witness, either by intimidation or improper inducement, not to give evidence, or not to tell the truth in any legal proceeding; offers an improper inducement or attempts to intimidate a judge, in order to secure a favourable verdict in any legal proceedings

(b) commits any other act with intent to divert the course of justice.

(2) Nothing contained in sub-section (1) shall prejudice any other criminal proceedings which may be initiated against any such person as is mentioned therein.

7. Cognizance of criminal contempt: In the case of a criminal contempt a superior court may take action;

(i) suo motu or

(ii) on the initiative of any person connected with the proceedings in which the alleged contempt has been committed; or

(iii) on the application of the law officer of a Provincial or the Federal Government.

8. Fair reporting:

(1) Subject to sub-section (2), the publication of a substantially accurate account of what has transpired in a court, or of legal proceedings, shall not constitute contempt of court.

(2) The court may, for reasons to be recorded in writing, in the interest of justice, Prohibit the publication of information pertaining to legal proceedings.

9. Personalized criticism:

(1) Subject to the provisions of this Ordinance, personalized criticism of a specific judge, or judges, may constitute **judicial contempt** save and except true averment if made in good faith and in temperate language in a complaint made,

(a) to the administrative superior of a judge of a subordinate court;

(b) to a Provincial government,

(c) to the Chief Justice of a High Court;

(d) to the Supreme Court;

(e) to the Supreme Judicial Council; or

(f) to the Federal Government for examination and being forwarded to the Supreme Judicial Council;

(2) Nothing contained in sub-section (1) is intended to deprive a judge of the right to file a suit for defamation.

10. Fair comments: The fair and healthy comments on a judgment involving question of public importance in a case which has finally been decided and is no longer pending shall not constitute contempt; provided that it is phrased in temperate language and the integrity and impartiality of a Judge is not impugned.

***Explanation***

As per law any conduct to influence witnesses, in any manner, or distort truth or not give testimony tantamount to contempt of court. If any offer of a nature is made to a judge to get a favorable judgment in any manner, it is also a contempt. The courts must maintain their dignity and must be allowed to go about their business without interference of any nature. Legislatures pass laws. But it is the task of courts to implement these laws. If anyone, no matter in which position, tries to influence court's decisions , they may well be held in contempt.

Criminal contempt notice may be taken by the Superior Court itself or by an individual connected in any way to the proceedings or by a Law Officer of provincial or Federal Govt. Suo motu, meaning "on its own motion," is a Latin legal term. When the Superior Court takes notice of an omission or a commission of an act, it will be deemed to be a suo moto action. Justice Shri V. R. Krishna Iyer of the Indian Supreme Court stated that such judicial activism shows that "the true strength and stability of our polity is the society's credibility in social justice, not perfect 'legalese.'"[200]

However, fair reporting of a legal proceeding is exempted from being contempt of court.

In addition, should the court feel that a particular legal proceeding should not be published or informed about, to public at large, it may duly pass an order to forbid so.

In such a case, should the journalist be guilty of doing so, it will be contempt of court.

However, this if done, is usually an exception, not a rule.

Personalized criticism of a specific judge or more than one judge, will be contempt of court. However, if a genuine observation to the superiors(hierarchy given in law) , is made and in a moderate or restrained choice of words. *The law ties this with a case that is no longer pending with the court.*

According to another definition of Criminal Contempt by ***Merriam-Webster***,

"Contempt that is committed in the presence of a court in session or a judge acting in a judicial capacity or so near to either of these as to interfere with the proceedings and that tends to belittle or insult the judge or to degrade or obstruct justice **:** a direct contempt not affecting a civil remedy of a party --- contempt that tends to interfere directly with a legislature or one of its committees exercising its lawful powers or that

[200] Dawn Newspaper, titled "Suo moto: Pakistan's chemotherapy?" by *Warris Husain* published 31st August 2011

constitutes disrespect for its authority in the course of its lawful proceedings."[201]

The responsibilities on the shoulders of a trial Judge are immense. He must evaluate all evidence on board, witnesses are not coerced, whether or not bail is to be allowed and if standards of fairness are met at the judgment delivered. For a Judge at the appellate level, responsibilities are no less, but different. They must see the validity of the legal issue raised in appeals. At no point, must his person may be brought in conflict except in a case of clear defamation, where he has the right to file a suit against the culprit.

***Judicial Contempt in the Ordinance*** is defined as:

11. Judicial contempt:

(1) A superior court may take action in a case of judicial contempt on its own initiative or on information laid before it by any person.

(2) Any person laying false information relating to the commission of an alleged judicial contempt shall himself be liable to be proceeded against for contempt of court.

(3) Judicial contempt proceedings initiated by a judge, or relating to a judge, shall not be heard by the said judge, but shall (unless he is himself the Chief Justice) be referred to the Chief Justice, who may hear the same personally or refer it to some other judge, and, in a case in which the judge himself is the Chief Justice, shall be referred to the senior most judge available for disposal similarly.

(4) No proceedings for judicial contempt shall be initiated after the expiry of one year.

***Explanation:***

Section(2) (c) defines judicial contempt as, "the scandalization of a court and includes personalized criticism of a judge while holding of office." Any effort to deliberately scandalize the court or/and personal criticism if a judge as he holds office is a judicial contempt. No one may falsify any information brought to the knowledge of the court. A court can

---

[201] Merriam-Webster –an Encyclopedia Britannica Company LINK: http://www.merriam-webster.com/dictionary/criminal%20contempt

take notice of any person indulging in judicial contempt on its own initiative or if knowledge is brought to court by a person. If the knowledge is incorrect, the person so falsifying will be held for contempt.

Utmost care must be taken to ensure that views or comments made about the court do not bring down the dignity or lower the esteem of the judiciary in any way . If views aired bring upon the court public scorn or/and ridicule it will mean causing scandalizing of the court.

***Waris Husain,*** in his article, "Armor of a Judge", states, "Generally, contempt proceedings are not only criticized for being based on the subjective attitude of the judge, but also due to contempt traps. While this is a newly developing legal defense, a review article by John Reidy, Michael Stephan, and Guha Krishnamurthi describes contempt traps as "a situation in which a government actor utilizes a judicial proceeding in order to create an opportunity for contempt in connection with matters not necessary, material, or otherwise germane to a legitimate investigation."[202]

He goes on to say, "Justice Markandey Katju explains, "The best shield and armor of a Judge is his reputation of integrity, impartiality, and learning. An upright judge will hardly ever need to use the contempt power in his judicial career. It is only in a very rare and extreme case that this power will need to be exercised, and that, too only to enable the judge to function, not to maintain his dignity or majesty."[203]

Last kind of contempt defined is the ***civil contempt***:

12. Civil contempt:

(1) Proceeding for civil contempt may be initiated suo motu or at the instance of an aggrieved party.

(2) The provisions contained herein are intended to be in addition to, and not in derogation of, the power of the court under any other law for the time being in force to enforce compliance of its orders, judgments or decrees.

13. Procedure in cases of contempt in the face of the court:

---

[202] *The Friday Times,* February 10-16, 2012 - Vol. XXIII, No. 51

[203] Ibid.

(1) In the case of a contempt committed in the face of the court, the court may cause the contemner/offender to be detained in custody and may proceed against him in the manner provided in sub-section (2); provided that if the case cannot be finally disposed off on the same day, the court may order the release of the accused from the custody either on bail or on his own bond.

(2) In all cases of contempt in the face of the court the judge shall pass an order in open court recording separately what was said or done by the accused person and shall immediately proceed against the offender or may refer the matter to the Chief Justice for hearing and deciding the case by himself or by another Judge.

14. Expunged material: No material which has been expunged from the record under the orders of

(i) a court of competent jurisdiction, or

(ii) the presiding officer of the Senate, the National Assembly or a Provincial Assembly;

shall be admissible in evidence unless it is otherwise ordered by the court.

15. Innocent publication: No person shall be guilty of contempt of court for making any statement, or publishing any material, pertaining to any matter which forms the subject of pending proceedings, if he was not aware of the pendency thereof.

16. Protected statements: No proceedings for contempt of court shall lie in relation to the following:

(i) observations made by a higher or appellate court in a judicial order or judgment;

(ii) remarks made in an administrative capacity by any authority in the course of official business, including those in connection with a disciplinary inquiry or in an inspection note or a character roll or confidential report; and

(iii) a true statement without intent to scandalize a judge regarding his conduct in a matter not connected with the performance of his judicial functions.

17. Procedure:

(1) Save as expressly provided to the contrary, proceedings in cases of contempt shall be commenced by the issuance of a notice, or a show cause notice, at the discretion of the court.

(2) In the case of a notice the alleged contemner may enter appearance in person or through an advocate, and, in the case of a show cause notice, shall appear personally; Provided that the court may at any time exempt the alleged contemner from appearing personally.

(3) If, after giving the alleged contemner an opportunity of a preliminary hearing, the court is prima facie satisfied that the interest of justice so requires, it shall fix a date for framing a charge in open court and proceed to decide the matter either on that date, or on a subsequent date or dates, on the basis of affidavits, or after recording evidence; Provided that the alleged contemner shall not, if he so requests, be denied the right of cross examination in relation to any affidavit, other than that of a judge, used in evidence against him.

18. Substantial detriment:

(1) No person shall be found guilty of contempt of court, or punished accordingly, unless the court is satisfied that the contempt is one which is substantially detrimental to the administration of justice or scandalizes the court or otherwise tends to bring the court or Judge of the court into hatred or ridicule.

(2) In the event of a person being found not guilty of contempt by reason of sub-section the court may pass an order deprecating the conduct, or actions, of the person accused of having committed contempt.

(3) Subject to the provisions of this Ordinance, truth shall be a valid defence in cases of contempt of court.

19. Appeal:

(1) Notwithstanding anything contained in any other law or the rules for the time being in force, orders passed by a superior court in contempt cases shall be appealable in the following manner:

(i) in the case of an order passed by a single judge of a High Court an intra-court appeal shall lie to a bench of two or more judges;

(ii) in a case in which the original order has been passed by a division or larger bench of a High Court an appeal shall lie to the Supreme Court, and

(iii) in the case of an original order passed by a single judge or a bench of two judges of the Supreme Court an intra-court appeal shall lie to a bench of three judges and in case the original order was passed by a bench of three or more judges an intra-court appeal shall lie to a bench of five or more judges.

(2) The appellate court may suspend the impugned order pending disposal of the appeal.

(3) The limitation period of filing an appeal shall be 30 days.

20. Repeal: The Contempt of Court Act, 1976 (LXIV of 1976) is hereby repealed.-APP

***Explanation***

Not obeying the order of the court in any matter as directed, will be taken as contempt of the court. A civil contempt is made on face of the court, thereby injuring the right of another, as an example, failure to pay child support when ordered by the court and not carried out, will result in a civil contempt. Civil contempt is also not fulfilling an undertaking given to the court. Right to initiate civil contempt proceedings will add to the powers of the court and are in addition to any other laws in force at the time being. Civil contempt will be heard in open court and shall be heard by Chief Justice or the procedure stated therein. Any material stuck off by relevant officers stated therein, will not be admissible in the case under hearing. Once again a reference to matter sub judice to the court. Any person publishing anything or making a statement about a subject regarding which case is pending in court will not be guilty of contempt of court if he was not aware of this fact that the matter was under hearing by the court.

Exception is also made to comments made in a higher court or in a court hearing an appeal with relation to the judgment or in an administrative capacity as stated in (ii) of 16 will not constitute a contempt, neither a fair comment without any intention to scandalize the judge. Nor, comments and observations made by a superior court in a judgment or a judicial order.. These are" protected statements".

In a judgment reported on 3rd July 2012,[204] Justice Shaukat Aziz Siddiqui (High Court Islamabad), initiated contempt of court proceedings against the Capital Development Authority(CDA), sent Director General Planning Ghulam Sarwar Sandhu to Adiala Jail.

While initiating the contempt of court proceedings against CDA DG, the order said, "The act of Sandhu is liable to punishment under section 5 (1) of the contempt of court ordinance 2003, for which formal proceedings are being ordered.[205]

"Advocate Abbas when trying to exonerate his client from the contempt of court case, Sandhu started staring at Justice Siddiqui which irked the judge who directed the police to arrest him.

"The learned judge in his order said: "It has been noted with great concern that mannerism of Ghulam Sarwar Sandhu was not only arrogant but unpalatable as well. He kept on staring at court with anger, as if he intended to give the message that he has no respect for court, judicial proceedings and any order passed therein. The court warned him to be careful but his persistent demeanor is tantamount to disturbing the order and decorum of the court."[206]He was later released. [207]

## *Why Amendment Bill of Contempt of Court 2012?*

This Ordinance was more comprehensive in terms of adding some clauses as exceptions to contempt of court compared with Article 204 of Constitution of Pakistan or Contempt of Court Ordinance 2003.

If I may add, there is never a dull moment in Pakistan. Prime Minister Yusuf Raza Gilani was dismissed as Prime Minister by the Supreme Court of Pakistan in June 2012. The Prime Minister was accused of having committed a contempt of court in April 2012 for not having written a letter to the Swiss authorities as directed by the Supreme Court to reopen a 1990 graft case against President Zardari. According to NDTV, "The ruling was a major escalation in a long-running confrontation between the judges and the government. Supporters of the government, and some independent commentators, accuse the court of pursuing a vendetta against Mr Zardari that threatens the country's nascent

---

[204] Malik Asad for Dawn Newspaper titled. "CDA DG sent to jail in contempt case"
[205] Ibid.
[206] Ibid.
[207] 3rd July 2012 Pakistan Today, titled, "IHC releases DG Planning CDA"

democracy. Mr Zardari's critics, on the other hand, say the court is the only institution standing up against the rampant graft - and ineptitude – in his administration."[208]

Not only was he disqualified as Prime Minister, he was also disqualified from holding a seat in the Parliament from date of his disqualification i.e. April 26th 2012. A nominal punishment of 30 seconds was awarded to former Prime Minister Gilani. Two groups have emerged. One who support the Supreme Court in the judgment and the other who think it was a harsher verdict than what was merited. Without going into opinions by both groups–I am sure this issue will be discussed for years to come– let us get to the outcome of the verdict . The new man in is Raja Pervez Ashraf. The new Prime Minister ushered in has been directed by the Supreme Court to write to the Swiss authorities and submit a compliance report to the Supreme Court by July 25th 2012. "A three-judge bench headed by Justice Asif Saeed Khosa on Thursday in its order warned the new PM, whose predecessor Raza Gilani was sent packing for defying court orders, that the court could take appropriate action if the letter was not written."[209]

What is largely seen as an effort to deflect the packing up of another Prime Minister , an Amendment Bill in Contempt Law was signed by President Zardari as reported on 12th July 2012.[210]

## *The Full Text of Amendment Bill in Contempt of Court Law 2012*

Whereas it is expedient to repeal and re-enact a law of contempt in exercise of the powers conferred by clause (3) of Article 204 of the Constitution of Islamic Republic of Pakistan; It is hereby enacted as follows:

Short title, extent and commencement:- (I) This Act may be called the Contempt of Court Act, 2012.

---

[208]Turmoil in Pakistan after Prime Minister Yousuf Raza Gilani dismissed: 20th June 2012 LINK: http://www.ndtv.com/article/world/turmoil-in-pakistan-after-prime-minister-yousuf-raza-gilani-dismissed-233668

[209] **The Nation 12th July 2012:** SC to take action against PM if Swiss letter not written till 25th

[210] The Express Tribune published on 12th July 2012: "Zardari signs contempt of court amendment bill"

(2) It extends to the whole of Pakistan.

(3) It shall come into force at once.

2. Interpretation:

(a) In this Act, unless there is anything repugnant in the subject or context. "judge" includes all officers acting in a judicial capacity in the administration of justice;

(b) judicial proceedings in relation to any matter shall be deemed to be pending from the time when a court has come to be seized of the matter in a judicial capacity, till such time as the appellate, revisional or review proceedings in respect of the matter have come to an end or the period of limitation for filing such proceedings has expired without any such proceedings having been initiated.

3. Contempt of court:

Whoever disobeys or disregards any order, direction or process of a court, which he is legally bound to obey; or commits a willful breach of a valid undertaking given to a court; or does anything which is intended to or tends to bring the authority of a court or the administration of law or the due course of any judicial proceedings, or to lower the authority of a court or scandalize a judge in relation to his office, or to disturb the order or decorum of a court, is said to commit "contempt of court".

Provided that the following shall not amount to commission of contempt of court- (i) exercise of powers and performance of functions by a public office holder of his respective office under clause (I)of Article 248 of the Constitution for any act done or purported to be done in exercise of those powers and performance of those functions;

(ii) fair comments about the general working of courts made in good faith in the public interest and in temperate language;

(iii) fair comments on merits of a decision of a court made, after the pendency of the proceeding in a case, in good faith and in temperate language;

(iv) subject to a prohibition of publication under section 9 or under any other law for the time being in force, the publication of a fair and substantially accurate report of any judicial proceedings;

(v) the publication of any matter, amounting to a contempt of court by reason of its being published during the pendency of some judicial proceedings, by a person who had no reasonable ground for believing that such judicial proceedings were pending at the time of the publication of the matter;

(vi) the distribution of a publication, containing matter amounting to contempt of court, by a person who had no reasonable ground for believing that the publication contained, or was likely to contain, any such matter;

(vii) a true averment made in good faith and in temperate language for initiation of action or in the course of disciplinary proceedings against a judge, before the Chief Justice of a High Court, the Chief Justice of Pakistan, the Supreme Judicial Council, the Federal Government or a Provincial Government;

(viii) a plea of truth taken up as a defence in terms of clause;

(vi) in proceedings, for contempt of court arising from an earlier averment unless it is false;

(ix) relevant observations made in judicial capacity, such as, those by a higher court on an appeal or revision or application for transfer of a case, or by a court in judicial proceedings against a judge;

(x) remarks made in an administrative capacity by any authority in the course of official business, including those in connection with a disciplinary inquiry or in an inspection note or a character roll or confidential report;

(xi) a true statement made in good faith respecting the conduct of a judge in a matter not connected with the performance of his judicial functions.

4. Punishment: (I) Subject to sub-section

(2) any person who commits contempt of court shall be punished with imprisonment which may extend to six months simple imprisonment, or with a fine which may extend to one hundred thousand rupees, or with both.

(2) A person accused of having committed contempt of court may, at any stage, submit an apology and the court, if satisfied that it is bonafide, may discharge him or remit his sentence.

Explanation. The fact that an accused person genuinely believes that he has not committed contempt and enters a defence shall not detract from the bona fides of an apology.

In the case of a contempt having been committed, or alleged to have been committed, by a company, the responsibility shall extend to the persons in the company, directly or indirectly, responsible for the same, who shall also be liable to be punished accordingly.

Notwithstanding anything contained in any judgment, no court shall have the power to pass any order of punishment for or in relation to any act of contempt, save and except in accordance with subsection (I).

5. Jurisdiction:

(I) A High Court or the Supreme Court, on its own information or on information laid before it by any person, may take cognizance of an alleged commission of contempt of the court.

(2) The Supreme Court shall have the power to take cognizance of any contempt of itself or of any judge of the Supreme Court alleged to have been committed anywhere and a High Court shall have the power to take cognizance of any contempt of itself or of any judge thereof or of any other High Court or of any judge thereof alleged to have been committed within the territorial limits of its jurisdiction.

(3) A High Court shall exercise the same jurisdiction in respect of contempt of courts subordinate to it or to any other High Court as it exercises in respect of contempt of itself.

(4) Nothing contained herein shall affect the power of any court to punish any offence of contempt under the Pakistan Penal Code.

6. Bars to taking cognizance: (I) No High Court shall take cognizance under this Act of a contempt alleged to have been committed in respect of a court subordinate to it where the said contempt is an offence punishable under the Pakistan Penal court

(2) No court shall take cognizance, as of a contempt of court, of any averment made before the Supreme Judicial Council in respect of which the Supreme Judicial Council has given a finding that the averment fulfilled the requirements of clause (vi) of the proviso to section 3.

(3) No court shall take cognizance of contempt of court arising from an averment made in due course in appellate, revisional review proceedings, till such proceedings have been finalized and no further appeal, revision or review lies.

(4) No court shall take cognizance of a contempt of court arising from an averment made by the Chief Justice of a High Court, the Chief Justice of Pakistan, the Supreme Judicial Council, the Federal Government or a Provincial Government--

(a) until the petition to which the averment relates has been finally disposed off ; or(b) otherwise than under the orders of the Chief Justice of the High Court, the Chief Justice of Pakistan, the Supreme Judicial Council, the Federal Government or the Provincial Government, as the case may be.

7. Procedure for Supreme Court and High Court:

(I) Whenever it appears to the Supreme Court or a High Court that there is sufficient ground for believing that a person has committed contempt of court and that it is necessary in the interest of effective administration of justice to proceed against him, it shall make an order in writing to that effect setting forth the substance of the charge against the accused, and, unless he is present in court, shall require by means of an appropriate process that he appear or be brought before it to answer the charge.

(2) The court shall inform the accused of the ground on which he is charged with contempt of court and call upon to show cause why he should not be punished.

(3) The court, after holding such inquiry and taking such evidence as it deems necessary or is produced by the accused in his own defence and after hearing the accused and such other person as it deems fit, shall give a decision in the case;

Provided that, in any such proceedings, before the Supreme Court or a High Court, any finding given in its own proceedings, by the Supreme Judicial Council about the nature of any averment made before it, that is relevant to the requirements of clause (vi) the proviso to section 3, shall be conclusive evidence of the nature of such averment.

(4) If contempt of court is committed in the view or presence of the court, the court, may cause the offender to be detained in custody and, at any time before the rising of the court on the same day, may proceed against him in the manner provided for in the preceding sub-sections;

(5) If any case referred to in sub-section (4) cannot be finally disposed off on the same day, the court shall order the release of the offender from custody either on bail or on his own bond.

8. Transfer of proceedings for reasons personal to the judge:

(1) Where, in a case in which a judge has made an order under sub-section (I) of section 7, not being a case referred to in sub- section (4) of that section, the alleged contempt of court involves scandalization personal to such judge and is not scandalization of the court as a whole or of all the judges of the court, judge shall forward the record of the case and such comments, if any; as he deems fit to make, to the Chief Justice of the court;

(2) On receipt of the papers, mentioned in sub-section (I), the Chief Justice, after inviting, if he deems fit, further comments, if any, from the judge first taking cognizance of the offence and making such inquiry in such manner as he deems fit, shall pass orders specifying which one of the following shall hear the case;

(a) another judge, which if the Chief Justice so orders, may be the Chief Justice;

(b) a Bench of judges set up by the Chief Justice, of which the judge first taking cognizance of the offence is not a member; and the case shall then be heard accordingly.

(3) If, at any stage of a case in which the Chief Justice has passed an order under clause;

(a) of sub section (2), the Chief Justice is of opinion that, in the interests of justice, the case shall be transferred to another judge, he may pass an order accordingly; and the case shall then be heard by such other judge.

(4) When, in pursuance of an order under sub-section (2), the Judge first taking cognizance of the case is not hearing the case;

(a) the other judge or, as the case may be, the Bench of judges hearing the case may invite or receive any further comments from the judge first taking cognizance of the offence and shall call and hear any witnesses whom such judge desires to be examined;

(b) all comments furnished by the judge first taking cognizance of the offence shall be treated as evidence in the case and such judge shall not be required to appear to give evidence.

(5) When in a case the first cognizance of the offence has been taken by the Chief Justice, the functions of the Chief Justice, under sub-section (I), (2) and (3) shall be performed by a Bench of judges composed of the two next most senior judges available.

9. Proceedings in camera and prohibition of publication of proceedings: In case of proceedings for transfer of a hearing under section 8 or of any proceedings in which truth is pleaded as a defence in terms of clause (vi) of the proviso to section 3, the court, if it deems it fit in the public interest, may hear the case or any part thereof in camera and prohibit the publication of the proceedings of the case or any part thereof.

10. Expunged material: No material which has been expunged from the record under the orders of--

(i) a court of competent jurisdiction; or (ii) the presiding officer of the Senate, the National Assembly, or a Provincial Assembly, shall be admissible in evidence.

11. Appeal and limitation for appeal: (I) From an original order passed by the High Court under this Act an appeal shall lie, if the order is passed by a single judge, to a Division Bench, and if it is passed by a Bench of two or more judges, to the Supreme Court.

(2) An appeal shall lie to the Supreme Court from an order passed by a Division Bench of a High Court in appeal against an order passed by a single judge.

(3) An intra-court appeal shall lie against the issuance of a show cause notice or an original order including an interim order passed by a Bench of the Supreme Court in any case, including a pending case, to a larger bench consisting of remaining available judges of the Court within the country:

Provided that in the event the impugned show cause or order has been passed by half or more of the judges of Court, the matter shall, on the application of an aggrieved person be put up for re- appraisal before the full court:

Provided further that the operation of the impugned show cause notice or order shall remain suspended until the final disposal of the matter in the manner herein before provided.

(4) An appeal under sub-section (I) or sub-section (2) shall be filed--

(a) in the case of an appeal to a Bench of the High Court, within thirty days; and

(b) in the case of an appeal to the Supreme Court, within sixty days, from the date of the order appealed against.

(5) An intra- court appeal or application for re-appraisal shall be filed within thirty days from the date of show cause notice or the order, as the case may be.

12. Power to make rules: The Federal Government may make rules, not inconsistent with the provisions of this Act, providing for any matter relating to its procedure.

13. Repeal: (I) The Contempt of Court Ordinance, 2003 (V of 2003) is hereby repealed.

(2) For removal of doubt it is hereby declared that the Contempt of Court Act, 1976(LXIV of 1976), Contempt of Court Ordinance, 2003 (IV of 2003) and Contempt of Court Ordinance, 2004 (I of 2004) stand repealed.

## Statement of objects and reasons

The contempt law is a blend of the power of the court to punish for its contempt and the rights of the citizens in a democracy for fair comments and criticism. It is therefore necessary that whereas the law may provide to the alleged accused to have fair trial including transparent procedure for right to appeal.

Right to appeal is being streamlined and other necessary provisions relevant to contempt proceedings are being incorporated in the Bill.[211]

## *Explanation*

Under the new law, contempt of court is defined as it has been defined initially in Article 204 itself. However, it clearly states, if someone does not comply with an order because it violates Article 248(dealing with indemnity awarded to certain public office bearers including the President), it may not be deemed as contempt of court. This is to fall within the exceptions of contempt of court. However, since Article 248 already exists, repetition of the same did not "increase its importance" so to speak. Former Prime Minister Gilani had repeatedly stated in answer to questions that "Article 248 awarded immunity to President under the Constitution and the charges of contempt against him are not of a criminal nor a moral nature." He said all those constitutional clauses that grant immunity to the president and the prime minister for doing any act in good faith stand fully operational, as even the opposition did not propose any amendment when 18th, 19th and 20th amendments were passed.[212]

Article 248 states:

**Protection to President, Governor, Minister, etc.**

(1) The President, a Governor, the Prime Minister, a Federal Minister, a Minister of State, the Chief Minister and a Provincial Minister shall not he answerable to any court for the exercise of powers and performance of functions of their respective offices or for any act done or purported to be done in the exercise of those powers and performance of those functions:

---

[211] 'Business Recorder' published 10th July 2012

[212] Irfan Ghauri for Express Tribune May 4th 2012, title, After Parliament nods, Gilani vows to continue as President"

Provided that nothing in this clause shall be construed as restricting the right of any person to bring appropriate proceedings against the Federation or a Province.

(2) No criminal proceedings whatsoever shall be instituted or continued against the President or a Governor in any court during his term of office.
(3) No process for the arrest or imprisonment of the President or a Governor shall issue from any court during his term of office.
(4) No civil proceedings in which relief is claimed against the President or a Governor shall be instituted during his term of office in respect of anything done by or not done by him in his personal capacity whether before or after he enters upon his office unless, at least sixty days before the proceedings are instituted, notice in writing has been delivered to him, or sent to him in the manner prescribed by law, stating the nature of the proceedings, the cause of action, the name, description and place of residence of the party by whom the proceedings are to be instituted and the relief which the party claims.

However, the Supreme Court did not accept this point for view. The text of Supreme Court judgment(short order) in this case, is shared as following:

"For the reasons to be recorded later, the accused Syed Yousuf Raza Gilani, Prime Minister of Pakistan/Chief Executive of the federation, is found guilty of and convicted for contempt of court, under Article 204 (2) of the Constitution of the Islamic Republic of Pakistan, 1973, read with Section 3 of the Contempt of Court Ordinance (Ordinance 5 of 2003) for wilful flouting, disregard and disobedience of this court's direction contained in paragraph number 178 of the judgment delivered in the case of Dr Mubashir Hasan versus the Federation of Pakistan (PLD 2010 SC 265). After our satisfaction that the contempt committed by him is substantially detrimental to the administration of justice and tends to bring this court and the judiciary of this country into ridicule.

"2. As regards the sentence to be passed against the convict, we note that the findings and the conviction for contempt of court recorded above are likely to entail some serious consequences in terms of Article 63 (1) (g) of the Constitution which may be treated as mitigating factors towards the sentence to be passed against him. He is, therefore, punished under Article 5 of the contempt of court ordinance (ordinance 5 of 2003) with imprisonment till the rising of the court today."[213]

[213] Published 26 April 2012 by DAWN titled, 'Text of SC Verdict'

The detailed judgment is uploaded by Dawn Newspaper, it was not possible to reproduce it here, but is available for viewing at: *http://dawncompk.files.wordpress.com/2012/05/sc-detailed-verdict-pm-gilani-case-with-add note.pdf*

***Exceptions to Contempt of Court Law 2012:***

Other exceptions to Contempt of Court remain as before and discussed earlier in the chapter under Article 204. The newer ones are :

- A holder of a public office who may take any action in light of clause (1) of Article 248 , or any act purported to be done in exercise of those rights. This offers an umbrella protection to certain public officials from public scrutiny. However, Article 248 is already a part of the Constitution. It is not a new injection. Therefore adding it here does not take it to "a higher legal pedestal."[214]
- Any comment that is fair and made After a case is decided upon, may not be deemed as contempt of court.
- A new exception is; a fair comment made in moderate and temperate language *during* a court proceedings. This may be deemed to be seen as an explanation/future deterrence to the defence put up by former Prime Minister Gilani.
- Publication of an accurate account of proceedings of the court will not be contempt. Here, a differentiation is made between objective reporting and subjective analysis.
- If a publication is made commenting on the proceedings while the hearing was underway–a person can prove, without reasonable doubt that he was unaware of the proceedings underway. The onus to prove so, will be on the defendant.
- Similarly if a person distributes some published material without the knowledge that it contained material commenting on proceedings underway in court will not be held in contempt. This too, has to be proved.
- If an affirmation or allegation is made in temperate language and good faith about initiation of disciplinary proceedings against a judge will not be said to be contempt of court. *Example:* In a paper titled, "Measures for the Effective Implementation of the Bangalore Principles of Judicial Conduct" (The Implementation Measures), adopted by the *Judicial Integrity Group* at its meeting held at Lusaka, Zambia, on 21-22 January 2010, Section 15 is titled "Discipline of Judges." It states that proceedings can be initiated against a

[214] Babar Sattar, "The Two Wrongs...Part I.. Legal Eye" The News published 27th July 2012

judge in serious cases of misconduct and a person suffering from this may lodge a complaint, It suggests a competent person of panel may be authorized to receive the complaint and deliberate if enough evidence and reason exists for initiating a disciplinary proceedings against the judge.

- Taking a plea in favor of (vi)is not contempt.
- Comments made by a superior court on observations to a junior court either in an appeal, revision of a case etc in judicial capacity is not contempt.
- If an authority during course of his official business, makes a comment in an administrative capacity, will not be construed as contempt.
- Last but not the least, if an individual makes a true comment on the conduct of the judge which has nothing to do with his judicial capacity or the functionary of the judicial system, this may not be deemed as contempt. This separates the Judge as a private person and one acting in a judicial capacity.

The new law(now struck down) did state that if offender offers a genuine apology to the court, and if the court is satisfied that it is a genuine apology, the punishment may be remitted ie surrendered or relinquished. The High Court can take suo moto notice of any contempt committed within its jurisdiction.

The procedure explained in the law is self-explanatory . However, the base of appeal was enhanced under the new law. In case of proceedings in the High Court, time was extended to 30 days and in case of Supreme Court to sixty days. Provision for intra-court appeal could be filed within thirty days of show cause notice or order. With the ushering in of this law, both Article 204 and Contempt of Court Ordinance 2003 stood repealed. However, this law had the shortest life ever, and was struck down on 3rd August 2012.

### *Amendment Bill in Contempt of Court Law 2012 struck down as null & void*

I would like to add here, I had written this chapter and was way ahead on this book when the new law was introduced. Therefore, this made it mandatory to revisit the chapter for inclusions. And then, at the eleventh hour, literally, the news broke on 3rd August 2012 that the Supreme Court has struck down the Amendment Bill in Contempt of Court Law 2012 declaring it as null and void. “While the Act was ultimately struck down in its entirety, the court did not find issue with all its clauses, but observed that keeping the remaining clauses wouldn't serve much purpose.

"After having found various provisions of Contempt of Court Act 2012 as ultra vires the Constitution, we are of the opinion that the remaining provisions of the impugned legislation, if allowed to stay on the statute book, would serve no purpose....," read the court order." [215]

The pages on this law have nonetheless been allowed to stand as it forms a part of the legal history of the country and no doubt will be debated for times to come. When contacted, ***Raza Rumi***[216]said, "One option could have been for the Supreme Court to revert the Bill for review to the Parliament marking its observations. The precedent for this exists as earlier too, the Amended Articles of the Constitution were sent to the Parliament for necessary review and changes. However, striking down the entire legislation is unprecedented in Pakistan's legal history."[217] Talking of precedents, the decision on this case will not have bearing on this one case only, but will act as a precedent for many more, in years to come. The courts are bound (to certain limits)by earlier decisions taken by superior courts. A precedent address and settles *similar questions* in latter cases. Precedence offers predictability and fairness in law. Predictability defines the rights and obligations of a person in a given set of circumstances. An individual can learn the precedents and know the outcome of his case beforehand. ***Justice Louis D. Brandeis*** emphasized the importance of this when he wrote, "Stare decisis is usually the wise policy, because in most matters it is more important that the applicable rule of law be settled than that it be settled right." (Burnet v. Coronado Oil & Gas Co., 285 U.S. 393, 52 S. Ct. 443, 76 L. Ed. 815 [1932]).[218]

"Yet another general principle the courts seek to apply when striking down primary legislation, is to attempt to spare as much of the statute as it possibly can – only those specific provisions which are in direct violation of the Constitution are struck down. A classic example is the judgment in *Rauf Bakhsh Kadri v The State*, where a bench of the Sindh High Court displayed clinical acumen in its interpretation of the then-NAB Ordinance, so as to preserve the statute while at the same time precluding the possibility of its use in an unconstitutional fashion. It is

---

[215] "Contempt Law: Outlawed" published in Express Tribune dated 4th August 2012

[216] A blogger & writer from Pakistan , based in Lahore

[217] Telephonic conversation on 3rd August 2012

[218] Example given in the definition of "Precedent" in The Free Legal Dictionary

surprising then, that within this well established historical context, the Supreme Court chose to strike down not merely the offending provisions, but the statute as a whole."[219] This is in an article by ***Yousuf Nasim.***[220]

Let me state here, when we start laying out too many conditions, correct though they may be, we tend to create a trap. The trap is to exclude multidimensional situations that are not covered in law, as, there can be many situations that cannot be catered for and covered in law. Simplification of laws is a beautiful thing. The purpose of law, must be ultimately for people like you and me to respect the law, especially the institutions that implement the law and are considered to be the bastions of justice. The more mazes we create, the more we get lost in the labyrinth.

***Do others Constitutions have Contempt of Court provisions? A brief comparison***

***The Contempt of Court Act 1971,*** of India is a comprehensive Act dealing with this wrong doing. The Act defines the contempt under Indian Law and limits powers of certain courts in punishing contempt. Section 2 of the Act defines a contempt as follows:

2. Definitions. In this Act, unless the context otherwise requires:

(a) "contempt of court" means civil contempt or criminal contempt;

(b) "civil contempt" means wilful disobedience to any judgment, decree, direction, order, writ or other process of a court or wilful breach of an undertaking given to a court;

(c) "criminal contempt" means the publication (whether by words. spoken or written, or by signs, or by visible representations, or otherwise) of any matter or the doing of any other act whatsoever which;

(i) scandalizes or tends to scandalize, or lowers or tends to lower the authority of, any court; or

---

[219] Analysis: Culling the Contempt Law published in DAWN newspaper

[220] Lawyer practicing in Karachi

(ii) prejudices, or interferes or tends to interfere with, the due course of any judicial proceeding; or

(iii) interferes or tends to interfere with, or obstructs or tends to obstruct, the administration of justice in any other manner;

(d) "High Court" means the High Court for a State or a Union territory, and includes the Court of the Judicial Commissioner in any Union territory.

This is more or less, a replica of the law under force in Pakistan under Article 204 Constitution of Pakistan 1973.

However, if a person publishes, portrays, says anything on an issue he had no reason to believe was a matter in court, it will not be deemed contempt of court. This applies to both civil and criminal proceedings. If an individual distributes anything stated above and was not aware it contained such matter, it will not be contempt. Further, anything stated in fair criticism of working of the court, or merits of a case is not contempt.

Publication of fair recount of proceedings of court is not contempt, neither is, publication of information relating to proceedings in chambers or in camera except for certain cases. The Act deals with contempt committed by companies and details of exceptions of publication of information of proceedings in chambers or in camera.

In an interesting report by ***Krishnadas Rajagopal,*** for ***The Indian Express,***[221] it states setting up of a Constitution Bench for reporting of cases led by Chief Justice of India, S. H. Kapadia, having expanded its reach to other spheres of journalism , ie ban on "Media Leakage", in a pending crime investigation, restricting sex and violence on TV and drafting norms for news coverage by electronic media.[222]

"A three-page order uploaded on the Supreme Court's official website on April 4 shows that four pending cases in the apex court regarding complaints of perceived media excess have been transferred to the Constitution Bench. It states that the Bench has given 'liberty' to parties concerned in these four matters 'to make submissions on issues relating to media coverage' on April 10, the next date of hearing.

---

[221] Titled, "SC spreads its media gaze from court to crime to contempt" published by The Indian Express Newspaper on 7th April, 2012

[222] Ibid.

"The four cases listed concern media reports in the Arushi double murder case and the contempt proceedings against former India Today magazine editor Prabhu Chawla and correspondent Mihir Srivastava in the Batla House encounter, apart from petitions seeking norms regarding presentation of sexual abuse and violence on TV as well as guidelines for TV news coverage."[223]

According to ***Sudhanshu Ranjan***, in ***Times of India***, in its 200th report, *Trial by Media: Free Speech vs Fair Trial under Criminal Procedure(Amendments to the Contempt of Courts Act 1971)*, has recommended a law to debar the media from reporting anything prejudicial to the rights of the accused in criminal cases, from the time of arrest to investigation and trial.[224]

Press excesses , in an age of media, invading in prohibited domains, is unfortunately becoming a norm.

### *Cases from around the World*

What is needed is to strike a balance between publishing and knowing where to stop. The 1981 Contempt of Court in UK deals with this violation which was a result of in part as a response to decision of Court of Human Rights in a case involving ***The Sunday Times.***[225] The law is not specific about what is allowed to be published and what is not, but lays down broad principles. It applies to all publications that create "a substantial risk" in the course of justice will be "seriously prejudiced". It is a question of judgment in each case as to what may create "substantial risk."[226] Publication during a trial is clearly problematic. In June 1999 ***The Sun*** published serious allegations about a defendant in a murder trial just as the jury were retiring; the charge was dropped and the Sun was fined £35,000. The collapse of an assault trial involving Leeds United footballers in April 2001, following publication of an interview with the victim's father in the Sunday Mirror (which some jury members had read while deliberating), resulted in its editor, Colin Myler, resigning; the paper was subsequently found guilty of contempt of court, fined £75,000 and ordered to pay costs of £100,000.[227]

---

[223] Ibid.
[224] Times of India published 26th Jan 2007
[225] By Gill Phillips: "Contempt of Court: a matter of legal judgment" published in *The Guardian* on 10th Jan 2011
[226] Ibid.
[227] Ibid.

Problems can obviously arise when media discusses, deliberates, speculates, calls politicians for discussions on TV shows and seeks opinions without facts on grounds and talking on the "ifs and buts" of a given scenario. This compromises the judicial trial and may result in influencing the outcome owing to media exposure.

In UK, the case, ***Her Majesty's Attorney General V Associated Newspapers Ltd and News Group Newspapers Ltd.[2011]***[228]was the very first case in UK and Wales to contemplate to determine if the online websites of the two national newspapers had committed contempt of court. The facts related to a murder. On the first day of the trial, the online website showed the accused in the case, holding a gun! This was Mail Online. The picture remained on the website for almost 5 hours. A jury member on his/her computer during those hours could have seen the picture. What a damaging, damaging projection! Ideally, the picture should have been cropped, deleting the gun. Contempt proceedings were brought against the papers by the Attorney-General.

Another case ***Her Majesty's Attorney General V MGN Ltd. And News Group Newspapers Ltd [2011].***[229] related to publicity surrounding arrest of one Chris Jefferies, the landlord of Joanne Yeates. The body of Yeates was found out of Bristol, and another man had confessed to the murder. The Sun carried a headline on 1st January 2011 after Jefferies had been arrested saying that he was "Obsessed by death."[230]

"In each case the court found the newspapers in contempt. In the former case the newspapers were fined £15,000 each and in the latter the Mirror was fined £50,000 and the Sun £18,000. The figure of £50,000 against the Mirror reflects the gravity of the offence. The previous highest penalty for contempt by the media was £75,000 imposed on the Sunday Mirror in 2002."[231]

Basically, journalists must guard against implying "guilt" of a person before a court for trial. This is crucifying him in some cases creating bias. Adding spice to a person's part adventurisms may be calling a person

---

[228] EWHC 418(Admin)LINK: http://uklawstudent.thomsonreuters.com/2011/12/duncan-bloy-contempt-of-court-and-media-publications/
[229] EWHC 2074(Admin) LINK: http://uklawstudent.thomsonreuters.com/2011/12/duncan-bloy-contempt-of-court-and-media-publications/
[230] Ibid.
[231] Ibid.

guilty of a crime because he erred in past which may well not be true. Journalists can give a factual account of court proceedings but, they may not brand him a criminal. This brings us to "substantial risk". What exactly in legal jargon would this term imply?***USLEGAL.COM*** defines it as, "... a strong possibility, as contrasted with a remote or even a significant possibility, that a certain result may occur or that a certain circumstance may exist. It is risk of such a nature and degree that to disregard it constitutes a gross deviation from the standard of care that a reasonable person would exercise in such a situation."[232]So if a journalist is covering an event with a strong possibility to lead the story to a desired reaction or creation of bias so that it interferes in the administration of justice, he will be indulging in contempt of court.

Two newspapers, ***Daily Mail*** and ***Daily Mirror*** were found guilty of contempt of court over their coverage following Levi Bellfield's conviction for the murder of *Milly Dowler*. The High court ruled that they had published "seriously prejudicial" articles in a case brought against them by attorney general Dominic Grieve. " The newspapers argued that what they published could not have created a substantial risk of serious prejudice because the jury already knew of Bellfield's guilt. But Grieve said after the decision: "This case shows why the media must comply with the Contempt of Court Act." "It is unfortunate that the deluge of media coverage following the Milly Dowler verdict, not only by these papers but also other media outlets, led to the judge discharging the jury before they had completed their deliberations on a charge of attempted kidnap, ultimately depriving Rachel Cowles of a verdict in her case."[233]The action was brought against Associated Newspapers, publisher of the Daily Mail, and MGN, publisher of the Daily Mirror. (The High Court has yet to decide on the penalty for the two papers, as we went into publication).[234]

In another recent case, ***The Spectator*** is to face charges over the murder of Stephan Lawrence trial. The magazine has admitted that it was guilty of publishing an article containing facts that were prejudicial and stated the magazine will not be contesting the case. "The charge relates to an article by the commentator Rod Liddle published last November during the trial of Gary Dobson and David Norris, who went on to be

---

[232] USLEGAL.COM LINK: http://definitions.uslegal.com/s/substantial-risk/
[233] BBC News 18th July 2012
[234] The Guardian UK Greenslade Blog. LINK: http://www.guardian.co.uk/media/greenslade/2012/jul/18/contempt-of-court-medialaw

convicted of murdering the black teenager. The Old Bailey judge warned jurors not to read the article."[235]

In an interesting case of contempt, quoted by ***Greek Reporter Europe,*** a Greek Psychology lecturer, from the University of Bedfordshire, on jury duty, was found guilty of contempt of court and sentenced to 6 months of jail . She had searched for the word GBH on the internet and in Luton, where she came across the information that the accused was accused of the very same mistake in the past too. She then proceeded to share this information with other members of the jury. The court stated she had sought facts of the case other than that presented in the court and thereby had interfered with course of justice.[236]

*Sky News,* a renowned TV channel, faced contempt of court charges over allegedly breaching an injunction taken out to protect the safety of the kidnapped British couple, Paul and Rachel Chandler. The court stated the news channel had been wrong in declaring details of the release of the couple by the Somali pirates at a juncture when they had not yet left the country.[237] They were thereby put at a security risk. "Sky News was accused of breaching an order prohibiting publication of the health and welfare of Mr and Mrs Chandler."[238]This incident received wide coverage internationally. *Lord Falconer,* Former Lord Chancellor told the BBC[239] that online news archives must not carry details of high profile cases. He felt that stories are written and these impact the eventual outcome thereby influencing the decision. Certain cases get a major pre-trial coverage. News organizations would have to remove stories from their archives that were written before an arrest was made and a case became active.

"If they refused to comply "it would be very strong evidence they'd committed contempt", he said."[240] Under Contempt Of Court Act 1981 if a journalist writes, projects, shows(on electronic media), depicts(via

---

[235] Reported by the Guardian UK 9th May 2012 by Owen Bowcott , titled, "Spectator magazine to face charges over article on Stephan Lawrence trial."

[236] Titled, "Juror Theodora Dallas Jailed for 6 months for Contempt of Court" by Stella Tsolakidou, published 23rd Jan 2012 . LINK: http://eu.greekreporter.com/2012/01/23/juror-theodora-dallas-jailed-for-6-months-for-contempt-of-court/ Also published Telegraph UK 23rd June 2012

[237] Titled, "Sky News Facing Court Over Chandlers Story" 21st November 2011 at news.sky.com

[238] Ibid.

[239] Titled " Net News Threatens court Cases" by Ruth Alexander, Reporter Law in Action, BBC Radio 4. Dated 19th Feb 2008

[240] Ibid.

picture), anything that may prejudice the outcome of a trial, he will be said to have committed contempt of the court.

This is indeed a concern, in light of growing dependency on the internet for research. The information is extraneous and not being presented in the court itself. Further what one gets from the internet on a given subject may or may not be factual . Prejudicial material can be easy to come by, appearing all over the web - on blogs and discussion boards, for example. As a result, Catrin Turner, a partner and online law specialist at solicitors Pinsent Masons, said "Removing a web page wouldn't necessarily remove the problem."[241]

***Times*** newspaper was ordered to pay costs over 27,000 GBP.[242] Seckerson, foreman of a jury in the case ***Seckerson and The Times Newspapers Ltd v The United Kingdom***[243] in the European Court of Human Rights was dismissed and decision of Court upheld. Seckerson , the foreman of jury at trial of a child minder found guilty of shaking a baby so hard in her care, that the child died a few days later after her mishandling of the infant. Jury passed a guilty verdict by a ratio of 10 out of 12. Once convicted in 2007, Seckerson got in touch with the Times Newspaper. The Times published two articles based on Seckerson.

In particular, the articles contained the following two quotes: "...the consensus was taken three minutes after the foreman was voted in. It was 10-2 against, all based on the evidence. After that, there was no going back" and "ultimately the case was decided by laymen and laywomen using that despicable enemy of correct and logical thinking, that wonderfully persuasive device, common sense."[244]

Since certain deliberations of the jury were disclosed and published, Times Newspaper was declared in contempt of the court.

---

[241] Ibid.

[242] Human Rights Europe Web Site news titled, "Judges Throw Out Times newspaper free expression complaint" published 8th Feb 2012 LINK: http://www.humanrightseurope.org/2012/02/judges-throw-out-times-newspaper-free-expression-complaint/

[243] (application nos. 32844/10 and 33510/10) in European Court of Human Rights.(Ibid)

[244] Human Rights Europe Web Site news titled, "Judges Throw Out Times newspaper free expression complaint" published 8th Feb 2012 LINK: http://www.humanrightseurope.org/2012/02/judges-throw-out-times-newspaper-free-expression-complaint/

Here, I would like to draw your attention towards a paradox. One is legally obligated to answer any question put forth by the court. It may include a question regarding the source of the journalist. Every journalist, to be a good journalist has to have sources. These sources must be protected. Who would like to share with a journalist who would expose him at the drop of a hat–or many hats? Particularly, in countries beset with corruption, lack of transparency in deals and inquiries, guarding of sources becomes a necessity.

There can be situations when the desire to protect the source comes into conflict with the law as it may be seen as interference in administration of justice.

In US, statutes give the journalists the privilege not to reveal sources. Legislatures were sensitive to this need in light of work ethics of journalists. Different states enacted laws at different stages. Maryland being the first state to do so in 1898. After a gap of 33 years, New Jersey was the second state to follow in Maryland's footsteps. Rest followed later.

A report by the ***Parliamentary Assembly of the Council of Europe,*** titled, "The protection of Journalist Sources," on 1st December 2010 prepared by the Committee on Culture, Science and Education,[245] discussed this right at length. The report raised many questions . For example how far can this right be recognized for journalists? Certain European countries limit the scope, they also award the right to journalists from certain media only. Is a journalist a *professional* journalist only or anyone who gathers information for news/views purposes? "Whistleblowers" are a mine of information for journalists. Yet law provides no specific provision for their protection.

These and many interesting views and questions, in particular relating to the electronic media and net communications are raised in this report.

The concept of protecting the right of protecting journalist sources is based on ***confidentiality.*** It has its root in the Latin word "trust". When an individual is trusted with something, like information, he is expected not to betray that trust.

---

[245] LINK:
http://assembly.coe.int/Main.asp?link=/Documents/WorkingDocs/Doc10/EDOC12443.htm

Confidentiality need, may have its roots in many or one reason(s). An informer may be afraid for his life or that of his family if it is discovered he leaked the information. The fear may be a fear of losing his job. The fear may be cultural stigma in some cases, so on and so forth. Confidentiality protects the society too, as without journalists' investigative work, much may not come to light which may be integral to shed light on issues of public interest for good governance.

The purpose of sharing so many shades and hues of contempt is to give the bigger picture of what contempt of court entails in its spiritual sense. The law has evolved to mean many things to many societies. It has developed into a law that guards the sanctity of the judgment of a court. Whereas, no one is above law, advertently or inadvertently, making a mockery of the court will not be allowed. Any degree of bias on the other hand, will bring in question, the decision of the court itself.

All societies rest their structures on pillars. These are the judiciary, executive and legislature. Some add media to the list. In countries where media is mature, and believes in responsible journalism, this contention may well be true.

Reflecting on the Law of Contempt of Court, I could not but ask myself: is this law a sword or a shield? Can it be used against the judiciary– a spook in the wheel or a whip to wield over practitioners of law at the highest forum? Or, is it a shield for the practitioners of law at the highest forums, from behind which they wag a finger at lesser mortals? Or , is it neither–but a double-edged sword? A moment of quiet contemplation.

### *Concluding Comments:*

For any society to develop, respect of the law is a basic ingredient. Whereas the courts are not an island within an island as we have seen, yet it is imperative that the courts are respected as institutions for dispensing justice. If this element is eroded, we will bring the very judgment in question thereby damaging the very institutions that dispenses justice. The interpretation can be as wide or as narrow as the Courts make it to be.

I cannot close this chapter without sharing Lao-tzu in "The Way of Lao-tzu," where he states, "The more law and order are made prominent, the more thieves and robbers there will be."

# *Chapter IV*

## *Defamation*

Defamation Laws spring from the Law of Torts, having its roots in English Common Law. ***Salmond*** defined tort as, "A civil wrong for which the remedy is common law action for unliquidated damages, and which is not exclusively the breach of contract, or the breach of trust."[246] The word "tort" comes from the Latin word *tortum,* implying "to twist", meaning thereby behavior or conduct that is tortuous or wrong. It corresponds with the English word *wrong* and the Roman word *delict*. When actions are twisted, this is in opposition to actions that are considered straight.

***Winfield*** defined Tort in the following words : "Tortuous liability arises from the breach of a duty primarily fixed by law; this duty is towards persons generally and its breach is redressible by an action for unliquidated damages."[247]

To be a tort, an act, whether commission of it, or omission of it, must be wrongful. This wrongful action must result in damage. The damage may be either in legal terms or actual terms. The cause of redress as a result of the act must lie in a legal remedy or in an action for damages. Damages are monetary claim to a damage suffered. The damage must be in real or legal terms . The party having complained must have suffered from a legal or real wrong committed by the act of another.

An empty threat is thus, not actionable.[248]

---

[246] Salmond, Jurisprudence, 12th ed. (1966)

[247] Winfield and Jolowicz on Tort, W.V.H. Rogers, 16th ed. Sweet and Maxwell A Thomas Company, London (2002), p.4

[248] (1941) OWN 864; AIR 1941 Oudh 572; 1941 OLR 542.

Law of Torts basically is based on a simple, understandable and logical principle that any and every harm to another individual is unlawful and thereby punishable. In these torts is a wrong that is deemed as a wrong *affecting one's reputation*. This is known as *defamation*.

Defamation is described as :

"An intentional false communication, either published or verbally spoken, that injures another's reputation or good name. Holding up of a person to ridicule, scorn or contempt in a respectable and considerable part of the community, may be criminal as well as civil includes both libel and slander. Defamation is that which tends to injure reputation, to diminish the respect, esteem, good will or confidence in which the plaintiff is held or to excite adverse, derogatory or unpleasant feeling or opinions against him. Statement that exposes person to contempt, hatred, ridicule or obloquy." [249]

Another definition sets it out as, " Defamation is a communication which exposes a person to hatred, ridicule or contempt, lowers him in the esteem of his fellows, causes him to be shunned, or injures him in his business or calling. Its categories are libel–broadly, printed or written material; and slander–broadly, spoken words."[250]

In the second definition of defamation above, please read written/published word as not only something written and/or published but in any form that creates a record and may be checked back for reference for example a TV programme, radio, computer online articles, so on and so forth.

Before the American Revolution, laws regarding defamation sprang from the Common Law of England, this resulted in libelous material published or slander committed was punishable with jail imprisonment. However, James Madison realized the need for freedom of speech , a press free of the shackles of government restraint . We see this value of freedom of speech reflected in the First Amendment of Constitution of America.

---

[249] Black's Law Dictionary Sixth Edition, Centennial Edition(1891-1991) Pg 417

[250] The Law of Mass Communications by *Harold L. Nelson and Dwight L. Teeter Jr Pg 56*

***Slander*** will be described as: "Speaking of base and defamatory words tending to prejudice another in his reputation, community standing, office, trade, business or means of livelihood ."[251]

So slander has certain basic ingredients; (a) it is defamatory (b) it is oral and (c) it must lead to damaging another's reputation.

If a doctor is shunned because of slander and his reputation thereby affected, damaging his practice as a result thereof, it will be deemed he has suffered due to baseless comments ie slander.

A person against whom slanderous comments/opinion is made is competent to file a case against the person committing the offence.

The onus to prove that slander was committed lies on the plaintiff. He must prove that the communication took place and that it's defamatory. It must not be a fair comment on the person or an institution. This, then, will not constitute slander. In slander, the person bringing about a case must prove that *special damage* has resulted owing to the slander.

In an interesting case of slander, ***Amanda Knox,*** an American, was cleared in the Italian Court for murder. She had put up a request that she may also be cleared of slander charges. She had made statements falsely implicating Patrick Lumumba for murder of her British housemate, one Meredith Kercher. Lumumba was initially arrested but later cleared of the charges. He sued Knox for slander after being cleared.[252]

In a high profile case, Former French Prime Minister Dominique de Villepin was acquitted of slander against his rival Sarkozy. The charges were brought about as a result of a smear campaign against Sarkozy. The case sprouted from a mysterious list that surfaced which contained the names of people who had secret accounts at a Luxembourg Clearing House. The article by ***The Independent*** goes on to state, "The accounts were purportedly created to hold bribes from a 1991 sale of warships to Taiwan, and other shady income. The list included names of prominent French public figures, including Mr Sarkozy, but was later deemed a hoax. Mr Villepin was given the fake list and asked a retired general to investigate its origins. The indictment said Mr Villepin should have

---

[251] Black's Law Dictionary Sixth Edition. Centennial Edition(1891-1991) Pg 1388

[252] Article by The Guardian titled, "Amanda Knox Appeals against slander conviction against Meredith Kercher case", published 7th Feb 2012

alerted judicial authorities to the scam earlier, and he was tried for complicity in slander. The appeals court judges explained today's acquittal, saying it had not been proven that Mr Villepin knew the lists were fake, nor had any role in the scam."[253]

In 1889 Parnellite MP William O'Brian sued the then UK Prime Minister Lord Salisbury(1830-1903 ) for slander. His claim was for £10,000 in damages for Lord Salisbury to have made comments about O'Brien's support for terrorism in Ireland. After two years had passed, the topic of coercion against Irish independence being the hot potato, *London Times* acquired some letters for which they paid a tidy amount, presumably written by Charles Parnell(1846-1891)to a Fenian Bomber. Parnell sued *London Times* and was awarded £5,000 damages plus costs. The letters turned out to be fake, written by one Pigott, a photographer, blackmailer and forger. Later, Pigott blew his brains out.

Proof of special damage is mandatory to prove slander or the court may not take action on it. However, there are a few exceptions to this. If words are used that charge the person with a criminal offence. Stating that "X" is a murderer, or "Y" committed a dacoity, or "Z" is a rapist. The court will not demand proof of special damages as it will deem that such serious allegations, if false, *will* have serious repercussions. Wrongfully accused people face trials and the charges may be fixed. Being innocent does not mean person accused *will* be acquitted. Most of us indulge in gossip and little realize its implications–unless we have ourselves been a victim. Oral defamation(slander) is often damaging. Each person's reputation is inviolate and thereby, no person may be accused of a criminal act he/she has not committed. In 2012, two ball boys had stated that Fine molested them when they were kids. They accused Syracuse's basketball coach, one Jim Boeheim, of being "out for money." What he tried to say was that both the men(then young boys) were not really sexually abused but were gunning at making money off the school. After 10 days, Jim Boeheim apologized for his harsh words. But it was too late. It was upsetting for the two men(also step brothers), to take lying down this accusation by Boenheim. The two men(Lang and Davis) have sued Boenheim.

"Boeheim's statements not only harmed Bobby Davis and Mike Lang, they also no doubt had a substantial chilling effect on other victims of

[253] "Ex-premiere Dominique de Villepin cleared in Slander case" published 14th September 2011

sexual abuse who already face so many obstacles to reporting," Wang wrote.[254]

Associating someone with a virulent disease is also actionable *per se* .Stating that "X" has venereal disease, or that "Y" is suffering from AIDS, are serious allegations and the court will not demand proof of damage in such cases.

If one brings in question the ability of a person as a professional in discharge of his duties this too shall be actionable *per se,* court will not ask to show proof of damage. If words to the effect prejudices a party and brings aspirations to his ability to effectively handle his job in question, proceedings lie against the offender.

***Ivan Hoffman***[255]***, B.A, J.D*** in his paper ***Defamation***[256] states, this kind of slander tends to "injure him in respect to his office, profession, trade or business, either by imputing to him general disqualification in those respects which the office or other occupation peculiarly requires, or by imputing something with reference to his office, profession, trade, or business that has a natural tendency to lessen its profits."[257]

***Buddha*** describes abstinence from slander as follows:

"The man who is committed to abstinence from slander avoids tale-bearing. He brings about reconciliation among those who are divided. His words strengthen the unity of those who are already united. He delights in seeing people in harmony. He loves harmony, so he will make only the remarks that tend to encourage harmonious relationships."

***Libel*** is the second kind of defamation. Here, the ingredients of libel are (a)words stated must be defamatory(b)it must be in form of a permanent record that can be referred back to, and(c)it must refer to the person of the plaintiff(complainant). ***Black's Law Dictionary*** defines libel as, "a method of defamation expressed by print, writing, pictures or signs. In its most general sense, any publication that is injurious to the

---

[254] *Syracuse.com* story by John O'Brien/The Post Standard, titled, "Bernie Fine's accusers ask Judge to let the slander suit against Jim Boenheim go forward", published 12th April 2012
[255] Attorney-at-Law
[256] LINK: http://www.ivanhoffman.com/defamation.html
[257] Ibid.

reputation of another. A false and unprivileged publication in writing of defamatory material."[258]

***Merriam-Webster*** defines libel as, "a written or oral defamatory statement or representation that conveys an unjustly unfavorable impression.... a statement or representation published without just cause and tending to expose another to public contempt: (2) defamation of a person by written or representational means: (3) the publication of blasphemous, treasonable, seditious, or obscene writings or pictures : (4) the act, tort, or crime of publishing such a libel."[259]

In a benchmark case, in 1934, ***Princess Irena Youssoupoff,*** niece of Russian Tsar Nicholas II, sued the ***Metro-Goldwyn Pictures.*** In the picture by the studio, *Rasputin and the Empress,* it was shown that the princess fell for the "mad monk" once he set out to seduce her. She was awarded US$125,000 at that time, the biggest libel judgment in England.

***Monson V Tussauds*** case that again is a milestone in the history of libel, took place in 1894. The Ardlamont Murder took place in Argyll, Scotland in 1893. It led to two cases. The HM Advocate Vs Monson and in 1894, a case of defamation by Monson against Madam Tussauds. John Monson was acquitted of the charge of the murder of Cecil Hambrough. Tussauds in the meanwhile had put up a waxen effigy of John Monson in its gallery of criminals. Monson sued Madam Tussauds for libel. Though Monson won the case and the lowest possible defamation costs were awarded, it did establish a new principle. The principle was *libel by innuendo.*

Innuendo will generally mean, "an indirect or subtle reference, especially one made maliciously or indicating criticism or disapproval."[260]

Yet another case I would like to state here is of UK Conservative MP ***Jeffrey Archer***. He was awarded £500,000 in damages and £700,000 in legal costs when he successfully sued the tabloid ***Daily Star*** in 1987. The tabloid accused Archer of paying a prostitute £2,000 pounds for services rendered and then having lying about it.

Another very interesting case law is quoted by a leading blog, reported in February 2012, Ecuadorean President Rafael Correa sued two

---

[258] Sixth Edition, Centennial Edition(1891-1991) Pg 915

[259] An Encyclopedia Britannica Company. LINK:http://www.merriam-webster.com/dictionary/libel

[260] The Free Dictionary by Farlex :LINK: http://www.thefreedictionary.com/innuendo

journalists, Juan Carlos Calderón and Christian Zurita. The journalists, in their 2010 book, *El Gran Hermano*, wrote that the President's brother Fabricio Correa, told them that "the President knew all about" the up to $120 million in federal construction contracts that firms tied to Fabricio were being awarded under a questionable bidding process (so questionable, in fact, that the President was eventually compelled to shut the policy down). Fabricio never denied telling the authors the President was aware of the possibly nepotistic contracts; in fact, Fabricio has since repeated it publicly."[261]As a result, Quito Judge María Mercedes Portilla ordered the journalists to pay the President $1 million each because, she ruled, their book had scarred his "honor, dignity and good name" and had caused him "spiritual damage." All this despite the fact that the authors themselves don't claim President Correa knew about his brother's contracts; rather, "we're quoting [Fabricio] as saying [the President] knew," Calderón told TIME in response to Portilla's decision.[262]

Quoting a case of Uzbekistan, early 2010 saw the conviction of known and acclaimed photographer and videographer, Umida Ahmedova, who was convicted on charges of slander and insulting the Uzbek people. Charges against Ahmedova were brought about in January 2010 on grounds that her book of photographs published in 2007 and a documentary film published in 2008–reflect the everyday life and gender inequality of the Uzbek people, but were found by the court to "discredit the foundations and customs of the people of Uzbekistan" and "offend [their] traditions."[263]

Libel is actionable per se . Claim of damages for publication of defamatory statement: "While determining damages due regard has to be taken of following factors: (a)nature of defamatory statement (b) conduct of person responsible for its publication (c) conduct of such person after issuance of notice and after institution of case (d) degree of care and caution exercised before publication of disputed statement. *(Majid Nizami Vs Sheikh Muhammad Rashid: PLJ 1997 Lahore 652=PLD 1996 Lahore 410)."*[264]

---

[261]*Global Spin* a blog of Time World, article by Tim Padgett, titled "Ecaudor's Correra wins Another Libel Case: Are the Latin American Media Being Bullied?" published February 10th, 2012

[262] Ibid.

[263] SITE for *Human Rights Watch* published 12th February 2010 LINK: http://www.hrw.org/news/2010/01/27/uzbekistan-drop-slander-charge-against-photographer

[264] PLJ Volume I 1996-7 Pg 754

Each time a slander or/and libel is repeated, it becomes an offence and the offender is liable to be brought to court for the offence. Every time it becomes cause for a new case. There are many grounds on which damages can be aggravated or mitigated in case of slander and libel. **Let us first examine how damages can be aggravated.**

Here, I would like to share an interesting case with the readers : "Ribereña Meléndez , was given a three-year suspended prison sentence on 7 November 2011 with the proviso that he would have to serve the sentence if he failed to pay the 30,000 soles (11,000 dollars) in damages demanded by the plaintiff. Alto Amazonas province Mayor Juan Daniel Mesía Camus brought about the lawsuit, over certain questions and reports about contracts by companies who had also supported his election campaign. The favorable decision in the Meléndez case was issued on 19 March by a criminal high court in San Martín province, which overturned his conviction on the grounds that it found no "aggravating" circumstances and that **insufficient evidence** was produced to demonstrate the defamatory nature of Meléndez's claims."[265]

**Language of the accused** will play an aggravating effect in awarding of punishment . If the language was violent, abusive, threatening, the damages payable will increase.

Similarly, the **nature of imputation** made will aggravate or mitigate damages. For example in case studies discussed earlier, we have observed charging someone with criminal offence has serious repercussions. It brings into suspicion the person accused, having him shunned by the society. If the defamation is deliberate and malicious, it will lead to enhancement of damages. **Failure to apologize** to the plaintiff after committing defamation will also be held against the person accused. The court will also consider if the attack was **unprovoked** and that the defendant was extremely negligent in the choice of words/publication.

## There are certain factors that mitigate the damages

There are many grounds on which damages against the offender can be mitigated. If the accused **apologizes at the first opportunity**, court

[265] News posted on CIMA (Center for International Media Assistance titled: "Peru: Court Quashes Defamation Conviction on Appeal ,Spares Journalist Jail Time" on 29th March 2012 LINK: http://cima.ned.org/peru-court-quashes-defamation-conviction-appeal-spares-journalist-jail-time

will take cognizance of the fact. If evidence falls short of justification ie if the case is not strong enough and does not prove guilt of the accused.

**Absence of malice** will also be an important factor in determining and adjudging damages. The court will also keep in mind if the plaintiff is in **the habit of libeling the defendant** and if, in reaction, the defendant libeled/slandered the plaintiff. If the defendant can prove that the plaintiff is into doing or saying something falling within the purview of defamation, against the defendant, this will be duly considered by the courts.

Also, **if the plaintiff has a far from clean reputation**, courts will take this into consideration. This does not mean to say that if someone has a doubtful reputation, anyone can get away by saying anything about his/her reputation. What it does mean is, if the plaintiff has a bad reputation, it is easy for another to be taken in by a negative news related to the plaintiff.

### *Accidental Defamation*

An interesting question arises here. Can it be possible to *accidently* defame a person? The answer is: yes. It is very much possible. In a leading case ***Newstead v. London Newspapers,***[266] in the case, a newspaper that was covering a bigamy case stated that the defendant was "one Harold Newstead, a 30-year old Camberwall man."[267]Although, the newspaper had its facts right, what it did not know was there was another 30 year old man by the same name, in Camberwall, a hairdresser by profession who sued the newspaper for defamation as there was a confusion of identities involved. Media must be careful when detailing facts about a person. If better details are given, or were given in the case discussed above, a case of defamation could have been avoided.

In yet another case of *"bad copy"* is ***Cassidy V. Daily Mirror Newspapers Ltd.***[268]In this case, the newspaper published a picture of Mr. C and Miss X with the following caption, "Mr. C, the racehorse owner, and Miss X, whose engagement has been announced."[269] The fact was, Mr. C was NOT engaged to Miss X and was already married to the plaintiff. The bad caption gave an erroneous impression that Mr. C was getting

---

[266] [1940] 1 KB 371. LINK: http://www.aibd.org.my/node/65#_ftn16
[267] Ibid.
[268][1929] 2 KB 331 LINK: http://www.aibd.org.my/node/65#_ftn17
[269] Ibid.

engaged to Miss X. She sued on a moral high ground stating that the report insinuated she had been living with Mr. C all this time without being married to him, thus making her a woman devoid of moral values.

***Some Questions Relating to Libel***

Another question rises here ; is the distributor of libel punishable and accountable under law? It will have a lot to do with to what degree did the concerned person know about the contents distributed. Therefore, if a newspaper contained material that was defamatory and thereby damaging, the newspaper agent may not be held liable if he can prove he was not aware of the story within. Of course just because he is an agent is no reason for him to have read the paper early morning before distribution. Or, if he can prove he does not know the language of the newspaper that he distributed. In Pakistan, this may well be likely in case the newspaper agent is not conversant with the English language, at least to the degree that he can fluently read it. He cannot however take a defense that he did not know the law. In the field of Jurisprudence, there is a legal principle, it states; ***Ignorantia juris non excusat or ignorantia legis neminem excusat*** *(Latin for ignorance of the law is no excuse or ignorance of law excuses no one).* It means a person may not escape liability on grounds he did not know a law existed as he had no awareness of its existence. This may on the face of it seem harsh but one is expected to know the law that governs his country. In case of committing a crime, a criminal may take refuge in the excuse he was ignorant of the law–this will allow the criminal to avoid the consequences of his action, every time.

An unacceptable proposition.

Another interesting question that arises is if a publication does not actually name a person, but details an incident or about the said event etc about him, is it construed as defamation? The answer is yes. It will be. If it can be proved to the court that people will recognize him in the piece, it will be deemed as defamation. Merely not taking the name alone will not bar the case being brought against the publication/medium of communication.

***Defenses to a case of Libel***

What are the defenses that are available to the defendant once defamation is committed?

First defense is ***Truth*** as justification. The roots of this justification lie in the Common Law of England. From here it was adopted by American courts. It appeals to logic and common sense. If a person is speaking the truth, there is no justification for penalizing him for being truthful. Media especially is supposed to state the truth. If anything is shown or published that is the truth, why must it not *if* it is the truth? It is service to social good to bring to light the truth about those who are in the limelight owing to their involvement with the common man/public. Some states in USA award full protection to the defendant under this law, others provide it is a defense if it is "published for good motives and for justifiable ends."[270]

The onus to prove that **the motives were good and for justifiable ends** will depend on the accused/defendant. It is a very heavy responsibility. It is possible that facts within may be true, and reasons good and to a good end. However, the difference between facts and fiction, in today's world of evaluation and over evaluation is a fine one and the line often merges. What will be the parameter to judge the story being libelous or not, in this situation? The person against whom libel is committed must prove that there was deliberate maliciousness on behalf of the accused/defendant. That the latter showed reckless disregard for the truth ***(New York Times vs Sullivan)***.[271]

Courts will not support the decision of an account being defamatory if there are minor inaccuracies in a bigger picture. In the case of ***Piracci vs Hearst Corp,***[272]plea of being truthful was accepted by the court when the newspaper in the aforementioned case stated the plaintiff was in police custody on the 16th of August though he was released on 15th of August.

Truth, or substantial truth IS a defense therefore, stating that what was being said was *merely an opinion* is not a good defense. If any person who offers an opinion is in a position to actually *know* the facts of the situation, his opinion, generally, will be viewed as a fact.

Yet another defense to defamation is that of a ***fair comment***." The journalist or the newspaper is free to make fair comment on all matters of public interest. The fact on which the comment is based must be true and

---

[270] Law of Mass Communications by Harold L. Nelson and Dwight I Teeter Jr.1978 Pg 152

[271]376 U.S. 254, 286 (1964); Gertz, 418 U.S. at 342; Hepps, 475 U.S. at 773

[272] 263 F. Supp.511 affirmed 371 F.2d 1016(4th Cir. 1966

the comment fair and without malice."[273]Fair comment is a legal term. It may be described as, "A form of qualified privilege applied to news media publications, relating to discussions of matters which are of legitimate concern to the community as a whole, because they materially affects the interests of community as a whole."[274]

A fair comment by the media is a qualified privilege being a *bona fide* comment with no maliciousness. A legitimate comment will not be deemed to be a tort. "Fair comment must be based on fact and these facts must be included in the communication, or indicated with sufficient clarity to lay a proper foundation for the comments being made."[275]

The words complained of being published or put across through any other medium of communication must be (a) fairly relevant to some matter of public interest (b) they must be expression of an opinion and not the allegation of a fact (c) they must not exceed the limits of fair comment and lastly (d) must not be published maliciously.[276]

However, defense of fair statement must fail if the basic facts are incorrect. According to legal definition, the matter discussed must relate to matters of State, Provincial Affairs, Issues relating to Good Governance, Public Institutions and Local Authorities, Institution of Justice, Theatres, Arts and other issues of public interest. As we see, this is a very wide platform.

Let's now turn to the third defense a person accused may take. This is the ***plea of innocence.*** This plea especially may be taken on grounds of a second publication. This defense may be invoked on three grounds as expressed in the established case of *Vizetelly v. Mudies Select Library*[277]:

"[It is a defense to] a person who is not the printer or main publisher of a work which contains a libel, but has only taken, what I may call, a subordinate part in disseminating it; if he succeeds in showing (1) that he was innocent of any knowledge of the libel contained in the work disseminated by him, (2) that there was nothing in the work or the circumstances under which it came to him or was disseminated by him that ought to have lead him to suppose that it contained a libel, and (3)

---

[273] "Journalism for All" by Dr Medhi Hasan and Dr Abdul Salam Khurshid 8th Edition 2004, Pg 202
[274] Black's Law Dictionary Sixth Edition, Centennial Edition(1891-1991) Pg 596
[275] *Kemsley v. Foot*,[1952] A.C. 345 at p.357)
[276] The Law of Torts by A. M Chaudhry published by PLD Publishers Pg 54
[277][1902] 2 Q.B. 170 at 180 (C.A.)

that when the work was disseminated by him it was not by any negligence on his part that he did not know that it contained the libel, then although the dissemination of the work by him was *prima facie* a publication of it, he may nevertheless, on proof of the before mentioned facts, be held not to have published it."[278]

In Pakistan slander is a civil crime whereas libel is both a civil & criminal defense. In 2002 President Pervez Musharraf passed a Defamation Ordinance that is reproduced and discussed for better understanding and application of the law in Pakistan.

**ORDINANCE NO. LVI OF 2OO2**
AN
**ORDINANCE**

To make provisions in respect of defamation

WHEREAS it is expedient to make provisions in respect of defamation and for matters connected therewith or incidental thereto;

AND WHEREAS, the President is satisfied that circumstances exist which render it necessary to take immediate action;

NOW, THEREFORE, in pursuance of the Proclamation of Emergency of the fourteenth day of October, 1999, and the Provisional Constitution Order No. 1 of 1999, read with the Provisional Constitutional (Amendment) Order No. 9 of 1999, and in exercise of all powers enabling him in that behalf, the President of the Islamic Republic of Pakistan is pleased to make and promulgate the following Ordinance; -

**Short title, extent and commencement.** – (1) This ordinance may be called the Defamation Ordinance, 2002.

(2) It extends to the whole of Pakistan.

(3) It shall come into force at once.

**Definitions.** – In this Ordinance, unless there is anything repugnant in the subject or context;

(a) "author" means the originator of the statement;

---

[278] Ibid.

(b) "broadcasting" means the dissemination of writing, signs, signals, pictures and sounds of all kind, including any electronic device, intended to be received by the pubic either directly or through the medium of relay stations, by means of,

(i) a form of wireless radio-electric communication utilizing Hertzian waves, including radiotelegraph and radiotelephone, or

(ii) cables, computer, wires, fiber-optic linkages or laser beams, and "broadcast" has a corresponding meaning;

(c) "Editor" means a person or operator having editorial or equivalent responsibility for the content of the statement or the decision to publish or circulate it;

(d) "newspaper" means a paper containing public news, intelligence or occurrences or remarks or observations or containing only, or principally, advertisements, printed for distribution to the public and published periodically, or in parts or members, and includes such other periodical works as the Federal Government may, by notification in the official Gazette, declare to be newspaper;

(e) "publication" means the communication of the words to at least one person after than the person defamed and includes a newspaper or broadcast through the internet or other media; and

(f) "publisher" means a commercial publisher, that is, a person whose business is issuing material to the public, or a section of the public, who issues material containing the statement in the course of that business.

3. **Defamation.** – (1) any wrongful act or publication or circulation of a false statement or representation made orally or in written or visual form which injures the reputation of a person, tends to lower him in the estimation of others or tends to reduce him to ridicule, unjust criticism, dislike, contempt or hatred shall be actionable as defamation.

(2) Defamation is of two forms, namely: -

(i) slander; and

(ii) libel.

(3) Any false oral statement or representation that amounts to defamation shall be actionable as slander.

(4) Any false written, documentary or visual statement or representation made either by ordinary form or expression or by electronic or other modern means or devices that amounts to defamation shall be actionable as libel.

4. **Defamation actionable.** - The publication of defamatory matter is an actionable wrong without proof of special damage to the person defamed and where defamation is proved, damage shall be presumed.

5. **Defences.** – In defamation proceedings a person has a defence if he shows that :

(a) he was not the author, editor, publisher or printer of the statement complained of;

(b) the matter commented on is fair and in the public interest and is an expression of opinion and not an assertion of fact and was published in good faith;

(c) it is based on truth and was made for public good;

(d) assent was given for the publication by the plaintiff;

(e) offer to tender a proper apology and publish the same was made by the defendant but was refused by the plaintiff;

(f) an offer to print or publish a contradiction or denial in the same manner and with the same prominence was made but was refused by the plaintiff;

(g) the matter complained of was privileged communication such as between lawyer and client or between persons having fiduciary relations;

(h) the matter is covered by absolute or qualified privilege.

6. **Absolute privilege.** – Any publication of statement made in the Federal or Provincial legislatures, reports, papers, notes and proceedings ordered to be published by either house of the

Parliament or by the Provincial Assemblies, or relating to judicial proceedings ordered to be published by the court or any report, note or matter written or published by or under the authority of a Government, shall have the protection of absolute privilege.

Explanation. – In this section legislature includes a local legislature and court includes any tribunal or body exercising the judicial powers.

7. **Qualified privilege:** Any fair and accurate publication of parliamentary proceedings, or judicial proceedings which the public may attend and statements made to the proper authorities in order to procure the redress of public grievances shall have the protection of qualified privilege.

8. **Notice of action:** No Action lies unless the plaintiff has, within two months after the publication of the defamatory matter has come to his notice or knowledge, given to the defendant, fourteen days notice in writing of his intention to bring an action, specifying the defamatory matter complained of.

9. **Remedies:** Where defamation shall be proved to have occurred, the court may pass an order directing the defendant to tender an apology, if acceptable to the plaintiff, and publish the same in similar manner and with the same prominence as the defamatory statement made and pay reasonable compensatory damages as general damages with a minimum of Rs. 50,000 (Rupees fifty thousand) or shall undergo three months imprisonment and in addition thereto, any special damage incurred that is proved by the plaintiff to the satisfaction of the Court.

10. **Code of Civil Procedure and Qanun-e-Shahadat Order to apply:** The Code of Civil Procedure, 1908 (Act. No. V of 1908) and the Qanun-e-Shahadat, 1984 (P.O. No. 10 of 1984) shall mutatis mutandis, apply to the proceedings under this Ordinance.

11. **Ordinance not to prejudice action for criminal defamation:** Nothing in this Ordinance shall prejudice any action for criminal libel or slander under any law for the time being in force.

12. **Limitation of actions:** An action against ;

(a) an author, editor, proprietor or publisher of a newspaper;

(b) the owner of a broadcasting station;

(c) an officer, servant or employee of the newspaper or broadcasting station; or

(d) any other purpose, for defamation contained in the newspaper or broadcast from the station or in publication otherwise shall be taken within six months after the publication of the defamatory matter came to the notice or knowledge of the person defamed.

13. **Trial of Cases:** No court inferior to that of the District Judge shall have jurisdiction to try cases under this Ordinance.

14. **Court to decide the cases expeditiously:** The court shall decide a case under this Ordinance within a period of six months.

15. **Appeal:** An appeal against the final order of the District Judge shall lie to the High Court within thirty days of the passing of such order; Provided that no appeal shall lie against an interlocutory order of the court.

16. **Power to make rules:** The Federal Government may, by notification in the official Gazette, make rules to carry out the purposes of this Ordinance.

***Explanation***

The law clearly defines what is meant by publisher, editor, newspaper, cable wires etc so there is no ambiguity as to whom the law relates to and how the law interprets the terms and definitions. Defamation in both its forms ie libel and slander have been discussed at great length earlier. The Ordinance interprets and explains defamation as per international standards. Also as per international standards, libel is made actionable per se(on the face of it) if any material published damages the reputation of the person defamed. A person accused may prove the defense, if any, that the statement is wrongly attributed to him, which is the cause of grief. If he can prove that it was made in good faith and in the interest of public good. If the plaintiff gave the explicit permission to publish something and later due to any external pressure or a change of heart, he has now brought about a suit of defamation. However, the onus to prove this will squarely lie with the defendant. If he agrees to publish a formal apology for the libel, thereby correct the wrong done, if the defendant had requested to publish the material and the plaintiff denied the permission and yet he went ahead and published it, thereby exposing the plaintiff to repercussions, dangers etc then the defendant may, as a defense offer to publish this fact thereby exonerating the plaintiff from any responsibility of the said publication. If a matter published was in nature of privileged information as between lawyer & client or doctor & patient or the issue has an umbrella cover by Qualified or Absolute Privilege.

I would like to share here, from Lord Denning in *British Steel Corporation v Granada Television Ltd* [1981] AC 1096 at 1129:

*"If they [newspapers] were compelled to disclose their source, they would soon be bereft of information which they ought to have. Their sources would dry up. Wrongdoing would not be disclosed. Charlatans would not be exposed. Unfairness would go unremedied. Misdeeds in the corridors of power – in companies or government departments – would never be known."*

Coming to the time bar according to Defamation Ordinance, a time duration of two months is explicitly stated during which plaintiff sends a written notice to the accused, giving him a notice of 14 days to respond or correct the wrong after which a suit against him can be instituted.

***Types of Privileges :***

The term privilege is used here, it will be pertinent to first determine what are these privileges available.

***Qualified Privilege:***

Statements that are created by law, constitutional or otherwise are protected by a Qualified Privilege. "The legal effect of the defence of qualified privilege is to rebut the inference, which normally arises from the publication of defamatory words, that they were spoken with malice. Where the occasion is shown to be privileged, the bona fides of the defendant is presumed and the defendant is free to publish, with impunity, remarks which may be defamatory and untrue about the plaintiff. However, the privilege is not absolute and can be defeated if the dominant motive for publishing the statement is actual or express malice." It is a right that will be available only if good faith is present, there is no malice and comments are made where facts justify the statement either spoken, or published, on in electronic media or social media. It is a privilege available to the law of libel and slander. For anyone to enjoy qualified privilege needs to checklist: (a) Fair and correct report/news of proceedings in public of legislature (b) An accurate and fair recount of proceedings before a court (c) An accurate and fair recount of any proceedings of an international organization or international conference (d) Accurate and fair account in public of any individual authorized to hold a public inquiry by legislature or government (e) A correct and true copy shared of a document that is by law open to public inspection (f) Any advertisement and/or notice published on direction of a court or an authorized officer(g) An accurate copy or extract of some matter published by any government or authority from another part of the world (h) copy or extract of correct matter published by any international organization or an international conference in any part of the world.

### *Absolute Privilege:*

Let us now turn to Absolute Privilege. Common Law lays down roots of the right in cases to speak openly and freely without the fear of being punishable under law. This deals with statements given in evidence and extending to judges, juries, and witnesses. Or, statements made in parliaments.

In ***Ducosin v. Mott***, 292 Or 764, 642 P2d 1168 (1982), the defendant called the county medical examiner and suggested that the plaintiff possibly administered inappropriate amounts of medication to her mother, resulting in the mother's death. The examiner notified the district attorney, who, in turn, ordered an autopsy. The autopsy revealed that the mother died of natural causes. The plaintiff then brought an action for defamation. The defendant claimed the defense of absolute privilege. The trial court rejected the defense and held for plaintiff. The Supreme Court reversed, holding once again that Ramstead and its progeny controlled:

"The public importance of disclosing that a death was caused by criminal means is at least as high on the scale of importance to society as the disclosure of unethical practice by a lawyer or the disclosure of the misdeeds of an applicant for a license as a medical director.

"Analogous cases are those in which the defendant made a defamatory complaint to the prosecuting attorney. “Although there is some authority to the contrary, the better view seems to be that an informal complaint to a prosecuting attorney or a magistrate is to be regarded as an initial step in a judicial proceeding, and so entitled to an absolute rather than a qualified immunity." Prosser, Law of Torts § 114, pp 780-81 (4th ed 1971). "Formal or informal complaints to a prosecuting attorney or other law enforcement officer concerning violations of the criminal law are absolutely privileged under the rule stated in § 587." Restatement of Torts (Second) § 598, Comment e. "We hold the statement made by the defendant was absolutely privileged."

## *Talking Defamation Cases from around the World*

The *Bloomberg Bussiness Week* [279] was a report of a controversial suit filed by Dr Vicky Belo, against one Argee Guevarra, the lawyer for one of Belo's former patients who accused her for doing a botched procedure years ago. In this case, Belo's General Manager, who was added to Guevarra's contacts on Face Book, spotted the alleged comments. Unfortunately, in Philippines, where this incident took place, a lawyer[280] when asked, commented that there is no law on Internet libel in the Philippines, where libel suits must involve defamatory statements that are made in print. It would be pertinent to note here that Pakistan is governed by Cyber Crime Ordinance and though, few are aware of how it operates, there are very few cases under this law to date. It falls under the wing of FIA.

In 2011, Supreme Court of India had directed ***Times Now TV Channel*** to deposit Rs 20 crore in cash and the rest in bank guarantee before it could accept an appeal verdict in a trial court in a case of defamation. Former Supreme Court Judge, Justice P.B Sawant had sued Times Now. The TV Channel, by error, displayed a picture of P. B Sawant on 10th September 2008. The story was of a person allegedly involved in a multi crore scam of Provident Fund. His name was phonetically similar to that of Judge Sawant. A Pune trial court decreed a suit for Rs 100 crore against the TV Channel.

Head of Times Now TV Channel, Arnab Goswami, when contacted by The Times of India(Newspaper), tendered an apology, stating, "We are extremely apologetic to Justice Sawant for the mistake and any personal

---

[279] Published under TECHNOLOGY titiled *"Phillipines Court Hears Face Book Libel case" dated 5th September 2009*
[280] Ibid.

damage done to his reputation because of the inadvertent error of running his picture instead of another judge. The picture ran for only about 15 seconds, and was a genuine oversight in the course of a broadcast. We deeply regret the mistake and assure Justice Sawant that it was not part of any intentional malice in reporting."[281]

Sawant's lawyer had argued that the day the news item appeared in September 2008, his secretary had called up the channel within hours but it hadn't taken corrective measures. Five days later, on September 15, Sawant sent another letter to the channel, which was received on September 19. However, the clarification started appearing only on September 23rd.[282]

Another interesting case of defamation filed was by veteran Indian politician ***Shashi Tharoor***. He filed a defamation notice against the *Sunday Indian Magazine* demanding a compensation of Rs 10 crore. He had demanded an apology from the said publication on a report that stated he had deposited money in Swiss accounts. The publicist had not responded leading to filing of the defamation case. The notice had stated that *Sunday Indian Magazine* withdraw the allegation and tender an unconditional apology. [283]

In an interesting report published 30th July 2010 in Sri Lanka[284] a British Tamil, Parameswaran, had fasted without break for 23 days, in 2009, supporting the Tamils demanding for a ceasefire, won a defamation case against two British tabloids ie *Daily Mail* and *SUN,* for having published unsubstantiating news about his fast. It stated, Parameswaran had burgers, on the sly while fasting. He filed a case of defamation in the High Court of Justice in London. The lawyers of the tabloids agreed they could not prove the claim and agreed to publish an apology to the effect. Also, a compensation of 77500 sterling pounds was awarded to Parameswaran.[285]

---

[281] Report published in Times of India, titled, *SC asks Times Now to deposit Rs 100 crore before HC takes up its appeal in defamation case :* dated 15th November 2011

[282] Published in The Indian Express on 15th November 2011 titled *"Apex Court declines Times Now plea in defamation case."*

[283] Published in Deccan Chronicle, titled Shashi Tharoor files defamation case against magazine dated 16th January 2012

[284] LINK: http://www.lankanewspapers.com/news/2010/7/58934_space.html SRI LANKA NEWS WITH DISCUSSIONS

[285] Ibid.

In Bolivia, in March 2012, a Bolivian news magazine editor was convicted for slandering a government lawyer. He has been sentenced to two and a half years in prison.[286] In Bolivia, Press Laws regulate the criminal cases that involve the media.

In Bangladesh, founder of Grameen Bank, was charged over comments made about the Bangladeshi politicians in 2007 media interview. He is said to have stated, " Politicians in Bangladesh only work for money. There is no ideology here." The case was filed by a local politician, who stated a strong cause for defamation, involving all politicians from Bangladesh.[287] The case against Prof Yunus was filed in January 2007. It followed a complaint from a politician hailing from Mymensingh. Muhammad Yunus is also a Nobel Peace Laureate.

A separate probe by the Government was also instituted into Grameen Bank after a Norwegian documentary claimed it had misused Norwegian aid. However, a Norwegian investigation has cleared Grameen Bank from any such misuse of funds.[288]

From the world of cricket: New Zealand cricketer Chris Cairns won a libel case for "match fixing" against Indian Lalit Modi. The case was filed in the London's High Court. Chris Cairns filed the case, spotting a tweet by Modi, accusing Cairns of match fixing. Justice Bean, presiding over the case, gave a favorable verdict to Cairns, ordering Modi to pay £90 000 in damages and £400 000 in costs. He also awarded an injunction restraining Modi from repeating the libel again.[289]

CBC News reports former B.C premier Bill Vander Zalm was found liable in a defamation case. He had defamed interest commissioner Ted Hughes from one of the provinces. A court in Vancouver delivered the verdict, ordering that Vander Zalm pay Hughes $60,000 damages. Hughes headed an inquiry in 1991 that found then-premier Vander Zalm had violated the province's conflict-of-interest regulations during the sale

---

[286] SITE for International Press Institute posted 23rd March 2012 titled Defamation Conviction in Bolivia Part of Wider Trend LINK: http://www.freemedia.at/index.php?id=288&tx_ttnews%5Btt_news%5D=6124&cHash=97ba561858

[287] BBC NEWS South Asia published 18th January 2011 titled "Grameen's Muhammad Yunus in court for defamation case."

[288] msn news published 18th January 2011 titled. "Nobel laureate in Bangladesh defamation case." LINK: http://news.ph.msn.com/top-stories/article.aspx?cp-documentid=4585600

[289] RADIO NEW ZEALAND NEWS: 27th March 2012 titled "Big Win for Cairns in Defamation Case."

of a theme park he owned. This prompted Vander's resignation as a premier.[290]

In one of the biggest defamation awards of the Victorian history and reported by the *Herald Sun,* is about the jury awarding $630,000 damages to a top silk who sued Phil Cleary and the publisher of the former Federal MP's book Getting Away with Murder. Dyson Hore-Lacy SC alleged Mr Cleary and publisher Allen and Unwin suggested in the book that he had provided a fabricated defense of provocation to wife killer James Ramage.[291]Mr Cleary, whose sister Vicki was killed by a man who claimed provocation, published *Getting Away with Murder* in 2005. It was said to be the true story of the death of Julie Ramage, who was strangled by her husband and then buried in a shallow grave. The defamation trial heard that after the killing Ramage called Mr Hore-Lacy, a family friend, and met him in the Harp Hotel, Kew, where he confessed."But in his evidence the silk said he refused to act as Ramage's lawyer and called in a solicitor to take over the case. He denied providing Ramage with the defence of provocation. Outside court Mr Hore-Lacy revealed that he offered to settle the case four years ago for $50,000 and an apology.

"I'm grateful that the jury has recognized this for the foul defamation it was," he said. "It's been a five-year struggle. I'm especially pleased about the $30,000 punishment damages which may induce publishers to be a bit more careful." Mr. Cleary said it was a disappointing outcome but he believed the book was about a murdered woman and not about Mr. Hore-Lacy. "It is a free speech issue in my mind," he said. "But we're not going to complain about the jury decision. We'll move on."[292]

One point I would like to state here is that in defamation cases, it is the court discretion to award the quantum of damages. Sometimes it may be nominal, and yet, in some cases as we have reviewed phenomenal. It may be sometimes difficult to ascertain the "actual damage" suffered by one, how can one determine the "level" of insult or injured person resulting from libel or slander?

---

[290] CBCnews posted 9th February 2012 titled, "Vander Zalm found liable in defamation case."

[291] Herald Sun published 22nd March 2010 titled, "Phil Cleary loses $630,000 defamation case over James Ramage claims."

[292] Ibid.

Basically, one may state the purpose of awarding damages in defamation to a plaintiff is to console him for the insult suffered. Even in the case of nominal awards, it still remains a moral victory.

In 2009, the Kenya High Court delivered a verdict against the *Times News Service,* owners of Kenya Times Newspapers . In the case, Kenya Times which published a story on misuse of the Constituency Development Fund (CDF) based entirely on details handed out in a press conference by a respected Non-Governmental Organization was found guilty of defamation and ordered to pay Kenya Shillings 6 million to a former MP[293]. In the article titled "How Fraud is bleeding CDF," the newspaper had alleged that in a report issued by the Centre for Law and Research International (CLARION) during a press brief, the MP had been found to have converted his building into a CDF office and was yet to be investigated on the claims.

The MP claimed that the article was false and malicious and was meant to paint him out to be a thief, corrupt and an embezzler of public funds. In its defense, the media house had called the writer of the article Mmbolo Mbulemi who had told the court that he had written the story based on a press statement from CLARION. In her ruling, Justice Mugo noted that the media house ought to have first investigated the claims made by CLARION during the press briefing before publishing them.[294]

In a rocking case in Switzerland on 17 April 2003, the Federal Tribunal, the supreme appeal court of Switzerland, had annulled the judgment pronounced on 13 January 2003 by the *Court de Justice* [cantonal appeal court] of Geneva against Pascal Diethelm, president of OxyGenève, and Jean-Charles Rielle, physician in charge, CIPRET-Genève, in the defamation case brought against them by Ragnar Rylander, professor emeritus and former director of the department of environmental medicine at Gothenburg University. Ragnar Rylander had filed a complaint against Pascal Diethelm and Jean-Charles Rielle, accusing them of defamation, following their press conference in March 2001 in which the two tobacco-control and public health specialists had revealed the professor's secret ties to Philip Morris and had indicated his implication for almost 30 years in a scientific fraud "without precedent"

---

[293] SITE: fesmedia Africa published 8th October 2009 titled "Kenya Times loses defamation case." :LINK:http://fesmedia.org/african-media-news/detail/datum/2009/10/08/kenya-times-loses-defamation-case/

[294] Ibid.

that consisted of the systematic and deliberate denial of the health hazards of passive smoking, of the creation of an artificial scientific controversy, and of the corruption of the scientific record with biased results.[295]The first instance court, the *Tribunal de Police*, judged the case on 24 May 2002 and found Pascal Diethelm and Jean-Charles Rielle guilty of defamation. The tribunal admitted as proven the fact that Rylander had secretly worked for Philip Morris and went as far as qualifying his links with the company as being "covert." However, the judges ruled that the evidence presented by the defendants was insufficient to prove that Rylander had been one of the most highly paid consultants of Philip Morris and that he had been involved in a scientific fraud "without precedent." The defendants were condemned to pay a fine of CHF 4'000.—each. The decision was immediately appealed. In its judgment of 13 January 2003, the *Court of Justice* confirmed the decision of the first instance tribunal, but significantly reduced the amount of the fine, down to CHF 1'000. Paradoxically, the judgment confirmed **all** the allegations of the defendants. The court considered as proven the facts that Rylander was "secretly employed by Philip Morris" and that he was "one of Philip Morris's most highly paid consultants."

Furthermore, the court concluded that Rylander "did not hesitate to deceive the general public in order to show himself favorable to the tobacco company that was paying him," and further observed that, in particular, "the study on respiratory diseases in children in which he altered the data base so that no link could be made between passive smoking and the frequency of respiratory infections, appears fraudulent." The court also determined that the "Rylander symposium" was favourable to the tobacco industry. But curiously, the court brought a new charge against the defendants, arguing that they had "given the impression" that Rylander's "whole career was nothing but a vast deception," indicating that "this kind of exaggerated statements cannot be tolerated," and confirmed the first condemnation and even deprived the appellants of the possibility of invoking their "good faith."

(See http://www.oxygeneve.ch/documents/acj_rylander_english.htm

---

[295] The Supreme Court of Switzerland annuls the judgment that found Pasal Diethelm and Jean-Charles Rielle guilty of defamation against Ragner Rylander (Communication by CIPRET-Genève and OxyGenève, 23 April 2003) LINK: http://www.prevention.ch/rycpeng230403.htm

for the full text of the judgment)[296]

On 22nd December 2009, a new defence for defamation was laid down by the Supreme Court of Canada. In the case titled *Grant v. Torster Corp.* called the "responsible communications defence." The defence provides greater protection in issues that are a matter of public interest. The court established several tests to this. These include: publication is on a matter of public interest, publisher actively worked to verify what's allegedly stated in the publication by public importance of issue under question, the seriousness of allegation published, the urgency(time sensitivity) of the matter in discussion, how reliable is the source quoted therein, whether the plaintiff was approached for his input before the matter alleged of was published, it was made in light of truth and any relevant facts that have an effect on the matter published.

In another case from Canada, *Malhab vs Diffusion Metromedia CMR* reported by the Business Law Blog on 4th March 2011, a radio show made accusations concerning Montreal taxi drivers whose mother tongue was Arabic or Creole. While observing about the taxi industry in Montreal, his accusations included those of them being arrogant, unclean, incompetent, corrupt and ignorant of official languages. A member of the group brought a case on behalf of the affected groups. The court determined by being member of a group against whom some statements have been made, does not entitle that individual to compensation. Each group member will have to establish clearly, that such "group comment" resulted in individual loss of reputation in each case.

Merely being a member of the group is just not enough. Unless, it can be proved beyond reasonable doubt that an ordinary person would have believed it completely, thereby resulting in actual damage to each member of the group. The court concluded that in this particular case there was no reason to believe that the reputation of Montreal taxi drivers speaking Creole and Arabic language has been damaged individually. Individual harm must be established to succeed in a defamation case.

In a truly startling report from Vienna, 2nd February 2012, the United Nations Human Rights Committee(UNHRC) found the conviction of a journalist hailing from Philippines, on charges of criminal defamation, was a violation of a journalist's right to free expression. The decision by UNHRC was clear that the five year punishment imposed on the journalist

---

[296] Ibid.

was against the Article 19 of the Universal Declaration of Human Rights. The name of the journalist was Alexander Adonis of Bombo Radyo. The case has its base in a 2001 broadcast. Adonis had reported an alleged affair between a married woman and a Philippine congressman. Prospero Nograles , the congressman, then speaker of the House, filed a libel complaint against Adonis. In 2007 Adonis was served a verdict by a Davao City Court. Besides the sentence, he was also ordered to pay as fine approximately 1,800 Euros to the congressman for "moral damages."

Filing with the UNHRC, Adonis contested that Sections 353 and 354 of the Philippine Revised Criminal Code unreasonably infringed upon the right to freedom of speech. UNHRC agreed with the submission. It demanded that Philippines must compensate for the years Adonis spent in jail. UNHRC also suggested that like punishments must not only be guarded against but also revisit it's libel legislation.

In Japan, in the case law ***Kiyomi Oguri v. Shigeo Kageyama,*** Oguri was blamed for having made political speeches, disseminated by the press and radio, charging his political and electoral opponent for a seat in House of Representatives; Kageyama, for receiving an eight million yen bribe in connection with a government contract. The trial court deemed this was unjustifiable and was an unjustifiable case of libel.[297]

In April 2012, a Texas couple who had filed a defamation case over three years ago were awarded $13.8 million dollars in a jury judgement. Mark and Rhonda Lesher of Clarksville, Texas, against anonymous commentators who accused them of being molesters and drug dealers. After the Leshers filed their suit, a Texas Judge ordered Topix, to turn in the information on the identity of the anonymous commentators . Topix being a web forum ; Topix.com the IP address or Internet Protocol, the number assigned to each computer was ordered to be disclosed. Six parties were indicted via their IP addresses as being the commentators and indicted for defamation.[298]

---

[297] Kageyama v Oguri, Decision of 4th July 1956, The Japan Supreme Court, the defendant was candidate from the Communist Party while plaintiff was the official candidate of the Liberal-Democratic Party.

[298] abc NEWS report by By KI MAE HEUSSNER and SUSANNA KIM LINK: http://abcnews.go.com/Business/jury-awards-13-million-texas-defamation-suit-anonymous/story?id=16194071#.T79bl9Ww-Bw

In Bahrain, a prominent activist was found guilty of defamation and sentenced to three months in jail for making anti-government comments on social media. The news of AP by Reem Khalifa and posted by Yahoo on 9th July 2012–made me laugh. Now of only, the ill-fated activist was in Pakistan, he could have criticised the government not only on social media but also in print and electronic media to his heart's content and got away with it. As it is, the "conviction involves one of several cases against Rajab, the president of the Bahrain Center for Human Rights. He has already been arrested and released twice since early May."[299]

***Concluding Comments***

With the rise of media, social media and electronic media, their desire to increase viewership ratings, it can become deceptively easy to fall in a trap of defaming others. Letting guards down and indulging in a "little gossip" can turn into a dangerous act of defamation.

Defamation, as we have seen, has many forms, a person's reputation is inviolate. We cannot take away the right of a 'good name', the right of 'good deeds' from anyone.

Unless and until it is proved beyond reasonable doubt.

Many cases from across cultures, across geographical and religious barriers, have been discussed . The Law of Defamation has an almost universal acceptance in the lives of a society . It can be seen as broadening of the base of civility. Just as a civil demeanour is expected in dealing with other members of the society, likewise, between individuals and individuals, between institutions and institutions, between individuals and institutions, the Law of Defamation governs our "exchange of civility."

Thomas Jefferson, in his letter to John Norvell, 1807, stated, and I would like to end the chapter on this note, "Defamation is becoming a necessity of life; inasmuch as a dish of tea in the morning or evening cannot be digested without this stimulant."[300]

Sad. But true?

---

[299] Lawyer: Bahrain activist convicted of defamation

[300] The Mirror Image Defamation Suit Against Cooley Law School:07/16/SBMBLOG: http://sbmblog.typepad.com/sbm-blog/2012/07/national-law-journal-describes-it-as-the-case-of-the-dueling-defamation-suits-jeff-kurzon-sued-last-year-in-ingham-county.html

# *Chapter V*

## Cyber Law

Cybercrime may be said to be crimes committed on the internet. Computer is the tool here to commit a violation against targeting another. All cybercrimes involve the person behind the computer as victim(s). Computers can be used against a person. For example, hacking will involve attacking someone's computer to access information, resources, private communication or financial information. When a person is a target of cyber-crime, the weapon used is the computer. This is used to damage him in the real world out there. The computer is a relatively new gadget therefore, harm by way of computers is a relatively new phenomenon. It can be as deadly, as hurtful, as defamatory and as financially ruining as any other crime. Cybercrime requires the knowledge of a technical nature. A high degree of technical knowledge, unfortunately, that has the potential to do more bad, than good.

"Hacker Tools" are available so that, once downloaded, they can also be used by those not having great computer skills. It's frightening to note that youngsters do a lot of silly things as a prank, not knowing this is a criminal offence and punishable as such.

" Cybercrime encompasses any criminal act dealing with computers and networks (called hacking) . Additionally, cybercrime also includes traditional crimes conducted through the Internet. For example, hate crimes, telemarketing and Internet fraud, identity theft, and credit card account thefts are considered to be cybercrimes when the illegal activities are committed through the use of a computer and the internet."[301]

---

[301] Webopedia LINK: http://www.webopedia.com/TERM/C/cyber_crime.html

It includes downloading illegal music files to stealing from others bank accounts to stealing people's pictures from Face Book to use it for blackmail. Stealing pictures itself is a crime, notwithstanding the purpose it is used for. The scope of cybercrimes is so broad that it is virtually impossible to encompass it in a definition.

This crime deals with the person attacked, facing a faceless assailant and is sometimes unaware of when the attack is made. The attack is disclosed when ramifications of the attack are known. With the increase of the use of computer, the crimes of computer have also increased.

"Generally refers to criminal activity where a computer or network is the source, tool, target, or place of a crime. These categories are not exclusive and many activities can be characterized as falling in one or more. Additionally, although the terms computer crime and cybercrime are more properly restricted to describing criminal activity in which the computer or network is a necessary part of the crime, these terms are also sometimes used to include traditional crimes, such as fraud, theft, blackmail, forgery, and embezzlement, in which computers or networks are used. As the use of computers has grown, computer crime has become more important.

"Computer crime can broadly be defined as criminal activity involving an information technology infrastructure, including illegal access (unauthorized access), illegal interception (by technical means of non-public transmissions of computer data to, from or within a computer system), data interference (unauthorized damaging, deletion, deterioration, alteration or suppression of computer data), systems interference (interfering with the functioning of a computer system by inputing, transmitting, damaging, deleting, deteriorating, altering or suppressing computer data), misuse of devices, forgery (ID theft), and electronic fraud."[302]

The salient clauses of Electronic/Cyber Crime Ordinance 2009, actionable under FIA, is being shared here.

Kindly note, few crimes have been reported so far. The ordinance comprises 49 sections and aims to criminalize various activities, involving the use and misuse of electronic data, equipment and systems.

---

[302] SITE:ZAFAR LAW ASSOCIATES: LLP: http://zallp.com/cybercrime.html

The law: "Prevention of Electronic Crimes Ordinance, 2009" (same as Prevention of Electronic Crimes Ordinance, 2007 & 2008) lapsed, which was promulgated by the President of Pakistan. The "Prevention of Electronic Crimes Ordinance, 2009" extended to the whole of Pakistan.

## *Prevention of Electronic Crimes Ordinance, 2008*

The ***"Prevention of Electronic Crimes Ordinance, 2008"*** will apply to every person who commits an offence under the said Ordinance irrespective of his nationality or citizenship whatsoever or in any place outside or inside Pakistan, having detrimental effect on the security of Pakistan or its nationals or national harmony or any property or any electronic system or data located in Pakistan or any electronic system or data capable of being connected , sent to, used by or with any electronic system in Pakistan.

The ordinance i.e. "Prevention of Electronic Crimes Ordinance, 2008" gives exclusive powers to the Federal Investigation Agency (FIA) to investigate and charge cases against such crimes.

The ordinance covers provision for illegal and criminal acts such as data access, data damage, system damage, electronic fraud, electronic forgery, spamming, spoofing, cyber terrorism etc.

***Chapter II of the "Prevention of Electronic Crimes Ordinance, 2008"*** deals with the Offences and Punishments. Punishments range from two years to death penalty. For the general guidance offences and punishments are mentioned below:

***Section 3*** of the "Prevention of Electronic Crimes Ordinance, 2008" deals with criminal access. The said section states:

***Criminal Access***: Whoever intentionally gains unauthorized access to the whole or any part of an electronic system or electronic device with or without infringing security measures, shall be punished with imprisonment of either description for a term which may extend to two years or with fine not exceeding three hundred thousand rupees, or with both.

Criminal Data Access is an Offence and Punishable.

***Section 4*** states:

***Criminal data access***: Whoever intentionally causes any electronic system or electronic device to perform any function for the purpose of gaining unauthorized access to any data held in any electronic system or electronic device or on obtaining such unauthorized access shall be punished with imprisonment of either description for a term which may extend to three years or with fine or with both.

***Section 5*** states:

***Data Damage***: Whoever with intent to illegal gain or cause harm to the public or any person, damages any data shall be punished with imprisonment of either description for a term which may extend to three years or with fine or with both.

***Section 6*** states:

***System Damage***: Whoever with intent to cause damage to the public or any person interferes with or interrupts or obstructs the functioning, reliability or usefulness of an electronic system or electronic device by imputing, transmitting, damaging, deleting, altering, tempering, deteriorating or suppressing any data or services or halting electronic system or choking the networks shall be punished with imprisonment of either description for a term which may extend to three years or with fine or with both.

***Section 7*** states:

***Electronic fraud***: Whoever for wrongful gain interferes with or uses any data, electronic system or electronic device or induces any person to enter into a relationship or with intent to deceive any person, which act or omissions is likely to cause damage or harm to that person or any other person shall be punished with imprisonment of either description for a term which may extend to seven years, or with fine, or with both.

***Section 8*** states:

***Electronic Forgery***: Whoever for wrongful gain interferes with data, electronic system or electronic device, with intent to cause damage or injury to the public or to any person, or to make any illegal claim or title or to cause any person to part with property or to enter into any express or implied contract, or with intent to commit fraud by any input, alteration, deletion, or suppression of data, resulting in unauthentic data with the intent that it be considered or acted upon for legal purposes as if it were authentic, regardless of the fact that the data is directly readable and intelligible or not shall be punished with imprisonment for a term which may extend to seven years, or with fine or with both.

***Section 9*** states:

***Misuse of electronic system or electronic device***: Whoever produces, possesses, sells, procures, transports, imports, distributes or otherwise makes available an electronic system or electronic device, including a computer program, designed or adapted primarily for the purpose of committing any of the offences established under this Ordinance or a password, access code, or similar data by which the whole or any part of an electronic system or electronic device is capable of being accessed or its functionality compromised or reverse engineered, with the intent it be used for the purpose of committing any of the offences established under this ordinance, is said to commit misuse of electronic system or electronic devices. Whoever commits the offence shall be punishable with imprisonment of either description for a term which may extend to three years, or with fine, or with both.

***Section 10*** states:

***Unauthorized access to code***: Whoever discloses or obtains any password, access as to code, system design or any other means of gaining access to any electronic system or data with intent to obtain wrongful gain, do reverse engineering or cause wrongful loss to any other unlawful purpose shall be punished with imprisonment of either description for a term which may extend to three years or with both.

***Section 11*** states:

***Misuse of encryption***: Whoever for the purpose of commission of an offence or concealment of incriminating evidence, knowledge and willfully encrypts any incriminating communication or data contained in electronic system relating to that crime or incriminating evidence, commits the offence of misuse of encryption shall be punished with imprisonment of either description for a term which may extend to five years or with fine or with both.

***Section 12*** states:

***Malicious code***: Whoever willfully writes, offers, makes available, distributes or transmits malicious code through an electronic system or electronic device, with intent to cause harm to any electronic system or resulting in the corporation, distribution, alteration, suppression, theft or loss of data commits the offence of malicious code.

Provided that the provision of this section shall not apply to the authorized testing, research and development or protection of an electronic system for any lawful purpose.

Whoever commits the offence shall be punished with imprisonment of either description for a term which may extend to five years, or with fine or with both.

***Section 13*** states:

***Cyber stalking***: Whoever with intent to coerce, intimidate, or harass any person uses computer, computer network, internet, network site, electronic mail or any other similar means of communication to communicate obscene, vulgar, profane, lewd, lascivious, or indecent language, picture or image, make any suggestion or proposal of an obscene nature, threaten any illegal or immoral act, take or distribute pictures or photographs of any person without his consent or knowledge, display or distribute information in a manner that substantially increases the risk of harm or violence to any other person, commits the offence of cyber stalking.

Whosoever commits the offence shall be punishable with imprisonment of either description for a term which may extend to seven years or with fine not exceeding three hundred thousand rupees, or with both.

Provided that if the victim of the cyber stalking is a minor the punishment may extend to ten years or with fine not less than one hundred thousand rupees or with both.

***Section 14*** states:

***Spamming***: Whoever transmits harmful, fraudulent, misleading, illegal or unsolicited electronic messages in bulk to any person without the express permission of the recipient, or causes any electronic system to show any such message or involves in falsified online user account registration or falsified domain name registration for commercial purpose commits the offence of spamming.

Whoever commits the offence of spamming shall be punishable with fine not exceeding fifty thousand rupees if he commits this offence of spamming for the first time and for every subsequent commission of offence of spamming he shall be punished with imprisonment of three months or with fine, or with both.

***Section 15*** states:

***Spoofing***: Whoever establishes a website, or sends an electronic message with a counterfeit source intended to be believed by the recipient or visitor or its electronic system to be an authentic source with intent to gain unauthorized access or obtain valuable information which later can be used for any lawful purposes commits the offence of spoofing.

Whoever commits the offence of spoofing specified shall be punished with imprisonment of either description for a term which may extend to three years, or with fine, or with both.

***Section 16*** states:

***Unauthorized interception***: Whoever without lawful authority intercepts by technical means, transmissions of data to, from or within an electronic system including electromagnetic system carrying such data commits the offence of unauthorized interception. The punishment for the offence of unauthorized interception shall be imprisonment of either description for a term which may extend to five years, or with fine not exceeding five hundred thousand rupees or with both.

***Section 17*** states:

***Cyber terrorism***: Any person, group or organization who, with terroristic intent utilizes, accesses or causes to be accessed a computer or computer network or electronic system or electronic device or by any available means, and thereby knowingly engages in or attempts to engage in a terroristic act commits the offence of cyber terrorism.

Whoever commits the offence of cyber terrorism and causes death of any person shall be punished with death or imprisonment for life, and with fine and in any other cause he shall be punishable with imprisonment of either description for a term which may extend to ten years or with fine not less than ten million rupees or with both.

***Section 18*** states:

***Enhanced punishment for offences involving sensitive electronic systems:***

Whoever causes criminal access to any sensitive electronic system in the course of the commission of any of the offences established under this Ordinance shall in addition to the punishment prescribed for that offence, be punished with imprisonment of either description for a term which may extend to ten years, or with fine not exceeding one million rupees, or with both.

***Section 19*** states:

***Of abets, aids or attempts to commits offence***: Any person who knowingly and willfully abets the commission of or who aids to commit or does any act preparatory to or in furtherance of the commission of any offence under this Ordinance shall be guilty of that offence and shall be liable on conviction to the punishment provided for the offence.

Any person who attempts to commit an offence under this Ordinance shall be punished for a term which may extend to one-half of the longest term of imprisonment provided for that offence.

***Section 20*** states:

***Other Offences***: Whoever commits any offence, other than those expressly provided under this Ordinance with the help of computer electronic system, electronic device or any other electronic means shall be punished in addition to the punishment provided for that offence, with imprisonment of either description for a term which may extend to two years, or with fine not exceeding two hundred thousand rupees or with both.

***Section 21*** states:

***Offences by corporate body:*** A corporate body shall be held liable for an offence under this Ordinance if the offence is committed on its instructions or for its benefit. The corporate body shall be punished with a fine not less than one hundred thousand rupees or the amount involved in the offence whichever is the higher provided that such punishment shall not absolve the criminal liability of the natural person who has committed the offence. Corporate body includes a body of persons incorporated under any law such as trust, waqf, an association, a statutory body or a company.

Much opposition was faced by the above stated law. Those who did not support it, did so with the view it would virtually make Pakistan a police state and a serious curb on the freedom of expression.

### *Some reported cases pertaining to Cyber Crime in Pakistan*

In a report published, on 7th January 2011, online harassment against women has increased, raising the number of reported cases to 68. According to FIA records, these cases mostly dealt with sending the women abusive, vulgar or/and obnoxious e-mails, or alleged hacking of mail accounts.[303] Sources added that 26 cases of cyber- crime were reported to the CCU in 2007, while 36 were reported in 2008. In 2009 the ratio was lower, but rose to 45 in 2010.[304]An FIR was also registered against a local varsity teacher, named Tanveer, who was involved in harassing a female employee of a local telecommunication company, by texting and sending her vulgar e-mails. The accused was arrested on 19th March.[305]

In an interesting report by Ericka Chicowski in December 2006, FIA made its first arrest for hacking into the e-mail systems belonging to CDPI(Centre for Development & Peace Initiative). One Waqas Abrar was apprehended by FIA. The accused gained illegal access, allegedly, to change the passwords, thereby denying access to company and demanded Rs 40.000 in order to restore company access. According to press reports,

---

[303] Daily Times: 68 cases of online female harassment registered in 2011 *By Ali Hassan* published 7th January 2011

295 Ibid.

296 Ibid.

the accused was allegedly working to do same to 20 other accounts and demand monies to restore access.[306]

Cybercrime in Pakistan has spiked with the increase of cyber terrorism, example of this, is the disappearance of the Wall Street Journal correspondent on 23rd Jan. 2002, from Pakistan's southern city of Karachi and his captors started sending e-mails to newspapers, then the investigators starting to trace the e-mails sent by the kidnappers. This was one of the important reason for establishing the National Response Center for Cyber Crimes in Pakistan to combat against cybercrimes.[307]

However, according to another report by *The Nation* there is an unwillingness of the victims of cybercrimes to come forward and report the at a crime has been committed.[308]

Another FIR was against a person named Noman Asif, who was working as a computer expert in a private company, and had been involved in creating fake, vulgar Facebook accounts of four females from the same family. The case was registered on the request of complainant Afzal Qureshi, who said that some unidentified person had created fake profiles and uploaded pictures of his wife and three daughters on the social networking site. Qureshi said that Asif's phone number along with those of his wife and daughters had also been posted on these fake profiles. He added that Asif had tried to portray his family members as call girls, while himself posing as their agent. The FIA arrested Asif in February last year.[309]

In the first ever cybercrime case heard by the Supreme Court, the Apex Court on 13thMay 2003 issued notices to Deputy Attorney General on a case reported by US Consulate Karachi.[310] US Consulate in Karachi reported to the Federal Investigation Agency that some Pakistanis are importing goods from America and other countries by misusing credit cards. The consulate identified about five Pakistanis and traced their

---

[306] SC Magazine news titled, "Pakistan makes arrests in ransom-hacking case" posted December 12th 2006.SITE: http://www.scmagazine.com.au/News/70021,pakistan-makes-arrests-in-ransom-hacking-case.aspx

[307] SITE:HackersMedia http://www.hackersmedia.com/2011/12/cplc-chief-says-pakistan-safe-heaven.html

[308] APP 24th May 2012 The Nation titled *Majority of cybercrime victims do not report*

[309] Daily Times 7th January 2012 by Ali Hassan titled 68 cases of online harassment registered in 2011"

[310] PPF RADIO NEWS NETWORK SITE. News posted on 13th May 2003 SITE: http://www.pakistanpressfoundation.org/news-archives/23708

phone numbers who were allegedly involved in the case and reported the matter to the FIA to take action against these persons .[311]

According to another case reported in *Express Tribune* FIA arrested a man for production of counterfeit credit cards and using them by hacking into card holders data. Tanveer Ahmed ,the accused, was suspected to have obtained computerized national identity cards data, possibly with the help of some NADRA officials. [312] Apparently, members of the gang hacked credit cards based on alleged illegal use of CNICs data, using them for large transactions. "Iqbal was reportedly caught red handed by a police team headed by Inspector Malik Tariq Masood while using the fake card. They also recovered two counterfeit credit cards, a laptop and an MSRW machine from him."[313]

### *A comparative analysis with cases from other countries*

The first case of cyber stalking in India was by the Delhi Police as reported by Shri Pavan Duggal, Cyber Law Consultant, President, CYBERLAWS.NET MEMBER,MAC, ICANN. [314] One Mrs Ritu Kohil informed the police that her identity was being used by one person to chat on the internet at a website **www.mirc.com** for the past 4 days.

Her complaint was that the offender was not only using her identity but had also given out her address and was using vulgar language. The person had also given out her number to other chatters giving permission to call her at all odd timings. Once the police started tracing IP addresses, one Manesh Kathuria was apprehended. He also pleaded guilty to the offence.

In another case lodged by M/S Pintach Technologies Ltd. (PTL),against one Mr Binoy, M/S Telequick and some of its employees. The case dealt with cheating and fraud, by theft and sale of proprietary data. M/S PTL had a concern in USA titled M/S Pintach Technologies Inc. Their business dealt with providing 'leads to Mortgage Originators'.[315] Mr Binoy was holding post of Senior Programme Manager." The accused,

---

[311] Ibid.

[312] *The Express Tribune* "Cyber Crime: Man arrested for credit card fraud" published 27th December 2011 by Asad Kharal

[313] Ibid.

[314] SITE for CyberLaw India : http://cyberlaws.net/cyberindia/2CYBER27.htm

[315] Cyber Law India: http://cyberlawdelhi.blogspot.com/2009/12/case-study-of-bpo-data-theft-case.html

Binoy had roped in two of his colleagues namely Abdul and Sanjeev who actively assisted him in his clandestine activities. [316] The three were reportedly arrested by a team of Police from Gurgaon and Faridabad.

In early 2011, UK cybercrimes cost £27bn a year according to government report. [317] This is reportedly a mid-level evaluation. In all probability, the actual losses are much higher. 'They are made up of £21bn of costs to businesses, £2.2bn to government and £3.1bn to citizens."[318] According to Guardian UK, cybercrime "costs UK £27bn a year."[319] 'The report, by information consultants Detica for the Cabinet Office, calculated that the theft of intellectual property – such as designs and formulas – from businesses costs £9.2bn.

Pharmaceutical, biotechnology, electronics, IT and chemicals firms are being hit hardest. Industrial espionage, including firms spying on each other, is said to cost £7.6bn. Cyber- crime also costs citizens £3.1bn a year and the government £2.2bn a year, the report said.[320]

In report by ***Michael Millar***[321]he states smaller firms offer better opportunity for cybercrimes. In his article published in BBC News , he quotes hacker, "They are often protected by insurance and it's very rare to see them going after a hacker for stealing their money, although with intellectual property it can be different" .[322] Millar states these hackers may be after an assorted information ie, data that may be resold(credit card numbers, login information & passwords, employee details). Malwares are uploaded to sites to attack visitors at site.

According to CSI/FBI Computer Crime and Security Survey 2000 quoted by bbc.co.uk[323]:

---

[316] Ibid.

[317] BBC NEWS UK politics posted 17th February 2011

[318] Ibid.

[319] By *Own Bowcott,* titled "Cyber Crime costs UK £27b a year" published 17th February 2011 in Guardian UK

[320] Ibid

[321] Michael Millar, Business Reporter for BBC News published 20th February 2012 titled, "Small Firms easy target for cyber- crime."

[322] Ibid.

[323] BBC.co.uk LINK:
http://news.bbc.co.uk/hi/english/static/in_depth/uk/2001/life_of_crime/cybercrime.stm

- ☐ 90% of US companies which responded to a Computer Security Institute survey said they had detected computer security breaches in the previous year
- ☐ 74% acknowledged financial losses as a result of the breaches of security
- ☐ 273 organizations quantified their financial losses: the total bill came to $265m
- ☐ 25% of respondents detected penetration from outside their company
- ☐ 79% detected employee abuse of the internet, for example downloading pornography or pirated software
- ☐ 85% detected computer viruses

***Misha Glenny*** writing for Guardian UK, in a report talks of an interesting case in Calgary, in Alberta, Canada. The system of a company dealing with pre-paid debit cards was hacked into. It targets a younger crowd who could otherwise not get credit via the regular channels. The gang that hacked into the system, used an ingenious method. They purchased a large number of pre-paid debit cards in different locations. Having done this, they placed a $15 on each card. He writes, " Once they had broken into the computer system of the company that issued them, they found the network area that dealt with the limits placed on each card. They sought out the cards they had purchased and, using the control they had established over the company's networked system, they electronically raised the spending limit on the cards from $15 to tens of thousands of dollars. Over one weekend, they extracted around $1m (£640,000) using the affected cards in ATM machines around the world."[324]

***Paul Sewers*** in a piece[325] quotes a BBC Report, that a team of Dutch experts have arrived at the conclusion that more than a million households in UK 's personal computers are linked to criminal networks called "botnets." He says, "....which are groups of Internet-connected

---

[324] Titled "cybercrime: Out of control?" By *Misha Glenny* 21st September 2011 in Guardian UK

[325] SITE TNW article titled "More than one Million UK Households are part of cyber-criminal botnets" LINK: http://thenextweb.com/uk/2011/12/05/more-than-one-million-uk-households-are-part-of-cyber-criminal-botnets/

computers that have been compromised by a third party and put to malicious use."[326]

He states that with around 6% of the UK's 19m Internet households thought to be part of a botnet, this helps criminals spread spam around the Web more effectively, whilst it can also be used to attack websites and even garner bank details from the unsuspecting public.[327]

In the same report he says and I quote , " The UK figure is placed at number 19 in the top 20 nations with the biggest botnet problem, but it's roughly in-line with the global average which sits at around 5-10% of domestic computers that are thought to be linked to botnets. Greece and Israel were way out on top, though, with around a fifth of all broadband subscribers thought to be unwittingly recruited into botnets."

Things are not exactly honky dory on this front in Canada. In a report for ***Financial Times***, ***Jameson Berkow*** quoting a study by *Symantec Corp.* in September 2011, shares that an average of about 14 Canadians are targeted every minute. He shares, "The 2011 Norton Cybercrime Report found more than 7.3 million Canadian Internet users fell victim to a cyber -attack of some kind in 2010, costing them $840-million in direct financial losses plus another $4.7-billion in lost productivity."[328]In 2010 cybercrime cost Canadians $5.5b states Berkow.

According to Berkow, men between the ages 18 to 31 who access their computer via their mobile phones were most likely to fall victim to cybercrime.

The **Toronto Sun,** reported that owing to a sharp increase in cybercrimes, over the recent period, Calgary Police is finalizing plan to create an investigative team exclusively to look into electronic crimes.[329]

***Kathleen Lau,*** in a piece for **it**World Canada[330] states that Canada has shot up to the sixth position from top in cybercrimes. This report was published in May 2011. Prior to this, it had maintained a position on the twelfth or the thirteenth slot. The report by *Lau* states and I quote,

---

[326] Ibid.

[327] Ibid.

[328] FINANCIAL TIMES TECH DESK, report by Jameson Berkow published 7th September 2011

[329] "Cops to launch cyber- crime squad" by Nadia Moharb published March 25th 2012

[330] LINK: http://www.itworldcanada.com/news/canada-shoots-to-sixth-place-in-global-cyber-crime-list/143097

"Canada's cybercrime landscape has undergone dramatic change in the last year, according to a new Websense Inc. report. Canada not only has ranked second in the world for hosting phishing sites from January to May of 2011, but it's also suffered a 319 per cent jump in the number of servers hosting those phishing sites."[331]

In USA, the cybercrimes have also peaked.

In a very interesting case reported on 8th October 2009, *Dan Goodin* reported the Egyptian and US authorities to have charged no less than 100 people for being guilty of conducting phishing operations that siphoned minimum $1.5m from thousands of accounts. Reportedly all the accounts were of Bank of America.[332]Operation Phish Phry, as the case was dubbed, marks the first joint cyber investigation between law enforcement agencies in those two countries. The case was filed in federal court in Los Angeles.[333]According to the indictment, the defendants who are Egypt-based, phished individual information and used this to access victims bank accounts.

**Pratap Chattarjee,** writing for *Guardian UK,* draws attention to need for a computer non-proliferation treaty.[334] He tells us by releasing *Stuxnet* and *Flame,* US has launched an arms race of weaponised viruses. " Operation Olympic Games a secret US intelligence operation that was shepherded into fruition by the Obama administration in collaboration with the Israeli government, is believed to have spawned two sophisticated computer viruses, one named Flame and the other, Stuxnet. The latter caused hundreds of nuclear centrifuges to spin out of control at Iran's uranium enrichment plant in Natanz, while the former attacked the country's oil industry."[335]

However, it is Germany that comes out at the top of the European cybercrime list .[336] "In its 16th annual Internet Security Threat Report, the US based software company paints a worrisome picture of growing cybercrime. Germany leads all other European countries in cybercrime.

---

[331] Ibid.

[332] SITE: The Register. Article "Feds net 100 phishers in biggest cybercrime case ever" by Dan Goodin posted 8th October 2009

[333] Ibid.

[334] Published 27th June 2012 by Guardian UK. Titled "The urgency of computer virus nonproliferation treaty."

[335] Ibid.

[336] automotiveIT.International 6th April 2011 LINK: http://www.automotiveit.com/germany-tops-european-cybercrime-list/news/id-002337

Symantec found 473,480 computers that had been infected by so-called Bots, programs that run automatically, most often without the computer's owner knowing about them. Symantec said one out of every five Bot-infected computers in Europe is in Germany. On average 1,946 Bots were active in Germany every day and Symantec said the country is a preferred 'logistics base' for people or companies distributing viruses, phishing emails or spam."[337]

***John Leyden*** in a report for ***The Register***,[338]German police have arrested several members of a hacking forum linked to the distribution of Trojan horse software that infected 80,000 computers. The www.codesoft.cc message board was being abused by cyber-crooks to exchange tips on ways to use malware and other means to create counterfeit credit cards.[339]

On June 20th 2011,***YahooNews*** shared that Germany federal police says there is a 20% rise in cybercrime over last year, causing euro 61.5million ($89 million) in damage. ***Matthew Allen,*** reporting from Switzerland, states that cybercrimes is now the second biggest threat to Swiss firms in year 2011, though Switzerland faces same nature of cyber-crimes as faced by other countries, it takes a delicate turn owing to the financial secrecy and banking secrecy laws in the country.[340]

***Liau Yun Qing,*** *on 27th January 2012* reported that Bangladesh has set up a cyber-crime watchdog unit to monitor "harmful content" on internet and mobile phones arena.[341]

This came on the heels of reports revealing a failed coup organized online and through mobile phones. The division is put in place under the Bangladesh Telecommunication Regulatory Commission(BTRC). " The Bangladeshi army said it had foiled an attempted coup last month organized by retired and serving officers. Citing General Muhammad Masud Razzaq, Reuters reported that Ziaul Haque had used Face Book

---

[337] Ibid.

[338] Posted in Malware 4th March 2009 titled "German cops bust cyberçrime forum" LINK: http://www.theregister.co.uk/2009/03/04/german_cybercrime_bust/

[339] Ibid.

[340] **Swissinfo.tech titled,** "Growing cybercrime menace hits unwary firms" on 29th Nov 2011 LINK: http://www.swissinfo.ch/eng/business/Growing_cybercrime_menace_hits_unwary_firms.html?cid=31665278

[341] LINK: http://www.zdnetasia.com/bangladesh-sets-up-cybercrime-watchdog-62303622.htm

and mobile phone to encourage fellow officers and ex-officers to join the movement."[342]

**PortTurkey.com** reports in 2012 that the number of cybercrimes in Turkey are on the rise. Bank fraud and credit card frauds rank the highest in the category of the cyber-crimes, reportedly.[343]Cyber Crimes Unit of National Police Department officials stated that Internet crimes totaled 2,357 in 2010 and 2,905 suspects have been identified in the investigations of these crimes. In 2009, a total of 2,871 incidents were reported to the police and 4,670 suspects were identified. Police officials noted that the estimated figures are much higher, but a remarkable number of cases are not reported to police.[344]

### *Concluding comments*

With the growing use and dependency on computers, the abuse of the medium is also increasing, cascading into a wide category of crimes. Most countries realize the need to curtail these crimes and recognize it as a field in its own. The list of crimes that can be committed through the computer are endless.

Criminal conduct that may appear to have no connection with computers can, in fact, be affected by technology. For example, stalking presents itself as a serious concern, growing with increased use of the Internet. Cyber-stalking generally involves the stalking of a person via the Internet or other electronic communication. [345]Precautions such as not sharing a password, keeping your computer on the "No Saving Password Option", using only one's own computer, not lending your computer to others, having effective firewalls and anti-hacking systems appointed are a few suggested steps to avoid any computer related crimes .

---

[342] Ibid.

[343] SITE for PortTurkey.com published 14th April 2012titled "Cyber Crimes are getting increased in Turkey" LINK: http://www.portturkey.com/internet/864-cyber-crimes-are-getting-increased-in-turkish-internet

[344] Ibid.

[345] LINK: http://www.encyclopedia.com/topic/Computer_Crime.aspx

# *Chapter VI*

## Psychological Warfare and Propaganda

Psychological warfare, also known as ***psywar***, is the use of propaganda against the enemy through a variety of options available. This is supported by means such as economics, military, or political measures. Although we look upon propaganda as a modern invention but is it really a modern invention? It has been used as early as Cyrus the Great against Babylon, Xerxes against the Greeks and Philip II of Macedon against Athens.

***Richard Alan Nelson*** defines propaganda as, "Propaganda is neutrally defined as a systematic form of purposeful persuasion, that attempts to influence the emotions, attitudes, opinions, and actions of specified target audiences for ideological political or commercial purposes through the controlled transmission of one-sided messages(which may or may not be factual ) via mass and direct media channels."[346]

It is not for nothing that it is said, "The pen is mightier than the sword." In a memo written to then-Secretary of State John Foster Dulles on 24th October 1953, former U.S ***President Dwight D. Eisenhower***, defined psychological war. According to him it is anything , *"from the singing of the beautiful anthem up to the most extraordinary kind of physical sabotage."* [347]

In 1902, ***Lenin***, in his renowned book, ***What is to be Done,*** expresses his definition of propaganda. He said that it is the use of historical and scientific arguments to indoctrinate the educated and intelligent masses. Agitation was described by him as the use of slogans,

---

346 "A Chronology and Glossary of Propaganda in the United States" by Richard Alan Nelson

347 *Psychological Operations/Warfare* by Major Ed Rouse(Retd)

stories, and selective half-truths to exploit the grievances of the uneducated and ignorant masses.

Very interestingly, we see him applying "marketing strategies" to the "target markets", understanding that not all are equal in terms of education and intelligence and suggesting two different strategies to deal with both.

In the twentieth century , propaganda gained a new dimension with ***Joseph Goebbels***, member of German's Nazi Party, who became the propaganda minister for Adolf Hitler in 1933. Goebbels worked with two objectives (a) To ensure that nothing was read or seen that was against the Nazi Party and (b) To ensure that Nazi views were put across to the people in a favorable manner. Books that did not conform to the Nazi ideology were burnt in public. Leni Riefenstahl, was given an open cheque in producing films–also controlled by the Nazis. She produced the well-known film, "Triumph of Will". This is considered as one of the greatest films of the era despite its contents. In order to ensure that the people could listen to all Hitler had to tell them, Goebbels had the ingenious idea to arrange for cheap and affordable radios . These were known as "Peoples Receivers."

In Nurembeg,1934, Goebbels stated , and some extracts are shared here: "Propaganda is a means to an end. Its purpose is to lead the people to an understanding that will allow them to willingly and without internal resistance devote themselves to the tasks and goals of a superior leadership. If propaganda is to succeed, it must know what it wants. It must keep a clear and firm goal in mind, and seek the appropriate means and methods to reach that goal. Propaganda as such is neither good nor evil. Its moral value is determined by the goals it seeks.

"Propaganda must be creative. It is by no means a matter for the bureaucracy or official administration, but rather it is a matter of productive fantasy. The genuine propagandist must be a true artist. He must be a master of the popular soul, using it as an instrument to express the majesty of a genuine political will. Propaganda can be pro or con. In neither case does it have to be negative. The only thing that is important is whether or not its words are true and genuine expressions of the people."[348]

Propaganda is a lethally powerful weapon that is used to work against an individual, group, ethnicity or nation. This is done by a powerful transmission of idea(s) to create a certain image. The perceived enemy can either be external or internal.

"All propaganda must be popular and its intellectual level must be adjusted to the most limited intelligence among those it is addressed to. Consequently, the greater the mass it is intended to reach, the lower its purely intellectual level will have to be."[349]

There were three types of propaganda developed during World War II. This was Black, White and Gray Propaganda. The Black Propaganda focused on conveying anything but the truth. White Propaganda conveyed mostly facts and was more forthcoming on truth. Gray Propaganda avoided sharing sources of the news shared and omitted on sharing full facts. Black propaganda was used to disseminate "false information in the enemy camp, military and civilian [...] aimed at undermining moral and generally sowing doubt, disquiet, and depression." White propaganda "aspires to uplift home morale with eyewitness accounts of military successes [...] it is based on truth, even if the truth is twisted a little." [350]

I cannot but be reminded here of the wonderful book ***Animal Farm*** by ***George Orwell.*** Written in 1940's before the beginning of the Cold War , Orwell discussed the thought as to how ideas may be compiled, projected and put forth implicitly affecting peoples beliefs. The story revolves around animals taking over governance under the leadership of the big pig named Napoleon. Another pig, called Squealer takes up the duty of being his minister of propaganda. His job was to ensure that animals understood that Napoleon's policies were not only fair, they were just too.

These pigs changed rules as they went along and used different methods against those who opposed. What is common between Animal Farm and many societies of today is people with no power are constant

---

[348] Der Kongress zur Nürnberg 1934 (Munich: Zentralverlag der NSDAP., Frz. Eher Nachf., 1934), pp. 130-141

[349] Smith III, Ted J. Propaganda. A Pluralist Perspective. New York: Praeger, 1989

[350] Rhodes, Anthony. Propaganda. The Art of Persuasion World War II. : New York: Chelsea House Publications, 1976

recipients of propaganda. Their views and perceptions on issues may be erroneous as they are subjected to constant propaganda. Basically, propaganda works to persuade and advocate an agenda.

"One of the most horrible features of war is that all the war-propaganda, all the screaming and lies and hatred, comes invariably from people who are not fighting."—George Orwell, *Homage to Catalonia*, 1938. Propaganda can be used to support a revolution, garner support for an agenda, even create war, raise and create hype for false "issues" and distort truth to play down "real" issues.

## *Characteristics of propaganda*

***Identifying the Audience & going through Enemy Resistance:*** What is the audience that must be targeted? This must be established first. Their likes, dislikes, attitudes towards issues, understanding of "glittering generalizations"(discussed in the chapter later) and aversions to some terms like "terrorist", "snitch" so on and so forth. Much like the advertiser , who must research his proposed target audience first by his determining what button(emotional or any other) of his consumer he must press to ensure a sale. Likewise, the propagandist too must do his homework to ensure the propaganda hits home. The propagandist must also keep in mind the time zone of propaganda, ie is he using this during war times or during peace times. A good propagandist must package his message beautifully, so that, his target, the people think, "Yes! That is EXACTLY what I have always believed in." Ideas in themselves can be timeless. They need to be altered according to given situations. Some kinds of propaganda can actually be the beginning of a movement. Therefore, words like "freedom" are emotional push buttons that are successfully used by the propagandist. The idea, seeds once thrown, must spread. It must not be restrictive to a certain selected group alone.

***Appeal to fear of the good people:*** *"I want to testify today about what I believe is a planetary emergency—a crisis that threatens the survival of our civilization and the habitability of the Earth."*[351]

***Appeal to Authority***: Citing support by prominent people. *"Just six weeks ago, the scientific community, in its strongest statement to*

---

[351] Al Gore's Propaganda: 27th Jan 2009 by Roy W. Spencer Ph. D LINK: http://www.drroyspencer.com/2009/01/al-gores-propaganda/

*date, confirmed that the evidence of warming is unequivocal. Global warming is real and human activity is the main cause."*[352]

***Bandwagon:*** The "inevitable victory" appeal, the persuasion tactic to convince people to join up or they will miss the bus. This is used by propagandist to convince the people that this is a movement everyone is joining up. This appeals to the common man's desire not to lose but to win–hence he must join the bandwagon to be on the winning side.

***Appeal to prejudice***: And we all have some. *"And to solve this crisis we can develop a shared sense of moral purpose."*(June 21, 2006, London, England).[353]

All of the above depends on one thing only: your understanding of your target audience. You can only push the different buttons if you know what makes them work. I would especially like to draw readers attention here to the role of entertainment in propaganda. Everyone likes to chill out. Hear music, soaps, movies. It reaches everyone, everywhere. More important, people are more receptive to a message since it is couched in entertainment, not an obvious effort at brain washing. Once , in Pakistan, cinema was the high point of family entertainment. The days of Waheed Murad, Mohd Ali, Zeba, Shabnum, Nadeem are long over. Pakistan cinema has gone into a decline. It has been replaced with home theatre, cable TV and with this has come an avalanche of Indian movie channels. TV has access to all groups, young and old, educated and uneducated, rich or poor. For this reason, it becomes a very effective tool in the hands of the propagandist. It evokes emotions, makes the recipient *accept* another culture more easily. For example a few decades ago, dance in weddings was marked with the traditional "luddi"(local dance) and "fun" dancing. This has today been replaced by following Indian steps on Indian popular film songs. The local news media gives coverage to Indian stars as if they are from the motherland. Though unintentional, and merely going by the popular interests, nonetheless, these actions play a role is changing perceptions and attitudes , replacing the cinema as the main family outing.

But then, countries also use propaganda for getting through to enemies. Of course, the enemy will control his area of influence. He will not give you easy access to his audience. If you do manage to get through,

---

[352] Ibid.

[353] Ibid.

you will be faced with ***counter-propaganda***. However, the world has turned into a global village today and mediums of communications have made it possible to transmit news and ideas at rocket speed. Another way to get past the enemy is to pretend friendship for the country against which force is to be used while secretly plotting its destruction. While a peaceful neighbor is in slumber, the propagandist is hard at work as we saw in the Nazi propaganda. The Nazi propaganda machine issued a barrage describing the great strength of the German army and air force and the folly of even trying to resist them. Nazi attacks discredited the doomed country's leaders, no matter how honest and sincere those leaders were. The "war of nerves" was unleashed.

"The Nazis were then ready to strike. All this required careful preparation and the cynical union of propaganda and terror. Before attacks were made on Austria, Czechoslovakia, Poland, Norway, the Netherlands, or, France, the Nazis planted their subversive agents in legations, consulates, and tourist bureaus, created Nazi party "cells" within a country's borders, and established espionage services which ramified all over the world. Treacherous persons already in the pay or under the influence of the Nazis—the "fifth columnists"—were ready to "sell one" when the time came for the Nazis to strike."[354]

***Captivating the Audience:*** The audience must "hold" with our propaganda. They must not be allowed to get away. The first step towards this goal is for the target audience to get over the distrust of the propagandist and accept it as truth. This is a huge block, once crossed, the rest becomes comparatively easier.

In order to do this the weakness in the enemy ranks must be spotted. This requires superior intelligence and understanding of enemy's key weaknesses. This is exaggerated and highlighted in the propaganda. For example, playing on schisms within the society, within ethnic group and between the civil and military. Exploiting these weaknesses and differences usually pays dividends. In some cases the propaganda is not blatantly obvious, here, insinuations may be raised, doubts created which are worked upon in later stages.

***Credibility of Propaganda:*** Propaganda to be effective must be credible. This does not mean it is necessarily true. However, the

[354] "What is Propaganda" : Constructing a Postwar World
http://www.historians.org/projects/GIRoundtable/Propaganda/Propaganda1.htm

propagandist must base propaganda on facts, even selective not on outright lies. The counter propaganda, otherwise will reveal the mistruths thereby causing future propaganda by the propagandist to suffer from serious lack of credibility. People of a nation develop perceptions and opinions about the other nations by virtue of their actions and conduct. This will have bearing on formation of opinion of the public at large depending upon their understanding and awareness of the agreements, treaties, understandings between the nations.

Credibility will depend on the source of propaganda. Who made a statement and what is the subject and crux of the statement. The supporting circumstances to the propaganda. If facts nullify what is being propagated, it may not stand or pass the test of credibility. The manner in which something is shared will make a difference. Something presented as news, has a veneer of impartiality. However, when views are presented, they take over a subjective cover. Who is writing or voicing an opinion will depend on *from where the person expressing the opinion is coming from.*

## *Tactics of Propaganda*

Let us now study the *tactics* of propaganda.

One interesting propaganda tactic is to make a ***selective selection*** while choosing a news item or a story. This then may be truth but only partial truth. It is not an impartial presentation of facts. Opinions and views formed on these selective stories is bound to be erroneous. No one for example gets up one day and decides to do an act generally known to be wrong and a danger to the life of the person doing it. This is usually a result of steady and gradual brainwashing to a point where the individual or a group of people start believing in the proposed act or belief (s)held-are willing to act on what is fed to them over a period of time.

In an interesting article by ***Jeff Cohen*** published 28th April 2008, he says and I quote, "But I'm also for keeping the focus and onus on CNN, FOX, NBC, ABC, CBS, even NPR – who were partners in the Pentagon's mission of 'information dominance.' And for us to see that American TV news remains so corrupt today that it has hardly mentioned the Times story on the Pentagon's pundits, which was based on 8,000 pages of internal Pentagon documents acquired by a successful Times lawsuit."[355]

---

[355] Article titled, "Military Propaganda pushed me Off TV" by Jeff Cohen, on blog War Is A Crime.org

Another tactic is the use of ***partial facts***. First is selective stories then a further breakdown into facts that are selective and may well miss out on many elements, that are intrinsic in projecting the truth. In his book, ***Journalism for All, Dr Mehdi Hasan***, talking of psychological warfare states,[356] "...He must be induced to overcome his distrust of the propagandist's activities before he can be considered open to influence. To overcome this distrust is to convince the enemy of the truth of what the propagandist says. Propaganda should be committed to a policy of truth. Here again, knowledge of the target audience is a prerequisite, but certain specialized techniques are also important."

The third tactic of propaganda is ***Reinforcing Reasons and Motivations.*** Repeating reasons to act in a manner, and reinforcing motivations to do a certain act, ***Harriet Braiker***[357] says these can be positive and negative both.

Positive reinforcement includes praise, charming those who are sought to be influenced by propaganda, gifts, public recognition. Negative reinforcement , creating fear of something "bad" happening, an imminent danger if something is not done. Motivation means to gravitate an individual or group of people towards a certain goal using propaganda. It makes the action suggested desirable and the end result a reward. ***Dr Mehdi Hasan***, in his book, ***Journalism For All***, says, "This means suggesting an idea to target and leading him to such a point where it is easy for him to draw the desired conclusion. The propagandist does not give the conclusion himself, but he does this indirectly, by shutting out all courses to his target but one."[358]

A very pertinent and interesting tactic is the ***Narrow Panel of Experts***. In order to add "expert" support to a propaganda, the propagandist uses experts. But the number of these experts is narrow and revolves around those experts who support and concur with the views of the propagandist and can help further the propaganda employed. It will not include experts who are more impartial in their view or those with an opposing view to that of the propagandist. The views of experts add weightage and credibility to the propaganda. It will project a one-sided view of a conflict.

---

[356] Journalism for All: published by Aziz Book Depot 1997 Pg 239
[357] Braiker, Harriet B. (2004). *Who's Pulling Your Strings ? How to Break The Cycle of Manipulation*
[358] Journalism for All: Dr Mehdi Hasan(1997)Pg 246

U.S Senator Hiram Johnson in 1917 correctly said, "The first casualty when war comes, is Truth."

"It is easier to dominate someone if they are unaware of being dominated. Colonized and colonizers both know that domination is not just based on physical supremacy. Control of hearts and minds follows military conquest. Which is why any empire that wants to last must capture the souls of its subjects" says *Ignacio Ramonet.* [359]

Talking of military conquests, one must not forget to share the view *of **Sun-Tzu**(400BC)'The Art of War. Strategic Assessments:"A military operation involves deception. Even though you are competent, appear to be incompetent. Though effective, appear to be ineffective."*

***Demonizing the enemy*** is yet another successful tactic. Any one not fighting the "right"(which of course is the propagandist's side) is an enemy. Bad. A demon. Must be fought tooth and nail. Hence, this is the most used tool when countries go to war against another country, or, in modern societies when war is declared on a school of thought vis a vis another school of thought.

Winston Churchill, British Prime Minister during World War II, said, "In wartime, truth is so precious that she should always be attended by a bodyguard of lies."

Battles are often fought on a narrow platform, the "good guys" or the "bad guys". Either you are with the good guys or with the bad guys. There is nothing in between. Nothing can be further from truth. We cannot overlook the shades of gray in between. I cannot but be reminded here of the words of American President ***George W. Bush Jr.*** "Either you are with us or against us." He was addressing a joint press conference with French President Jacques Chirac, in reference to War on Terror.[360]

Wartime propaganda using false accusations all the time, partial truths, projecting your actions as a reaction to your opponents reinforces the "good" and the "bad" theory. The purpose is to destroy the morale of the enemy and boost that of your own.

---

[359] *Le Monde diplomatique, May 2000 "The Control of Pleasure."*

[360] CNN.Com/U.S: "You are either with us or against us." Posted 6th November 2011

In a very interesting article by ***Anthony DiMAGGIO***, titled ***Seven Years of Wartime Propaganda***,[361] the writer shares his research on the ground realities in Iraq post US Iraq invasion. He writes, 'The American press has systematically ignored, marginalized, or buried deep within their pages casualty reports indicating that hundreds of thousands, perhaps over one million Iraqis died during the occupation. What little reporting has been done on casualties focuses more on American lives. An analysis of the 2003-2005 period finds that the New York Times covered American casualties three times more than Iraqi civilian casualties."[362]

In his concluding paragraph he states, "This study has merely skimmed the surface of the bi-partisan deceit that drives media and political rationalizations for the war."

The next tactic in propaganda is ***using a narrow range of discourse***. Opinions are formulated on a narrow range. Often things are not simple. There are questions within issues, however, these are ignored to make the issue simple and easily targeted by the propagandist. The narrow focus, ignoring the bigger picture, suits the propagandist.

*"To the rulers of the state, then, if to any, it belongs of right to use falsehood, to deceive either enemies or their own citizens, for the good of the state: and no one else may meddle with this privilege..."* (**Plato**).

**Let us now look at some interesting angles of propaganda**

First, why does propaganda work? One because it helps people / governments justify what they do. In a detailed article in *New York Times*, titled, *"Secret 'Kill List' Proves a Test of Obama's Principles and Will"*[363] by ***Jo Becker & Scott Shane***, speaks of the drone strategy. We have constantly read of the militants killed by the drones in Pakistan. The strategy has created a huge backlash resulting in anti-American sentiments owing to civilians being killed in the process. In this article, the shocking propaganda claiming militants killed is revealed by the authors, "One guy gets knocked off, and the guy's driver, who's No. 21, becomes 20?" Mr. Daley said, describing the internal discussion. "At what point are you just filling the bucket with numbers?" He goes on to say, " It is also because Mr. Obama embraced a disputed method for counting

[361] Published in "counterpunch" dated 29th Feb-2nd March 2009

[362] Ibid.

[363] New York Times published 29th May 2012

civilian casualties that did little to box him in. It in effect counts all military-age males in a strike zone as combatants, according to several administration officials, unless there is explicit intelligence posthumously proving them innocent." The article shook the world. This is in contradiction to all we have been told over the years about militants being killed in their safe havens in Pakistan.

To give another example, In an article carried by **Information Clearing House,** titled, *Journalism vs Propaganda* [364] by **Glenn Greenwald,** I share an extract here, "Almost immediately after a suicide bomber killed five Israeli tourists in Bulgaria on Wednesday, Israeli officials, led by Prime Minister Benjamin Netanyahu, blamed Iran, an accusation uncritically repeated by most Western media outlets even as Bulgarian investigators warned it would be a 'mistake' to assign blame before the attack could be investigated. Now, Israel, along with the U.S., is blaming Hezbollah and, therefore, Iran for the attack. Today's *New York Times* article by Nicholas Kulish and Eric Schmitt – headlined 'Hezbollah Is Blamed for Attack on Israeli Tourists in Bulgaria' – uncritically treats those accusations as confirmed fact despite no evidence being offered for it: American officials on Thursday **identified** the suicide bomber responsible for a deadly attack on Israeli vacationers here as a member of a Hezbollah cell that was operating in Bulgaria and looking for such targets, **corroborating** Israel's assertions and making the bombing a new source of tension with Iran.

"One senior American official said the current American intelligence assessment was that the bomber, who struck Wednesday, killing five Israelis, had been 'acting under broad guidance' to hit Israeli targets when opportunities presented themselves, and that the guidance had been given to Hezbollah, a Lebanese militant group, by Iran, its primary sponsor. Two other American officials **confirmed** that Hezbollah was behind the bombing, but **declined to provide additional details**.

"The attacks, the official said, were in retaliation for the assassinations of Iranian nuclear scientists, for which Iran has blamed Israeli agents — an accusation that Israel has neither confirmed nor denied. 'This was tit for tat,' said the American official, who spoke on condition of anonymity because the investigation was still under way. . . .A senior Israeli official said on Thursday that the Bulgarian attack was part of an intensive wave of terrorist attacks around the world carried out by

---

[364] 21st July 2012 LINK: http://www.informationclearinghouse.info/article31948.htm

two different organizations, the Iranian Quds Force, an elite international operations unit within Iran's Islamic Revolutionary Guards Corps, as well as by Hezbollah."

"By "identified," "confirmed" and "corroborated" Iranian and Hezbollah responsibility, what The New York Times means is this: American officials asserted that this was so, even as they "declined to provide additional details" and even though "the investigation was still under way." Indeed, this accusation is, as the NYT sees it, "confirmed" and "corroborated" even though "no details yet about the bomber like his name or nationality" are known; even though their anonymous American source "declined to describe what specific intelligence — intercepted communications, analysis of the bomber's body parts or other details — led analysts to conclude that the bomber belonged to Hezbollah"; even though "the Bulgarians are still trying to figure out how the bomber entered the country, how he traveled around and where he stayed"; and even though the Bulgarian Foreign Minister said: "We're not pointing the finger in any direction until we know what happened and complete our investigation." All The Paper of Record knows is that US and Israeli officials have blamed Iran and Hezbollah, and — as usual — that's good enough for them. Identified, Confirmed and Corroborated."[365]

Another reason for the propaganda to work is the fear of the unknown. The fear of upsetting the values that are dear, upsetting the order one cherishes. These values can be justice, freedom, right to fundamental rights.

Propaganda presents facts that may bring forth these fears, making them seem likely, and through the techniques discussed earlier, making the propaganda seem so logical that it whips people to accept the propaganda hook, line and sinker. Media management and public relations has become developed, advanced and very professional. I would like to mention here briefly the propaganda used in advertisements. Certain versions of truth may be given in advertisements, while others can be completely misleading. Ethics of advertising forbids misguided and wrong claims. Propaganda is also used in election campaigns in the more recent years, "image building."

I would like to quote here, ***Adolf Hitler***, who stated, *"All propaganda must be so popular and on such an intellectual level, that*

---

[365] Ibid.

*even the most stupid of those towards whom it is directed will understand it.... Through clever and constant application of propaganda, people can be made to see paradise as hell, and also the other way around, to consider the most wretched sort of life as paradise."*

In a very interesting article titled, *Payola Pundits for War*[366], **Justin Raimondo,** talks about the role of public relation firms in "selling" wars. This is a focus on the role of propaganda by these firms in certain issues. He says, "Public relations spending doubled under the Bush administration – to at least $88 million in fiscal 2004, for a grand total of $250 million during the first term –and it is safe to say that not all of that money was allocated to purely domestic programs."

He continues, "The use of public relations agencies to sell wars as one would soap or any other product has a long and inglorious history reaching all the way back to the first Gulf War, and the infamous lies told by Hill and Knowlton. H&K, with numerous and close ties to the Bush family, contracted with the Kuwaiti government to sell the American public on the war: their "Citizens for a Free Kuwait" Astroturf group flooded the country with war propaganda, including an appearance before a congressional committee sponsored by Democratic congressman Tom Lantos ......."[367]

And yes, Public Relation firms do put out press stories in the press.

In September 2006, it was reported[368] that "at least 10 local journalists had accepted US government pay from programs on Radio Marti or TV Marti. El Nuevo Herald fired two of them Thursday for conflict of interest."[369] The article goes on to say. "Jesús Díaz Jr., president of the Miami Herald Media Co. and publisher of both newspapers, expressed disappointment, saying the payments violated a 'sacred trust' between journalists and the public." It further states, "Even the appearance that your objectivity or integrity might have been impaired is something we can't condone, not in our business," Díaz

---

[366] Antiwar.com published 29th Jan. 2005 LINK: http://original.antiwar.com/justin/2005/01/28/payola-pundits-for-war/

[367] Ibid.

[368] **VLEEPTRON_Z posted 9th September 2006:tittled'**Miami Herald fires reporters for taking pay from US government's Radio/TV Martí'. LINK: **http://vleeptronz.blogspot.com/2006/09/miami-herald-fires-reporters-for.html**

[369] Ibid.

said. "I personally don't believe that integrity and objectivity can be assured if any of our reporters receive monetary compensation from any entity that he or she may cover or have covered, but particularly if it's a government agency." The article furthers shares the names of journalists paid, amounts of payments involved and how it was discovered, " Radio and TV Martí are US government programs created to promote democracy and freedom in Cuba. Their programming cannot be broadcast within the United States because of anti-propaganda laws. Radio and TV Martí have received $37 million this year. The payments to journalists were discovered in documents recently obtained by The Miami Herald as a result of a federal Freedom of Information Request filed on Aug. 15."

Propaganda aims to rally public support for an agenda, an issue, a conflict. It therefore uses all tools at its disposal, including, half-truths, false promises, outright lies, exaggeration et al to achieve the end. For the propagandist, the end justifies the means. I am fairly certain it was Vladimir Lenin who said that treaties are like pie crusts, made to be broken. To tell the truth, it is a pretty bourgeois habit, but to lie and lie convincingly, is a sign of superior intelligence.

In dictatorships, propaganda may be more open, press laws more stringent in publishing any opposing views. In a democracy it has to be more planned, more sophisticated. French Author ***Anatole France***, wrote, "Democracy is run by unseen engineer."

***Arthur Ponsonby*** said, "It has been rightly said that the injection of the poison of hatred into men's minds by means of falsehood is a greater evil in war-time than the actual loss of life. The defilement of the human soul is worse than the destruction of the human body." [370]

Before delivering his request for a declaration of war to Congress President Wilson had predicted: "Once lead this people into war, and they'll forget there was ever such a thing as tolerance; to fight you must be brutal and ruthless, and the spirit of ruthless brutality will enter into the very fibre of our national life, infecting Congress, the courts, the policeman, the man in the street."[371]

Propaganda **does** change perceptions, especially if it is subtle.

---

[370] "Falsehood in Wartime"(London 1928)Pg 10

[371] FROM: *This Fabulous Century: Sixty Years of American Life*, vol. 2, *1910-1920* (New York: Time-Life Books, 1969), pp. 235-38

***Alvin and Heidi Toffler*** in their book, **War and Anti-War**[372] discuss six methods used in wartime propaganda. The very same principles, if we water them down, apply to everyday situations as well:

***Atrocity Accusations:*** Accusing the other of being responsible for sub human acts, that are shocking and challenge the very values that are cherished and admired by a decent, honor loving individual. This in turn justifies the actions of the propagandist. There is shock, hue and cry, and people rally behind the cause propagated. Bombing places where civilians are killed, women, men, little children can result in a huge backlash, fanned by egging on by the propagandist. After 9/11, Muslims are increasingly over a period of time subject to suspicion. **Brian Kilmeade**,[373] co-hosts a show ***Fox & Friends***, on ***Fox.*** On 15th October 2010 edition of Fox News Radio 's *Kilmeade & Friends* he stated, "Not every Muslim is an extremist, a terrorist, but every terrorist is a Muslim. You can't avoid that fact." On the 18th edition of Kilmeade clarified that he had not meant to hurt anyone's feelings when he said not all Muslims are terrorists but all terrorists are Muslims.

On the October 15 edition of *Kilmeade & Friends*, Kilmeade said: "From what we've seen from the Khobar Towers to the Cole bombing to the embassy bombings to the Times Square, the shoe bomber, do you think Americans have a right to look at moderate Muslims and say, 'Show me you're not one of them.' "[374]

Words and concepts to such effect can and do have an impact on the public. Everyone who hears, reads, or sees is not intelligent and educated to discern between the truth and the false. Between generalities that are self-defeating and specifics in a situation. Now a person making such statements may actually believe them at times, to be true and not propaganda at all.

***Hyperbole Inflations:*** Alvin & Heidi offers that the second method of propaganda is hyperbole inflations. Exaggeration of an act. Using one incident as an occurrence and project it as if it happens all the time, thereby building fear in the hearts towards whom propaganda is

---

[372] Published by Little, Brown and Company 1993

[373] Kilmeade also co-hosts *Brian and the Judge*, a talk-news radio show on Fox News Radio, with Judge Andrew P. Napolitano. He also hosts the Fox News Radio program *Kilmeade and Friends*

[374] MEDIA MATTERS FOR AMERICA .Posted: 18th October 2010 LINK: http://mediamatters.org/research/201010180007

directed. Or/and making the act or words of one person representative of the group to which he or she belongs.

***Demonization & Dehumanization*** : Another tool stated is to make those who are to be the victims of the propagandist to come out smelling bad. To make them look completely rotten in every respect. Framing them as proposed destroyers of all held dear ie the values, that we, the honorable people may cherish. "Dehumanization is the psychological process whereby opponents view each other as less than human and thus not deserving of moral consideration."[375]

Dehumanization attributes horrific acts to the enemy, the Nazi extermination of European Jews is an example and the genocide rape of Bosnian Muslim women. Dehumanization, essentially is used in wartime zone. In a letter retrieved from a war zone, the author, ***Augustin Cochin*** wrote against the Germans in WWII;

"Dreadful, dreadful race; the more we see them from close up, the more we loathe them...It is annoying to get killed behind the parapet by such animals. They have a peculiar, powerful odor."[376]

“Us vs Them” defines the strategy of demonization & dehumanization. “They” are demons, capable of all wrong and the very base acts, “we” are the good people driven to defend our honor and save the people from wrongs “they” may commit further.

***Polarization:*** Polarizing the two: “they” and “us”. Our men in war are glorious heroes, “theirs” are villains deserving the worst treatment at our hands as they are just up to no good.

On 12th January 2012, ***Daniel Bates & Lee Moran,*** [377]in their article write, “ The 'disgusting' and 'highly reprehensible' 40-second clip shows four men in combat gear standing over the three corpses with their genitals exposed as they relieve themselves.

---

[375]Michelle Maiese. "Dehumanization," (July 2003) 9 Dec. 2007 <http://www.beyondintractabilit.org/essay/dehumanization>

[376]Michael W. Brough, "Dehumanization of the Enemy and the Moral Equality of Soldiers," - Rethinking the Just War Tradition, (Albany, 2007):151

[377] Mail Online published 12th Jan 2012 titled, ”Disgusting Video is recruitment tool for the Taliban: Outrage across the world after footage emerges showing U.S troops urinating on Afghan dead bodies.”

The men can be heard joking 'Have a great day, buddy', 'Golden like a shower' and 'Yeahhhh!' as they groan with relief whilst urinating." They write in the same piece, "Pentagon spokesman Navy Captain John Kirby said the video was deeply troubling: 'Whoever it is, and whatever the circumstances, which we know is under investigation, it is egregious behavior."

In AlJazeera newspaper[378] an article states and I quote, "Al Jazeera has obtained exclusive material of a course taught on a US military base implying that Hamas has influenced the US government at the highest levels. The course is called 'Understanding the Threat to America'. And in it are hundreds of slides that claim to link the Muslim Civil Liberties Advocacy Organisation (CAIR) and other American Muslim groups to the Palestinian group Hamas. It was taught to senior military officers at a base in the state of Virginia.

"The Pentagon suspended the course in late April when a student objected to the material. The FBI also changed some agent training last year after discovering that it, too, was critical of Islam." [379]

Propaganda tactics result in hatred, creating a wedge between different groups, countries, religions.

***Divine Sanction:*** Giving an impression, that those higher in divinity support your thought process. This especially works when the issue is religion related. Reinterpreting scriptures is one way.

***Meta-propaganda:*** Use of propaganda to rebut propaganda. Projecting "their" messages as propaganda and "ours" as clear messages based on truth. It can be showed that "they" have control of media, and by showing video footage(selective of course)to support "our" claims.

"... there is not a living soul in any country who does not deeply resent having his passions roused, his indignation inflamed, his patriotism exploited, and his highest ideals desecrated by concealment, subterfuge, fraud, falsehood, trickery, and deliberate lying on the part of those in whom he is taught to repose confidence and to whom he is enjoined to pay respect." [380]

---

[378] Published 12th May 2012 titled "The US military anti-Islamic classes"
[379] US military course taught officers "Islam is the enemy" Guardian UK published 11th May 2012
[380] Arthur Ponsonby in "Falsehood in Wartime" (LONDON 1928)

**Let us look at the mediums of propaganda**: According to ***Aliya Hyot***[381] TV, radio, internet, print medium. ie newspapers, posters, brochures etc. According to Professor M. Lane Bruner, broadcast propaganda -- communicated through television, radio and film -- is the most dangerous kind. These messages are developed and broadcast by producers, directors, writers and news anchors or disc jockeys whose personal beliefs creep into ideas that are viewed and heard by a massive audience. Since the audience has little or no opportunity to respond or provide feedback to these messages, they become fact in the minds of many. "Furthermore," Bruner says, "given the wide range of choice of programs, people oftentimes only tune in to the programs that reinforce their own beliefs."[382]

Cartoons are a potent way of conveying propaganda. For example, a caricature in "The New Yorker" of 2008 presidential hopeful Barack Obama and his wife Michelle reinforced persistent African-American stereotypes. And when a Danish newspaper published political cartoons with images of Mohammed in 2006, tensions were ignited between Muslims who considered the images sacrilegious, and members of the European press. The cartoon raised the question of whether or not propaganda is permissible by free speech. Bruner says yes, it is: "Basically, most propaganda, as long as it does not transgress the current legal limitations on speech, is protected speech."[383]

Internet is yet another medium of communication. Increasingly, people are relying more and more on internet for research, communication and reading materials. It is a good way to convey opinions. However, computer has become a hub of exchange of communication between people from different parts of the world, Twitter, Face Book are very popular as are blogs and yahoo, google groups. Owing to this fast exchange of communication, opinions formed may be uninformed. Interestingly, in order to cash on this medium of communication, it is reported, that a certain country invests a lot of funds, in its "Front Desk" of the Foreign Affairs Department, The individuals employed there operate through many fake IDs. The main purpose is to enter chats with Pakistanis, open blogs under pseudonyms,

---

[381] "How Propaganda Works" LINK: http://history.howstuffworks.com/historians/propaganda2.htm

[382] Bruner, M. Lane, Ph.D. Associate Professor of Rhetoric & Politics, Department of Communication, Georgia State University. Personal interview conducted by Alia Hoyt. Sept. 8, 2008

[383] Ibid.

and write / float pieces that are based on propaganda. The basic purpose is to spread disenchantment and disinformation in the Pakistani society.

Radio too, is a very effective method of propaganda, since the visual element is missing, it is more difficult to decipher if a lie or half-truth is being propagated as the body language, the facial expressions, are missing.

Is name calling common in propaganda? Why, yes. It usually is.

Name calling has led men and women to do great deeds, enter into war with other nations, gripped with a feeling of such great righteousness that they are willing to die, even. To commit murder too.

This angle; linking a person by name, calling him or her to a much hated symbol is highly successive in besmirching the reputation of that person. Amongst younger people, especially going to Public Schools in Pakistan, the worst thing you could call another is a "snitch". Once labeled so, you are finished. A snitch you would remain for the rest of your life, a pariah, an outcast from "the" group.

Ouch!

As I see the world today, calling someone a Fascist, since the killing of many due to the drone strategy; a supporter of the strategy, you are definitely not viewed as a patriot. Another word used to label someone with is a 'Terrorist."

Propagandists use ***glittering generalities***. Using words loosely, to convey an image to others. Different words mean different things to different people. According to Institute of Propaganda Analysis (1938):

'The Glittering Generality is, in short, Name Calling in reverse. While Name Calling seeks to make us form a judgment to reject and condemn without examining the evidence, the Glittering Generality device seeks to make us approve and accept without examining the evidence. In acquainting ourselves with the Glittering Generality Device, therefore, all that has been said regarding Name Calling must be kept in mind..." [384]

Interestingly the increased use of propaganda in coming years was predicted by Mark Twain, " Next the statesmen will invent cheap lies,

---

[384] Reference: http://www.propagandacritic.com/articles/ct.wg.gg.html

putting the blame upon the nation that is attacked, and every man will be glad of those conscience-soothing falsities, and will diligently study them, and refuse to examine any refutations of them; and thus he will by and by convince himself that the war is just, and will thank God for thc better sleep he enjoys after this process of grotesque self-deception."[385]

A propagandist uses false connections. Using testimonials by people that is not relevant to the issue at hand. For example using a known sportsman to tell the public whom to vote for. Two unrelated things altogether.

By controlling thoughts of the public, using the mediums of communications discussed earlier, the propagandist can control the thoughts of the public. In 1921, American journalist Walter Lippmann said that the art of democracy requires the manufacture of consent. Propaganda is to democracies what violence is to dictatorships.

### *Limitations of Propaganda*

Propaganda has tremendous power to sway the public opinion. However, it can be a fallacy to over rate the impact of propaganda. The people exercise their own judgment as well. They do not swallow everything dished out to them by the propagandist.

The field must be ripe, a schism must exist to the propagandist to exploit. In a superb article by ***Glenn Greenwald***,[386] titled "*Media, drones and rank propaganda*"[387], he states, "As usual, the leading spokespeople for government policies are disguised as the nation's Adversarial Watchdog Press". He goes on to state, 'This morning, I witnessed one of the most flagrant and repellent examples of rank government propaganda masquerading as objective journalism that I have ever seen, when I saw on Andrew Sullivan's Blog this four-minute, sleek video produced by *Newsweek* and *The Daily Beast*, starring *Newsweek* reporter (and its former Managing Editor) Daniel Klaidman. It's literally painful to watch..."[388]

The article carries the link of the video above. Greenwald continues, "Did I exaggerate, or was that every bit as manipulative and repulsive as I

---

[385] Mark Twain in 1916

[386] American lawyer, columnist, blogger, and author. Writes for Salon.com

[387] 8th June 2012 published by Salon. Com

[388] Ibid.

suggested? How is it remotely justifiable — using the standards of 'objective journalism' that these media outlets incessantly invoke — for Newsweek to produce a video that has little purpose other than to justify, glorify, and defend Obama's drone attacks on other countries? Is this not one of the most glaring examples ever demonstrating that 'objective journalists' like Newsweek's Daniel Klaidman are barred from expressing opinions — unless the opinion expressed is that the actions of the U.S. Government are justified and noble? That's why Chris Hedges was forced out of The New York Times for opposing the attack on Iraq while John Burns was venerated and made the chief war correspondent after he supported the attack: opinions are perfectly permissible from American journalists only to the extent that they defend official actions. In what conceivable way is it the proper role of Newsweek and its national security 'reporters' to produce melodramatic agitprop which vigorously takes the U.S. Government's side in ongoing, highly divisive political controversies?"[389]

It is opined, propaganda is more easily accepted if it is in line with what people want to accept. Hitler's propaganda sought ready acceptance because German people craved supremacy. People use creams that promise fair complexion in days because they want to accept this. This is what they desire. The promise to have your lover at your feet, if you do certain acts promised by the soothsayer.

The propagandist must remember, that certain opinions are born of events, these are distinct from opinion created by propaganda. Dr Shakeel Afridi's case falls within the purview of opinion based on events. Dr Shakil Afridi helped the CIA by running a fake vaccination programme that allowed him to collect the DNA of Bin Laden's children from the family compound in Abbottabad.

Sample analysis confirmed the terror leader was probably there and triggered the deadly mission by US Navy SEALS last May .[390]Last year, 198 cases of polio were recorded in Pakistan, making it the country among the largest to fall prey to this disease. ***Hedi Larson*** reports for ***The Guardian UK*** , "The news of Dr Afridi's role did not emerge until a Guardian article in July 2011, when it shook the immunization world. Although Dr Afridi had pretended to provide a hepatitis B vaccination, not

---

[389] Ibid.

[390] MailOnline published 23rd May 2012 titled "White House accused of 'outing' Pakistani doctor who led U.S to Bin Laden's hideout as he is jailed for 33 years for treason as punishment for humiliating his country"

normally a door-to-door delivery, the news had a particularly strong impact on those working in polio eradication, where door-to-door vaccination is the norm. Anxieties and distrust about the polio vaccine and its western providers were rampant in some communities, and suspicions about CIA links with the polio vaccination campaigns, and rumors they were a front for the sterilizing of Muslims, had been around for a decade after 9/11. After years of working to dispel myths about CIA links to the polio eradication efforts – from northern Nigeria to Pakistan and India, all of the work seemed fruitless."[391] She further states, "But deep-seated suspicions about the motives of those who provide polio vaccines have persisted in some circles from Nigeria to Pakistan, and the CIA's choice of immunization as a strategy to find Bin Laden has only given credence to the conspiracies."

To quote another example, ""The studies of George Gallup, since World War II started, reveal a similar relation between events and attitudes. In the early spring of 1940 only 7 Americans out of 100 voted 'yes'- in response to Dr. Gallup's question as to whether the United States should declare war on Germany. A month later, after the battle of Flanders, 16 out of 100 said they would vote for war if a national referendum were called. Dr. Gallup went on to say that 'events and actions are infinitely more potent factors in influencing the formation of public opinion than a mere desire (for example) to imitate one's fellow citizens.'"[392]

Heredity and environment also play a role in limiting the influence of propaganda. A great number of people follow the beliefs of their parents, political and otherwise, though ongoing events and peer pressure too, may change the opinion later. " The public opinion polling experts believe that sex, age, place of residence, and income are all of some importance in influencing attitudes, and that on some issues, race, religion, and party affiliations also enter."[393]

A man's knowledge on a subject can also deflect propaganda irrespective of the source it comes from.

---

[391] Titled "The CIA's fake vaccination drive has damaged the battle against polio" published 27th May 2012

[392] "Some Limitations of Propaganda" LINK: http://www.historians.org/Projects/GIroundtable/Propaganda/Propaganda6.htm

[393] Ibid.

## *Counter Propaganda*

Counter propaganda is described as [394] propaganda to offset or nullify unfriendly or enemy propaganda. I share a definition by ***Garth Jowett*** and ***Victoria O'Donnell*** who define propaganda as, "The deliberate, systematic attempt to shape perceptions, manipulate cognitions, and direct behavior to achieve a response that furthers the desired intent of the propagandist. "[395] Counter propaganda contains all the elements contained within propaganda, ie research, understanding of the people towards whom it is targeted. To be effective, counter propaganda must react swiftly to wash away the impact of propaganda. It must address the questions: who is the target of propaganda?

How many people have been subject to the propaganda? What is the intent and desired effect of the propaganda? What are the exaggerations, inaccuracies, deliberate mistruths of the propaganda? What facts, arguments must be employed to deflect the propaganda?

"During the months leading up to the 1984 Summer Olympics hosted by Los Angeles, the Soviet Union circulated forged Ku Klux Klan leaflets threatening the lives of non-white athletes. The Soviet Union sent the leaflets specifically to the African and Asian Olympic Committees. The U.S. State Department released a public statement, accusing the KGB of producing the leaflets and notified each Olympic committee that the leaflets were forgeries. The result was no single Olympic committee refused to attend the games and the Soviets were revealed as the origin of the propaganda."[396]

In an interesting piece by **AlJazeera** titled, "*Counter-Propaganda is still propaganda*"[397] it says in May the story broke by Associated Press(ran on abc news)[398] stating the Secretary of State had "hacked" into the "tribal sites of Yemen Al Qaida". It stated, "Secretary of State Hillary Clinton explicitly acknowledged that the US government hacked into websites run by al-Qaeda's affiliate in Yemen."[399] In fact, as *Wired's* Kim

---

[394] Dictionary.com

[395] [Garth Jowett and Victoria O'Donnell, *Propaganda and Persuasion*, 4th ed. Sage Publications, 7

[396] [Herbert Romerstein, "Counterpropaganda: We Can't Do Without It,"] in Waller, ed.,*Strategic Influence: Public Diplomacy, Counterpropaganda and Political Warfare* (IWP Press, 2008), 135

[397] Published 13th June 2012 by Jillian C. Cork

[398] Hilary Clinton: U.S Hacked Yemen Al-Qaida sites on 23rd May 2012 LINK: http://news.yahoo.com/secretary-hillary-clinton-hacked-yemen-al-qaeda-sites-020500553--abc-news-topstories.html

[399] AlJazeera , published 13th June 2012 by Jillian C. Cork

Zetter reports, State officials did not hack the websites, but rather placed anti-al-Qaida ads to replace those that were running. According to State Department spokesperson Victoria Nuland, the ads were placed for free, though Nuland admits that State does pay for counter-ads on sites like YouTube where extremist material is placed.[400]

The article goes on to state the following:

"In addition to this latest news, a *Washington Post* article on the matter also noted that the US Central Command (CENTCOM) has a digital engagement team that monitors blogs and forums and engages with those who are 'moderate in tone'. While in theory this might sound like a good idea, previous reports about CENTCOM's efforts claimed that the project used 'fake online identities' to engage with online supporters of terror, something which journalism professor Jeff Jarvis lambasted as "clumsy". In the *Post* article, counter-terrorism expert Evan Kohlmann also questioned the effectiveness of such efforts in a place like Yemen, where internet penetration is approximately 1.8 per cent."[401]

The picture that emerges, with all these messages from vested interests floating, the use of mediums of communications that are bloated with propaganda and counter propaganda. A horrific proposition indeed. Which is an outright lie? What is an exaggeration? Which message does one trust? To what degree? How much is true? What is the interest within interest here? Enter the spin doctor!

### *What is a spin?*

Let's take a closer look at the concept of Spin . It is an art in itself in the world of media exposure we live in today. Spin is a type of propaganda, an interpretation, subjective of course, to persuade public opinion in favor of, or against, an individual, a group, an issue or a nation. It can employ manipulative and deceptive tactics. In the US, spin tactics were used to get public support for Iraq war. In a stunning article by ***Jeffrey Phelps***[402]for a well- known site examiner.com , he recounts the spin by the media. He says, "Possibly one of the most deceitful operations in the history of the USA, the run-up to the Iraq War was carried out by a totally corrupt band of thieves and liars. Every day the media would propagandize for the Bush White House and its minions, who fed

[400] Ibid.
[401] Ibid.
[402] Writer for DENVER CONSPIRACY EXAMINER

Americans a steady diet of terror threats that kept many in a constant state of fear."[403]

He continues damningly, " As the so-called war progressed, however, questions emerged. Americans had been drowned with WMD propaganda and everyone was naturally expecting to see the evidence as it surfaced. But it never came......Nevertheless, an army of propagandists echoed the mantras of the establishment and the people were told what they needed to hear, so those in charge could proceed with their operations without impedance by the American people."[404]

Later, on 14th December, 2005, *George W, Bush Jr.* took responsibility for "wrong intelligence" leading to invasion of Iraq.[405]"It is true that much of the intelligence turned out to be wrong," Bush said during his fourth and final speech before Thursday's vote for Iraq's parliament. "As president I am responsible for the decision to go into Iraq. And I'm also responsible for fixing what went wrong by reforming our intelligence capabilities. And we're doing just that."[406]

The wrong intelligence that led to the death of over 1,000,000 innocent Iraqi civilian deaths .[407]

An interesting site I came across during my research was aptly titled, SpinWatch(MONITORING PR AND SPIN)[408] which covered a long list of Public Relations pieces and spin made for a very interesting read. On the ending note, I have to share with you, crickey investigation in Australia on spin.[409]Spinning the Media is an investigation in conjunction with the University of Technology (UTS) Sydney into the role PR plays in making the media.....[410]

**Crickey** in this article by Bacon and Pavey writes:

---

[403] Titled "Twisted new WMD Spin" published 23rd June 2012
[404] Ibid.
[405] Titled "Bush takes responsibility for invasion intelligence on CNN SITE." LINK: http://articles.cnn.com/2005-12-14/politics/bush.iraq_1_iraq-wrong-intelligence-nation-building?_s=PM:POLITICS
[406] Ibid.
[407] Examiner.com Titled "Twisted new WMD Spin" published 23rd June 2012 by Jeffrey Phelps
[408] LINK: http://www.spinwatch.org/
[409] 15th March 2010 "Over half of our news is spin" LINK: http://www.crickey.com.au/2010/03/15/over-half-your-news-is-spin/
[410] Ibid.

*"Our investigation strongly confirms that journalism in Australia today is heavily influenced by commercial interests selling a product, and constrained and blocked by politicians, police and others who control the media message."*

## *Concluding Comments*

So what have we learnt here? Basically I would be disillusioned if I were the reader. Are we fed a whole wad of lies? Partial lies? Spin? How do we discern lies from propaganda? Can we do it at all? Who should be trusted? Is there at all, a Code of Conduct for Journalists to adhere to? Yes? No?

"It is worthy of remark that a belief constantly inculcated during the early years of life, whilst the brain is impressible, appears to acquire almost the nature of an instinct; and the very essence of an instinct is that it is followed independently of reason."—**Charles Darwin**, *The Descent of Man*, 1871.

Should media be allowed to run unchecked, unbridled, with its truth, partial truth, spin and propaganda? Or should it be reined in, just enough to stop damage by this "freedom of expression"?

***Eric Margolis***[411]posted the following on his Face Book:

"Media reporting on Syria continues to be highly inaccurate, reflecting government policies rather than facts. A great deal of exaggeration or plain old disinformation. We are in the middle of a media/propaganda blizzard where truth has been long ago blown away."[412]

Technology has given us space. Anyone can open a web site. Anyone with a phone and computer can start expressing on online forums. Photoshop has developed into an art, it can convey "realities" we see with our own eyes. There is another problem. With easy access to a computer, there is the issue, often encountered of "cut-paste". Not a deliberate effort many a time to spread propaganda, nonetheless, spin posted is easily spread and through it disinformation, by this way. Sometimes people cut paste as it is. Sometimes sentences may be changed, adding or deleting

---

[411]An American born journalist ad writer .He was Contributing Editor to Toronto Sun. He contributes to Huffington Post and frequently appears on TV. He is a syndicated columnist.

[412] 28th July 2012

some that might completely change the very meaning of what was conveyed in the original piece.

"In early 2004, John Kerry's presidential campaign drew fire when conservative web critics—and several gullible newspapers—published a composite photograph of him and Jane Fonda, one of the right wing's favorite targets. Kerry and Fonda, in a photo that turned out to have been doctored, were shown "together" at a 1970s rally protesting the Vietnam War.244 It was unclear who created the fake picture, but the willingness of many people to trust this picture spoke volumes about how easy it is to manipulate public opinion." [413]

Nothing ever taught in media schools justifies outright lies or mistruths. The difference however between incorrect doctoring and improving image is thin and not really as clear as we think or want it to be. Does this justify improper doctoring? The answer is no, it is not. Then there are talk shows online. " But Big Media, as it participates in the new conversation online, takes on risks that could hurt credibility even more." [414] This trend, can play a huge role in creating damage. Statements going on air, live, unverified can spread panic faster than anything else, if untrue.

I know I am posing more questions in my concluding comments but media practitioners must study them closely . Departure from ethical practices can have a cascading effect on the society. Media must not forget, it has the role of being a watchdog for society–not an extended arm of vested interests.

[413] Dan Gillmor in "We The Media" LINK: http://www.authorama.com/we-the-media-10.html
[414] Ibid.

# Chapter VII

## Electronic Media

Electronic media is defined as, " Broadcast or storage media that take advantage of electronic technology. This may include television, radio, Internet, fax, CD-ROMs, DVD, and any other medium that requires electricity or digital encoding of information. The term 'electronic media' is often used in contrast with print media." [415]

Electronic media, today, has huge ingress into the homes and minds of the people. Even if one lacks the literacy to be able to read a newspaper, everyone can switch on the radio or/and TV to listen to a programme of his or her choice. Any equipment used in the electronic communication process (e.g. television, radio, telephone, desktop computer etc) may also be considered electronic media.

Electronic media enables reaching out to a bigger segment of population as compared to any other medium of communication. Hearing something or better still, watching pictures moving(TV/Film) leaves an impact hardly any other medium of communication can hope to, making the mediums of communication a weapon in the hands of the those who wield it. It can be used to educate, form opinions and spread cultural ideology via entertainment. Or, it can be used for spin, propaganda as we discussed in detail in the last chapter. Or a genuine effort to educate and acquaint the viewer with "truth".

Protecting national interests and avoiding sensationalism takes new dimensions with electronic media. Growing competition, race to improve

---

[415] BusinessDictionary.com LINK: http://www.businessdictionary.com/definition/electronic-media.html

ratings and win commercials based on higher viewership makes self-regulation a distant goal.

In Pakistan, the base of PEMRA Ordinance 2002(Pakistan Electronic Media Regulatory Authority), lies in the EMRA(Electronic Media Regulatory Authority) Ordinance passed during the Government of Malik Miraj Khalid by his Information Minister Mr Irshad Ahmad Haqqani . The Ordinance allowed radio and television(this is before private TV channels were allowed by then President Musharraf) to create news, political issue programmes. However, the Ordinance lapsed as it was not ratified by the later Government of Nawaz Sharif.

General Pervaiz Musharraf, who came in power in 1999, and his then Information Minister, formed the PEMRA Ordinance 2002 the text of which is shared as under .The Ordinance is being shared here , from the PEMRA website.[416]

***PAKISTAN ELECTRONIC MEDIA REGULATORY AUTHORITY ORDINANCE 2002***

AS AMENDED BY THE

PAKISTAN ELECTRONIC MEDIA REGULATORY AUTHORITY (AMENDMENT) ACT, 2007

(ACT NO.II OF 2007)

AN

ORDINANCE

to regulate electronic media in Pakistan

WHEREAS it is expedient to provide for the development of electronic media in order to – improve the standards of information, education and entertainment; enlarge the choice available to the people of Pakistan in the media for news, current affairs, religious knowledge, art, culture, science, technology, economic development, social sector concerns, music, sports, drama and other subjects of public and national interest; facilitate the devolution of responsibility and power to the grass-roots by improving the access of the people to mass media at the

[416] http://www.pemra.gov.pk/pemra/images/docs/legislation/Ordinance_2002.pdf

local and community level; and ensure accountability, transparency and good governance by optimizing the free flow of information;

AND WHEREAS, the President is satisfied that circumstances exist which render it necessary to take immediate action;

NOW, THEREFORE, in pursuance of Proclamation of Emergency of the fourteenth day of October, 1999 and the Provisional Constitution Order No.1 of 1999 read with the Provisional Constitution (Amendment) Order No. 9 of 1999, and in exercise of all powers enabling him in that behalf, the President of the Islamic Republic of Pakistan is pleased to make and promulgate the following Ordinance:-

PRELIMINARY

1. Short title, extent and commencement.— (1) This Ordinance shall be called the Pakistan Electronic Media Regulatory Authority Ordinance, 2002.

(2) It extends to the whole of Islamic Republic of Pakistan.

(3) It shall come into force at once.

2. Definitions.- In this Ordinance, unless there is anything repugnant in the subject or context,-

(a) "advertisement" means a set of visual and audio messages for the projection of a product, service, or idea with the object of propagating sale, purchase or hire of the product, service or idea for creating other related effects;

(b) "Authority" means the Pakistan Electronic Media Regulatory Authority (PEMRA) established under section 3;

(c) "broadcast media" means such media which originate and propagate broadcast and prerecorded signals by terrestrial means or through satellite for radio or television and includes teleporting, provision of access to broadcast signals by channel providers and such other forms of broadcast media as the Authority may, with the approval of the Federal Government, by notification in the official Gazette, specify;

(ca) "broadcast station" means physical, technical and software infrastructure for the operation of radio or television and also includes satellite uplinking from ground, repeaters and all such other accessories;

(d) "broadcaster" means a person engaged in broadcast media except broadcast journalists not actively involved in the operation, ownership, management or control of the broadcast media;

(da) "cable TV" means reception of broadcast and pre-recorded signals from different channels and their distribution to subscribers through a set of closed transmission paths;

(e) "Chairman" means the Chairman of the Authority;

(ea) "Chairperson" means the head of a Council of Complaint;

(f) "channel" means the set of frequencies that a broadcast station occupies for broadcasting;

(fa) "channel provider" means a vendor who represents local or foreign channels and provides access of their signal to a distribution service;

(g) "company" means a company as defined in the Companies Ordinance 1984 (XLVII of 1984);

(h) "copyright" means copyright as defined in the Copyright Ordinance 1962 (XXXIV of 1962);

(ha) "Distribution Service" means a service which receives broadcast and pre-recorded signals from different channels and distributes them to subscribers through cable, wireless or satellite options and includes Cable TV, LMDS, MMDS, DTH and such other similar technologies;

(hb) "DTH" means Direct to Home distribution of audiovisual signals received via satellite to small dish antennas across the foot-print of the satellite to subscribers;

(hc) "electronic media" includes the broadcast media and distribution services;

(i) "foreign company" means a company or body corporate organized, and registered under the laws of a foreign government;

(j) “frequency” means the frequency of the electromagnetic wave number measured in Hertz per second and used for transmission;

(k) “FAB” means the Frequency Allocation Board established under section 42 of the Pakistan Telecommunication (Reorganization) Act, 1996 (XVII of 1996);

(ka) “illegal operation” means the broadcast or transmission or distribution of, or provision of access to, programmes or advertisements in the form of channels without having a valid licence from the Authority;

(kb) “LMDS” means local multipoint distribution service to transmit audio-visual signals through wireless devices, on a higher frequency range for the provision of cable television service;

(l) “media enterprise” means an enterprise concerned with the publication of a printed newspaper or a broadcast media or distribution service;

(la) “MMDS” means multi-channel multi-point distribution service to transmit audio-visual signals through wireless devices, to multiple subscribers, after receiving such signals from other channels of communication;

(m) “licence” means a licence issued by the Authority to establish and operate a broadcast media or distribution service;

(n) “licensee” means a person to whom the Authority has issued a licence;

(na) “newspaper” means a newspaper as defined by the Press, Newspapers, News Agencies and Books Registration Ordinance,2002 (XCVIII of 2002);

(o) “member” means a member of the Authority;

(p) “national broadcaster” means the Pakistan Broadcasting Corporation, the Pakistan Television Corporation and the Shalimar Recording and Broadcasting Company;

(q) "PTA" means the Pakistan Telecommunication Authority established under the Pakistan Telecommunication (Reorganisation) Act, 1996 (XVII of 1996);

(r) "person" includes an individual, partnership, association, company, trust or corporation;

(s) "prescribed" means prescribed by the rules or regulations made by the Authority;

(t) "programme" means the systematic broadcasting of visual or sound images by a broadcast station but does not include an advertisement;

(ta) "regulations" means the regulations made under this Ordinance;

(u) "rules" means the rules made under this Ordinance;

(v) "Teleport" means a facility with installed equipment used or required in the process of uplinking or downlinking of audio-visual programmes and signals between an earth station and a satellite; and

(w) "uplinking" means transmission of audio-video signal from ground transmission facility to a satellite, in order to transmit any programme within or outside Pakistan.

**3. Establishment of the Authority.-**

(1) As soon as may be, after the commencement of this Ordinance, the Federal Government shall, by notification in the Official Gazette, establish an authority to be known as the Pakistan Electronic Media Regulatory Authority (PEMRA) for carrying out the purposes of this Ordinance.

(2) The Authority shall be a body corporate having perpetual succession and a common seal with powers subject to the provision of this Ordinance to hold and dispose of property by the said name, sue and be sued.

(3) The principal office of the Authority shall be at Islamabad and it may set up offices at such place or places in the country as it may deem appropriate.

(4) No act or proceeding of the Authority shall be invalid by reason only of the existence of a vacancy in, or defect in the constitution of, the Authority.

**4. Functions of the Authority.**

(1) The Authority shall be responsible for regulating the establishment and operation of all broadcast media and distribution services in Pakistan established for the purpose of international, national, provincial, district, local or special target audiences.

(2) The Authority shall regulate the distribution of foreign and local TV and radio channels in Pakistan.

(3) The Authority may, by notification in the official Gazette, make regulations and also issue determinations for carrying out the purposes of this Ordinance.

**5. Power of the Federal Government to issue directives. –**

The Federal Government may, as and when it considers necessary, issue directives to the Authority on matters of policy, and such directives shall be binding on the Authority, and if a question arises whether any matter is a matter of policy or not, the decision of the Federal Government shall be final.

**6. Members of Authority.-**

(1) The Authority shall consist of a Chairman and twelve members to be appointed by the President of Pakistan.

(2) The Chairman of the Authority shall be an eminent professional of known integrity and competence having substantial experience in media, business, management, finance, economics or law.

(3) Out of twelve members one shall be appointed by the Federal Government on full time basis and five shall be eminent citizens chosen to ensure representation of all provinces with expertise in one or more of the following fields: media, law, human rights, and social service. Of the five members from the general public, two members shall be women.

(4) Secretary, Ministry of Information and Broadcasting, Secretary, Interior Division, Chairman, Pakistan Telecommunication Authority and Chairman, Central Board of Revenue shall be the ex officio-members.

(4A) The remaining two members shall be appointed by the Federal Government on need basis on the recommendation of the Chairman.

(5) The members shall receive such fee and expenses for each meeting as may be prescribed.

(6) A member, other than an ex officio member, shall be deemed to have vacated his office if he absents himself for three consecutive meetings of the Authority without the leave of the Authority.

**7. Tenure of members.-**

(1) The Chairman and members, other than ex officio members, unless earlier removed for misconduct or physical or mental incapacity, shall hold office for a period of four years and shall be eligible for re-appointment for a similar term or as the Federal Government may determine:

Provided that the Chairman and a member shall retire on attaining the age of sixty-five years.

Explanation.- For the purposes of this section the expression "misconduct" means conviction for any offence involving moral turpitude and includes conduct prejudicial to good order or unbecoming of a gentleman.

(2) The Chairman or a member may, by writing under his hand, resign his office.

**8. Meetings of the Authority, etc.**

(1) The Chairman or, in his absence, the member elected by the members for the purpose, shall preside at a meeting of the Authority.

(2) One-third of the total members shall constitute a quorum for meetings of the Authority requiring a decision by the Authority.

(3) The members shall have reasonable notice of the time and place of the meeting and the matters on which a decision by the Authority shall be taken in such meeting.

(4) The decisions of the Authority shall be taken by the majority of its members present, and in case of a tie, the member presiding a meeting shall have a casting vote.

(5) All orders, determinations and decisions of the Authority shall be taken in writing and shall identify the determination of the Chairman and each member separately.

**9. Remuneration, of Chairman and members.-**

(1) The Chairman and members shall be paid such emoluments as the President of Pakistan may determine and shall not be varied to their disadvantage during their term of office.

10. Chairman and members not to engage themselves in certain business, etc.-

(1) The Chairman shall not, during his term of office, engage himself in any other service, business, vocation or employment, or enter into the employment of, or accept any advisory or consultancy relationship with any person or entity engaged in applying for a licence from the Authority or operating a broadcast station established within the purview of the Authority or in providing services or products to the Authority on any of the projects, schemes, proposals or plans undertaken, executed or supervised by the Authority or any related undertaking of such aforesaid person or entity.

(2) The members shall not have any direct or indirect financial interest, or have any connection with any such person, entity or related undertaking as mentioned in sub-section (1) of this section associated in any way with the licensee of a broadcast station for so long as they are members and hold office.

**11. Officers, employees, etc. –**

To carry out the purposes of this Ordinance, the Authority may, from time to time, appoint members of its staff, experts, consultants, advisers and other officers and employees on such terms and conditions as it may deem fit.

12. Officers, etc. deemed to be public servants. –

The Chairman, members, members of its staff, other officers and employees of the Authority shall be deemed to be public servants within the meaning of section 21 of the Pakistan Penal Code (Act XLV of 1860).

**13. Delegation.-**

The Authority may, by general or special order, delegate to the Chairman or a member or any member of its staff, or an expert, consultant, adviser, or other officer or employee of the Authority any of its powers, responsibilities or functions under this Ordinance subject to such conditions as it may by rules prescribe:

Provided that the delegation of such power shall not include the power to grant, revoke or cancel a broadcast media or distribution service licence except Cable TV.

**14. Fund.-**

(1) There shall be established a fund to be known as "PEMRA Fund" which shall vest in the Authority and shall be utilized by the Authority to meet charges in connection with its functions including payment of salaries and other remunerations to the Chairman, members, employees, experts and consultants of the Authority.

(2) The Fund shall consist of.-

(i) Seed money by the Federal Government;

(ii) fees for issuance and renewal of licences for establishing and operating broadcast or CTV stations;

(iii) loans obtained with the special or general sanction of the Federal Government;

(iv) foreign aid obtained with sanction of and on such terms and conditions as may be approved by the Federal Government; and

(v) all other sums received by the Authority from any other source.

(3) The Authority may open and operate one or more accounts in local, or foreign currency, in any scheduled bank.

(4) The Authority may invest its funds in such investments as it may, from time to time, determine.

**15. Budget.-** The Authority shall, in respect of each financial year, prepare its own budget and submit it to the Federal Government three months before the commencement of every financial year for information.

**16. Accounts and Audit. –**

(1) The Authority shall maintain complete and accurate books of accounts of its actual expenses and receipts in such form as the Federal Government may, in consultation with the Auditor General of Pakistan, determine.

(2) The Authority shall cause to be carried out audit of its accounts by one or more auditors who are chartered accountants within the meaning of the Chartered Accountants Ordinance, 1961 (X of1961).

(3) Notwithstanding the audit provided in sub-section (2) the Auditor-General shall have the power to audit or cause to be audited the accounts of the Authority.

**17. Annual report. –**

The Authority shall compile and submit an annual report on its operations and accounts for each financial year to the President of Pakistan and shall also arrange for its publication and circulation to the media and the public.

**18. Categories of licences:-**

The Authority shall issue licences for broadcast media and distribution service in the following categories, namely:-

i. International and National scale stations;

ii. Provincial scale broadcast;

iii. Local Area or Community based Radio and TV Broadcast;

iv. Specific and specialized subjects;

v. Distribution services; and

vi. Uplinking facilities including teleporting and DSNG.

(2) The Authority may further sub-categorize the categories specified in sub-section (1) as it may deem fit.

**19. Licence to broadcast or operate.-**

(1) The Authority shall have exclusive right to issue licences for the establishment and operation of all broadcast media and distribution services, provided that this exclusive right shall be used by the Authority in conformity with the principles of fairness and equity applied to all potential applicants for licences whose eligibility shall be based on prescribed criteria notified in advance and that this shall be done through an open, transparent bidding process:

Provided that the bidding shall be held if the number of applications exceeds the number of licences to be issued by the Authority.

(2) No person shall engage in any broadcast media or distribution service except after obtaining a licence issued under this Ordinance.

(3) Every licence shall be subject to such terms and conditions as may be prescribed.

(4) The Authority shall have the power to determine number of licences to be issued in each category or sub-category and charge fees at such rates as the Authority may fix from time to time for the grant of a licence and for its annual renewal

(5) The Authority shall devise a Code of Conduct for programmes and advertisements for compliance by the licensees.

20. **Terms and conditions of licence.-** A person who is issued a licence under this Ordinance shall-

(a) ensure preservation of the sovereignty, security and integrity of the Islamic Republic of Pakistan;

(b) ensure preservation of the national, cultural, social and religious values and the principles of public policy as enshrined in the Constitution of the Islamic Republic of Pakistan;

(c) ensure that all programmes and advertisements do not contain or encourage violence, terrorism, racial, ethnic or religious discrimination, sectarianism, extremism, militancy, hatred, pornography, obscenity, vulgarity or other material offensive to commonly accepted standards of decency;

(d) comply with rules made under this Ordinance;

(e) broadcast, if permissible under the terms of its licence, programmes in the public interest specified by the Federal Government or the Authority in the manner indicated by the Government or, as the case may be, the Authority, provided that the duration of such mandatory programmes do not exceed ten per cent of the total duration of broadcast or operation by a station in twenty-four hours except if, by its own volition, a station chooses to broadcast such content for a longer duration;

(f) comply with the codes of programmes and advertisements approved by the Authority and appoint an in-house monitoring committee, under intimation to the Authority, to ensure compliance of the Code;

(g) not broadcast or distribute any programme or advertisement in violation of copyright or other property right;

(h) obtain NOC from Authority before import of any transmitting apparatus for broadcasting, distribution or teleporting operation and

(i) not sell, transfer or assign any of the rights conferred by the licence without prior written permission of the Authority.

## 21. Consultation with Provinces

(1) The Authority shall, except where applications for the issuance of a licence relates to Islamabad Capital Territory, invite the comments of the Government of the Province concerned, with regard to the proposed location of the Radio, TV or MMDS station for which the application has been made, and if the concerned Provincial

Government has any reservation to the issuance of the licence, the Authority shall invite the representative of the Provincial Government and consider its viewpoint before taking a decision on the issuance of a licence:

Provided that where the Provincial Government objects to the issuance of a particular licence, the applicant shall be provided an opportunity to be present at the meeting of the Authority and given an opportunity of being heard with regard to the observations made by the Provincial Government.

(2) Where the signal of a radio, TV or MMDS station has the potential to cover an area outside the limits of the Province in which the unit is proposed to be located, the Authority shall invite one or more representatives from the concerned Provincial Governments to express their viewpoint, if any, on the inter-Provincial dimensions of the signal.

22 Duration for consideration of the application for a licence. The Authority shall take decision on the application for a licence within one hundred days from the receipt of the application.

**23. Exclusion of monopolies.-**

(1) No person shall be entitled to the benefit of any monopoly or exclusivity in the matter of broadcasting or the establishment and operation of broadcast media or distribution service or in the supply to or purchase from, a national broadcaster of air time, programmes or advertising material and all existing agreements and contracts to the extent of conferring a monopoly or containing an exclusivity clause are, to the extent of exclusivity, hereby declared to be inoperative and of no legal effect.

(2) In granting a licence, the Authority shall ensure that open and fair competition is facilitated in the operation of more than one media enterprise in any given unit of area or subject and that undue concentration of media ownership is not created in any city, town or area and the country as a whole:

Provided that if a licensee owns, controls or operates more than one media enterprise, he shall not indulge in any practice which may impede fair competition and provision of level playing field.

24. Licence, application, issuance, refusal and validity.-

(1) Any person desirous of obtaining a licence for establishment and operation of broadcast media or a distribution service shall apply to the Authority in such manner and form as may be prescribed.

(2) The Authority shall process each application in accordance with prescribed criteria and shall hold public hearings in the respective provincial capitals of each Province, or as the case may be, in Islamabad, before granting or refusing the licence.

(3) Each application shall be accompanied by such fee as the Authority may prescribe.

(4) A licence shall be valid for a period of five, ten or fifteen years subject to payment of the annual fee prescribed from time to time.

(5) The Authority may renew a licence on such terms and conditions as may be prescribed and in case of refusal to renew a licence reasons shall be recorded in writing.

25. Certain persons not be granted licence.- A licence shall not be granted to—

(a) a person who is not a citizen of Pakistan or resident in Pakistan;

(b) a foreign company organized under the laws of any foreign government;

(c) a company the majority of whose shares are owned or controlled by foreign nationals or companies whose management or control is vested in foreign nationals or companies; or

(d) any person funded or sponsored by a foreign government or organization.

26. Council of Complaints.-

(1) The Federal Government shall, by notification in the Official Gazette, establish Councils of Complaints at Islamabad, the Provincial capitals and also at such other places as the Federal Government may determine.

(2) Each Council shall receive and review complaints made by persons or organizations from the general public against any aspects of programmes broadcast or distributed by a station established through a licence issued by the Authority and render opinions on such complaints.

(3) Each Council shall consist of a Chairperson and five members being citizens of eminence from the general public at least two of whom shall be women.

(3A) The Councils shall have the powers to summon a licensee against whom a complaint has been made and call for his explanation regarding any matter relating to its operation.

(4) The Authority shall formulate rules for the functions and operation of the Councils within two hundred days of the establishment of the Authority.

(5) The Councils may recommend to the Authority appropriate action of censure, fine against a broadcast or CTV station or licensee for violation of the codes of programme content and advertisements as approved by the Authority as may be prescribed.

27. Prohibition of broadcast media or distribution service operation :-

The Authority shall by order in writing, giving reasons therefore, prohibit any broadcast media or distribution service operator from;

(a) broadcasting or re-broadcasting or distributing any programme or advertisement if it is of the opinion that such particular programme or advertisement is against the ideology of Pakistan or is likely to create hatred among the people or is prejudicial to the maintenance of law and order or is likely to disturb public peace and tranquility or endangers national security or is pornographic, obscene or vulgar or is offensive to the commonly accepted standards of decency; or

(b) engaging in any practice or act which amounts to abuse of media power by way of harming the legitimate interests of another licensee or willfully causing damage to any other person.

28. Suspension of broadcast media or distribution service:--

A broadcast media or distribution service operator shall not cease or suspend broadcasting except on account of force majeure or with the prior approval of the Authority.

29. Power to authorize inspection:-

(1) The Authority may authorize any of its officers or its nominees to enter the premises of a broadcast media or distribution service operator for purposes of inspection.

(2) A broadcast media station or distribution service premises shall, at all reasonable times, be open to inspection by an authorized officer under sub-section (1) and the licensee shall provide such officer with every assistance and facility in performing his duties.

(3) The authorized officer shall, within forty-eight hours of the inspection, submit his inspection report to the Authority.

(4) The Authority may authorize any of its officers to undertake investigation, in the manner it may prescribe, in any matter with regard to its functions and to seek any specific information, from any person, which the Authority may deem useful in order to enable it to determine and dispose off such matter.

(5) The Authority or as the case may be the Chairman, after issuing show cause notice to broadcast media or distribution service may seize its broadcast or distribution service equipment, or seal the premises, which is being used in contravention of the provisions of this Ordinance or the rules made thereunder or any other law:

Provided that the equipment shall be returned to the holder of a valid licence after imposing on him such penalty as the Authority may determine.

(6) The Authority may, after the licensee has been, given reasonable opportunity to show cause, impose fine up to one million rupees on a licensee who contravenes any of the provisions of this Ordinance or the rules or regulations made thereunder.

29-A. Dues to be recovered as arrears of land revenue:-

All dues including outstanding licence fee, annual renewal fee or any other charges including fine as imposed by the Authority shall be recoverable as arrears of land revenue.

30. Power to vary conditions, suspend or revoke the licence:-

(1) The Authority may revoke or suspend the licence of a broadcast media or distribution service by an order in writing on one or more of the following grounds, namely:-

(a) the licensee has failed to pay the licence fee, annual renewal fee or any other charges including fine, if any;

(b) the licensee has contravened any provision of this Ordinance or rules or regulations made thereunder:

Provided that in the case of revocation of a licence of a broadcast media an opinion to this effect shall also be obtained from the Council of Complaints;

(c) the licensee has failed to comply with any condition of the licence; and

(d) where the licensee is a company, and its shareholders have transferred a majority of the shares in the issued or paid up capital of the company or if control of the company is otherwise transferred to persons not being the original shareholders of the company at the time of grant of licence, without written permission of the Authority.

(2) The Authority may vary any of the terms and conditions of the licence where it deems that such variation is in the public interest.

(3) Except for reason of necessity in the public interest a licence shall not be varied, suspended or revoked under sub-section (1) or (2) unless the licensee has been given reasonable notice to show cause and a personal hearing.

30A. Appeals:-

Any person aggrieved by any decision or order of the Authority may, within thirty days of the receipt of such decision or order, prefer an appeal to the High Court:

Provided that PEMRA shall make available a copy of its decision or order of revocation of licence within twenty-four hours after decision to the licensee for referring an appeal to the High Court.

31. Uplinking Facilities:-

(1) No person shall carry out uplinking without a valid Teleport or Satellite TV licence from the Authority;

(2) The Authority may, subject to fulfillment of such conditions, as may be prescribed, issue permission in writing to any party to carry out temporary uplinking from a ground transmission facility to a satellite in order to transmit any programme within or outside Pakistan.

32. Power to grant exemptions:- The Authority may grant exemptions from any provisions of this Ordinance, where the Authority is of the view that such exemption serves the public interest and the exemptions so granted shall be supported by recording the reasons for granting such exemptions in writing provided that the grant of exemptions shall be based on guidelines and criteria identified in the Rules and that such exemptions shall be made in conformity with the principles of equality and equity as enshrined in the Constitution.

33. Offences and penalties:-

(1) Any broadcast media or distribution service operator or person who violates or abets the violation of any of the provisions of the Ordinance shall be guilty of an offence punishable with a fine which may extend to ten million rupees.

(2) Where such broadcast media or distribution service operator or person repeats the violation or abetment, such person shall be guilty of an offence punishable with imprisonment for a term which may extend to three years, or with fine, or with both.

(3) Where the violation, or abetment of the violation of any provision of this Ordinance is made by a person who does not hold a licence, such violation shall be punishable with imprisonment for a term which may extend to four years, or with fine, or with both, in addition to the confiscation of the equipment used in the commission of the act.

(4) Whosoever damages, removes, tampers with or commits theft of any equipment of a broadcast media or distribution service station

licensed by the Authority, including transmitting or broadcasting apparatus, receivers, boosters, converters, distributors, antennae, wires, decoders, set-top boxes or multiplexers shall be guilty of an offence punishable with imprisonment which may extend to three years, or with fine, or both.

33A The Officers of Federal, Provincial and Local Government to assist Authority:- The officers of Federal Government, Provincial Governments and Local Governments including the Capital Territory Police and the Provincial Police shall assist the Authority and its officers in the discharge of their functions under the provisions of this Ordinance and the Rules and Regulations made thereunder;

33B. Warrants for search:-

(1) Where on information furnished by the Authority, the Court has reason to believe that any unlicensed broadcast media or distribution service is being owned, controlled or operated or its equipment is being kept or concealed, it may issue a search warrant and the person to whom search warrant is directed, may enter the premises where such unlicensed broadcast media or distribution service is being owned, controlled, operated or provided or its equipment is being kept or concealed, or carry out search and inspection thereof and seize all or any equipment therein.

(2) Any equipment of a broadcast media station seized under sub-section (1) having no ostensible owner shall vest in the Authority.

34. Cases to be initiated on complaint:- No court shall take cognizance of any offence under subsection (1) or (2) of section 33 of this Ordinance except on a complaint in writing by the Authority or any officer authorized by it.

34-A. Offences to be compoundable and cognizable:

The offences under sub-section (3) and subsection (4) of section 33 of this Ordinance shall be compoundable and cognizable.

35. Cognizance of offences etc:- (1) No court inferior to that of a Magistrate of the first class shall try an offence punishable under this Ordinance.

(2) Notwithstanding anything contained in section 32 of the Code of Criminal Procedure, 1898 (Act V of 1898), it shall be lawful for any Magistrate of the first class to pass any sentence authorized by this Ordinance even if such sentence exceeds his powers under the said section 32.

36. Offences by companies:-

(1) Where any offence under this Ordinance has been committed by a person who at the time the offence was committed was in charge of, and was responsible to the company for the conduct of the business of the company as well as the company itself shall be deemed to be guilty of the offence and shall be liable to be proceeded against and punished accordingly.

(2) Where the person guilty of an offence under this Ordinance, is a company, corporation or firm, every director, partner and employee of the company, corporation or firm shall, unless he proves that offence was committed without his knowledge, or consent, shall be guilty of the offence and shall be liable to be proceeded against and punished accordingly.

37. Ordinance overrides other laws:- (1) The provisions of this Ordinance shall have effect notwithstanding anything to the contrary contained in any other law for the time being in force, or any contract, agreement or any other instrument whatsoever:

Provided that –

(a) the national broadcasters, namely the Pakistan Broadcasting Corporation shall continue to be regulated by the Pakistan Broadcasting Corporation Act 1973 (XXXII of 1973) and the Pakistan Television Corporation and Shalimar Recording and Broadcasting Company Limited shall continue to be administered under the provisions of the Companies Ordinance 1984 (XLVII of 1984); and

(b) other existing private broadcasters or CTV operators who had been granted respective monopolies in multi-modal distribution system, cable TV and in FM radio shall henceforth be regulated by this Ordinance except in respects where specific exemptions are granted by the Authority.

38. Indemnity:- No suit, prosecution or other legal proceeding shall lie against the Federal Government or any Provincial Government or local authority or any other person exercising any power or performing any function under this Ordinance or for anything which is in good faith done or purporting or intended to be done under this Ordinance or any rule made thereunder.

39. Power to make rules:-

(1) The Authority may, with the approval of the Government, by notification in the official Gazette, make rules to carry out the purposes of this Ordinance.

(2) In particular, and without prejudice to the generality of the foregoing power, such rules may be provided for all or any of the following matters, namely:-

(a) to prescribe the forms for the licences for working, installing, operating, or dealing in transmission broadcast or distribution apparatus and the manner in which applications for the licences shall be granted;

(b) to prescribe the terms and conditions of the licence including fee to be charged in connection with the issuance of licences and related matters,

(c) to prescribe standards and measures for the establishment of broadcast media stations, installation of broadcasting, distribution service or teleporting equipment, transmitters, receivers, boosters, converters, distributors and common antennae;

(d) to prescribe terms and conditions for the broadcast media or distribution service operators who own, control or operate more than one media enterprise; and

(e) to define the circumstances constituting undue concentration of media ownership and abuse of powers and anti-competitive practices by media companies.

40. Removal of difficulties:- If any difficulty arises in giving effect to the provisions of this Ordinance, the Authority may make such order, not inconsistent with provisions of this Ordinance, as may

appear to it to be necessary for the purpose of removing the difficulty.

***The Ordinance is in easy English and quite understandable***

The allowance of private TV channels had some objectives ie improve the standards of information, education and entertainment. This is the first objective stated. Whereas it was a huge leap forward, under then President Musharraf to open doors for privatization of the electronic media, putting an end to government monopoly , a much needed step to encourage freedom of expression, whether or not it achieved this ,is arguable. I remember the plays of Fatima Surraya Bajiya; piece of art. Drama serials like Khuda Ki Basti, Tanhayee'yan, Aangan Terha and many, many others. I remember, how in Karachi, the shutters of the shops at Tariq Road, would drop close before 8pm as the much awaited weekly play went on air, expecting no clients, and the traffic would be negligible. Today, they are replaced with more glamour. No doubt, technologically, the plays today are way ahead, but whether the same can be said of the plots and themes, a mirror to our culture, can be argued. Also discernable, is the heavy influence of Indian soaps on many of our plays. Replaced by the tongue-in-cheek, classy acts of Bushra Ansari and other respectable names is loud, bawdy and "humor". We also increasingly see Bollywood news as a part of "News". Many local channels show Indian soaps and films instead of locally based entertainment programmes, in spite of many existing Indian entertainment channels, thereby damaging the cultural fabric of the country. The influence of growing Indian culture by a plethora of channels is something to be concerned about.

A very important role of media is to educate the masses. Another is to improve standards of information. However, with the proliferation of more and more channels, the competition to survive and with a desire to attract higher viewership, aiming for higher ratings and thereby enabling attraction of advertisers and a stronger position as opinion makers, the original object has truly suffered. Sensationalism has taken the place of objective reporting on many occasions while informing the public on ongoing issues.

**Philip K. Dick,** [417] said and I quote, "Because today we live in a society in which spurious realities are manufactured by the media, by governments, by big corporations, by religious groups, political groups... So I ask, in my writing, What is real? Because increasingly we are bombarded with pseudo-realities manufactured by very sophisticated people using very sophisticated electronic mechanisms. I do not distrust their motives; I distrust their power. They have a lot of it. And it is an astonishing power: that of creating whole universes, universes of the mind. I ought to know. I do the same thing." [418]

The second object was to enlarge the choice available to the people of Pakistan in the media for news, current affairs, religious knowledge, art, culture, science, technology, economic development, social sector concerns, music, sports, drama and other subjects of public and national interest. Without question, the choices have increased. This opening up of choices is interlinked to a question. Whether this increased choice has led to greater good of the society? The media is at the end, answerable to the society. It must discharge it's social responsibility. ***Ayesha Siddiqa***[419]in her article states, " There is an oversaturation in both electronic and print media. It is stunning to see so many new newspapers and an ever increasing number of TV channels when the market is so limited. Second, the media industry (both electronic and print) is increasingly dominated by non-professionals such as owners, anchors, column writers, news service walas (and even touts). Third, the dominance of non-professionals has shifted the emphasis from news-making to opinion-making where even reporters want to now comment and analyse rather than report."[420]

Another object of free media is to ensure accountability, transparency and good governance by optimizing the free flow of information. Ideally the open discussion on an issue, pointing out the missteps by governing individuals and institutions, should be the responsibility of the media. Problems occur when bias and partisanship enters into discussion of issues. This bias may be by the anchorpersons or,

---

[417] In 1952, he began writing professionally and proceeded to write numerous novels and short-story collections. He won the Hugo Award for the best novel in 1962 for The Man in the High Castle and the John W. Campbell Memorial Award for best novel of the year in 1974 for Flow My Tears, the Policeman Said. In addition to 44 published novels, Dick wrote approximately 121 short stories, most of which appeared in science fiction magazines during his lifetime

[418] http://www.goodreads.com/quotes/tag/media

[419] The writer is an independent social scientist and author

[420] "The Myth of a Journalist" in Express Tribune published 22nd June 2012

affiliations to political groups by the media outlet owners. Issues are then, not presented objectively to the public. Having selective information, the general public can form completely misdirected opinions and views on matters pertaining to public interest. Who can blame them for this? **David F. Wells**[421] states, "In our postmodern culture which is TV dominated, image sensitive, and morally vacuous, personality is everything and character is increasingly irrelevant." [422] A comment on the power of opinion making capabilities of an anchor person.

The clauses within the Ordinance, originally, were more administrative in nature ie number of members in PEMRA, license grant, fees, revocation, the right of Federal Government to the PEMRA in policy matters that will be binding, so on and so forth. I would however, like to direct your attention to Section 20 that deals with some sections of *Terms of License,* what the licensee is supposed to adhere to upon getting the license. The first states it ensure preservation of the sovereignty, security and integrity of the Islamic Republic of Pakistan. If readers recall, this is straight out of Limitations on Freedom of Expression, Article 19, Constitution of Pakistan. The second is ensure preservation of the national, cultural, social and religious values and the principles of public policy as enshrined in the Constitution of the Islamic Republic of Pakistan.

The concept here is, the media must be in synchronization with the Constitution of Pakistan. It must not run on a parallel agenda that can only lead to chaos and disenchantment within the society.

Next is to ensure that programmes and advertisements do not contain or encourage violence, terrorism, racial, ethnic or religious discrimination, sectarianism, extremism, militancy, hatred, pornography, obscenity, vulgarity or other material offensive to commonly accepted standards of decency.

However, we have seen , videos of terrorists addressing the people being released on TV, statements by some people in the public eye that was repeatedly aired, leading to bloodshed and sectarian violence in a certain province, religious discrimination and discussions that have created hatred between different religious or ethnic groups. Media has a great swaying power on the opinions of the masses. This power must be

---

[421]Writer, a famous book, *"No Place for Truth: Or, Whatever Happened to Evangelical Theology"*
[422]http://www.goodreads.com/quotes/tag/media

exercised with great caution and restraint. Failing which, media fails to be socially responsible.

It talks about "broadcast, if permissible under the terms of its licence" programmes in the public Interest specified by the Federal Government or the Authority in the manner indicated by the Government or, as the case may be, the Authority......"

The term public interest needs to be discussed.

Public interest may be defined as "the welfare or well-being of the general public."[423]Journalists must apply any story they wish to cover to this acid test. Let me clarify a point here: what the public may be interested in may be very different from what is in public interest. Public interest deals with the concept of "common wellbeing" or "general welfare." The public interest would be in having s peaceful , healthy society, mutual respect for different religious, ethnic groups within and a society where different institutions work together towards the development of the society as such. Media, particularly electronic media can play a vital role in a country like Pakistan with a low literacy rate but a huge exposure to radio and TV.

***Chris Elliot,*** [424] in ***The Guardian***, raised a very pertinent question, "What defines the public interest? ...... It's an important principle that can be used to defend journalistic activities that go beyond what is normally considered acceptable behavior – such as the use of subterfuge – to obtain a story, where complex moral and legal arguments are at stake. However, it is also often stretched to cover activities that many find thoroughly objectionable, not even of interest to the public."[425]

In the months and years that followed the creation of private owned electronic media, we saw TV going way overboard on reporting issues. I would like to discuss some events that led ,in 2007, to PEMRA (Amendment) Ordinance 2007. A copy of the same published by **The Nation** on 4thNovember 2007 is part of this book, added as ***'Annexure 'A'*** at the end of the book.

"The crisis that Pakistan's broadcast journalism is going through is deeper than it appears and certainly not confined to one ratings-hungry

[423] Sictionary.com LINK: http://dictionary.reference.com/browse/public+interest

[424]Chris Elliott is the Guardian readers' editor

[425] Published in The Guardian UK 15th May 2012 titled, "What do you think public interest means?"

anchor, or one revenue-thirsty channel. At the heart of this crisis lies a fundamental question, which at one time or the other has been asked in almost all media markets across the world: 'What is journalism for?'"

***Fahd Husain***[426]continues in his piece, " This is what John Paul II said in 2000: 'With its vast and direct influence on public opinion, journalism cannot be guided by economic forces, profit, and special interest. It must instead be felt as a mission in a certain sense sacred, carried out in the knowledge that the powerful means of communication have been entrusted to you for the good of all.' He further states, 'The operative part is the "good of all". In essence then, journalists have a wider responsibility to the citizenry at large, a responsibility which hinges on them to uphold the sacred public trust by telling their readers/viewers the truth. Truth itself may be open to many philosophical interpretations, but in the context of journalism, it can simply mean protecting information from all external agendas and saying it as it is.'"[427]

I would like to state at the onset as we discuss the situation at that time, that it is purely from the point of view of media coverage, not taking any positions on the issues itself . Basic facts are penned for those who may not be aware of the issues as they developed.

The first was the **Lal Masjid** incident. Code named *Operation Silence,* in July 2007, the nation saw a confrontation between the Islamic Fundamentalists and the Government, then headed by President Musharraf and Prime Minister Shaukat Aziz. *Operation Silence* focused on Lal Masjid and the Jamia Hafsa Mosque in Islamabad, Pakistan. Reportedly, since January 2006, Lal Masjid and the adjacent Jamia Hafsa Mosque was operated by Islamic militants led by two brothers. The organization supported imposition of Shariah Law in Pakistan. The organization was in conflict with the authorities in Islamabad 18 months prior to the operation. "In early January 2007, the Lal Masjid administrators had demanded the immediate rebuilding of eight illegally-constructed mosques that had been knocked down by the CDA."[428] Demonstrations were held, and as it may happen in most demonstrations, certain sections within become violent. Properties were destroyed and armed clashes with authorities took place. It was only after Ministry of

---

[426] The writer is the host of "Tonight with Fahd" on Waqt News

[427] "Who will watch the watchdogs" by Fahd Husain published in Express Tribune on 31st January 2012

[428] Lal Masjid: Rewarding an insurrection by Pervez Hoodbhoy published 21st May 2012.in Express Tribune

Environment was set on fire and Army Rangers attacked who were on guard there that the siege of Lal Masjid began. The complex was besieged from 3rd July to 11th July 2007. Negotiations failing, the complex was stormed and taken over by authorities.

Having stated bare facts, let's move to our subject matter ie the coverage of the event on TV. I recall, watching with horror, bile rising, as TV reporters in the Lal Masjid , after the operation was over, showed splashes of blood. Some even held up a human finger found of a man killed. Nowhere in the world could I recall such unprofessional coverage. The minute by minute coverage had Pakistanis glued to the TV for days. Lal Masjid was turned into a media circus, with discussions upon discussions on the incident. By taking sharp sides, media was responsible for even deeply etching the divide within the society that has emerged over time, rather than trying to bridge it. Maybe I am being a simpleton when I express my deep regret at maintaining this position. Media ideally is not supposed to take over the role of a party and take positions on issues.

In an article in ***DAWN***, titled, "Lal Masjid and Television",[429] **Zubeida Mustafa** writes, "The performance of the electronic media on the week-long siege of the Lal Masjid in Islamabad has given rise to mixed reactions. With viewers' fatigue setting in, many felt that some of the TV channels had gone overboard in providing coverage to Operation Silence. There was not always some 'breaking news' to present although that is how most channels portrayed their reports. Even events that had taken place hours earlier and had been very comprehensively reported were telecast as being a new development. This could be as misleading as showing old footage without giving dates. Similarly TV came under attack for the repeat telecast of images that could incite rather than inform. The electronic media's potential to inform the public and educate the people by providing a forum for experts to voice their opinion and knowledge on issues of current importance is definitely immense. In this context its role has been to quite an extent a positive one in times of crisis. But when the cables start resorting to sensationalism and competing to get a scoop, they are treading on dangerous ground. They tend to exaggerate news or twist the truth to make it exciting and, unlike the print media, the correction might not rectify the initial error and put the record straight. Take the case of a channel which reported that authorities had asked Edhi to supply 800 shrouds after Operation Silence was over. A few minutes later it put

[429] Published 19th July 2007

in a correction that the number was 80. But the error of an extra zero failed to register and the figure of 800 was bandied around internationally. Similarly when long hours were spent in waiting for action or when the media was not given access to the 'war zone', if it may be called so, there was a lot of speculative broadcasting. After all, a reporter with a mike in his hand and the camera focused on him, is expected to speak something, isn't he? Isn't it time our channels did some soul searching on what they envisage their role to be and what role they can possibly play in our circumstances where the freedom of expression cannot be taken for granted."

I was very pleased to see that she said what I feel and stated earlier, that media should try to bridge the gap in the society not to polarize it further. She concluded the article by stating, " True, television coverage will always be controversial when society is polarised. But it is time its reporters and cameramen realized that while they are reporting and capturing images they should remain scrupulously unbiased and objective. They will have to learn to leave their prejudices behind when they go for a professional assignment."[430]

Another incident that happened , media coverage of which propelled us towards the PEMRA Amendment 2007, was the Lawyers Movement. The Chief Justice was asked to resign or face "charges of misconduct" on 9th March 2007. This resulted in his sacking by the then President Pervez Musharraf. The "charges of misconduct" were based on a letter by Advocate Naeem Bokhari. In an article by Nasir Iqbal for Dawn[431],"But members of the legal fraternity point out that the turning point came with the appearance of a so-called 'open letter' by a lawyer-cum-television personality, Naeem Bokhari in which Justice Iftikhar Chaudhry was accused of a series of doing favors and violating judicial norms and practices. He was accused by Mr Bokhari of running a 'slaughter house' in the name of courtroom, and warned of a 'rebellion' if he did not change his style and behavior."

The move to make Justice Iftikhar Chaudhry "nonfunctional" was immediately followed by yet another decision by the president to send a

[430] Ibid.
[431] Published 10th March 2007

reference under Article 209 of the Constitution to the Supreme Judicial Council to investigate allegations of misconduct against him. This led to what came to be known as the "Lawyers Movement". Rallies and protests were organized nationwide, political parties, human-right activists, members of the civil society joined together to reinstate him. On 20 July 2007, Iftikhar Chaudhry, was reinstated to his position as Chief Justice in a ruling by the thirteen-member bench of Pakistan Supreme Court headed by Justice Khalil-ur-Rehman Ramday.

Having established the basic facts, let us turn again to our subject matter ie the TV coverage of the Movement.

***Mazhar Arif***[432] writing in *Viewpoint* on 29th June 2012, says, "Since the lawyers' movement, media, judiciary and so-called civil society, representing the urban educated middle class, are complementing each other in promoting particular ethno-religious and political interests besides promoting the state ideology or at least the ideology of some sections of the society sponsored and patronized by the state based on jingoism, xenophobia, sectarianism, hatred and exclusion." He goes on to say, "The media are the methods of mass communication and entertainment which have developed into vital political forces...At the same time there has grown serious concern that such media can themselves be methods of social control, and political influence."(The Penguin Dictionary of Politics) ."[433]

The media, more especially TV played a huge role in reinstatement of Chaudhry Iftikhar. In a ***Daily Times Editorial*** of 10th April, 2008[434], it says, "One can say with confidence that without TV coverage the deposed Chief Justice of Pakistan Mr Iftikhar Muhammad Chaudhry would not have become a national figure. " The 24/7 reporting on the event, creating a "now or never" situation, it was a live drama so to speak for the public. When "experts" are invited by every channel, each channel trying to up the other in ratings, there is bound to be views that may neither be informed, nor unbiased. In case of "live coverage" such cannot be corrected either on divergent issues. ***Thomas Houlahan Report***, by a Washington based expert on Pakistan's Judicial Crises and lawyers

---

[432] Mazhar Arif is a senior journalist, media critic, researcher, writer and people's rights activist presently working as Executive Director, Society for Alternative Media and Research (SAMAR), an organization seeking space for voices of the voiceless in the media and engaged with promoting media literacy to enable readers, viewers and listeners to understand and analyze media contents

[433] From the article in Viewpoint

[434] Titled, "Media and the lawyers"

movement, states, "I've noticed that much of the 'analysis' has been pretty hysterical and that many of those offering the opinions on the situation seem grossly ill-informed. It therefore struck me that it might be a good idea for someone to inquire as to what exactly has transpired between President Musharraf and the Supreme Court. At least it would provide a set of facts for commentators to work off."[435] Houlahan has penned a 47 page report on the subject.

These are just two of the ongoing events strongly projected by television channels.

In a powerful article **Yawar Abbas**,[436] in ***Daily Times***, says, "During the last decade, Pakistan's media has contributed positively to the cause of democracy in the country and also played an active role in the restoration of the judges through round the clock coverage of the famous Lawyers' Movement. Nonetheless, serious doubts and conflicting views regarding the media's role in the country have also accompanied these wide-scale developments. Some of these views rise from concerns that the media is strictly averse to the idea of even the most modest regulation by the government and that it refuses to abide by a unanimously agreed code of conduct or ethics. The media groups in the country have grown into big mafias; they own print as well as electronic media — a situation that is almost unprecedented anywhere in the world. Critics also maintain that the Pakistani media is creating an environment of despair and hopelessness by presenting a very bleak picture of the country. This constant fear mongering and pessimistic outlook on such a broad scale can have its own psychological ramifications for Pakistani society in the future."[437]

The good, the cultural, the beautiful has all been relegated to the back burner. All that is projected is the bad, the ugly, the destructive. Talk shows talking of doomsday scenario, seem to have replaced entertainment and any good things related to Pakistan. This has on one hand created despondency in the local population, on the other hand, it has effectively created a consistently negative view of Pakistan for the rest of the world.

The coverage of the two incidents(there were many others), made authorities realize that in the PEMRA Ordinance 2002 much that needed

---

[435] WORLD LAW DIRECT: http://www.worldlawdirect.com/forum/international-law-issues/10118-pakistans-judicial-crises-lawyers-movement.html

[436] *The writer is in the Foreign Service of Pakistan*

[437] Daily Times, published 24th March 2011 titled, "Is Media fanning extremism?"

to be included, had not been included. The coverage and its drawbacks owed largely to a fledgling electronic medium, just hatched, largely untrained and to a certain degree, unaware of the impact of its power on formation of opinions. On 4th November 2007, PEMRA(Amended)Ordinance was carried by most national newspapers. The copy of the same added here as ***'Annexure A'*** was published on that date by *The Nation*.

The purpose of adding and discussing here the leading clauses within the amendment separately and deliberating upon it, is to bring greater focus on the need to address the looming issues we see in the electronic media. Although in November 2007, a petition was filed in the Supreme Court challenging the Amended Ordinance, 'The amended ordinance places unreasonable restrictions on the citizens of Pakistan in the exercise and enjoyment of the fundamental rights of freedom of speech, expression and free flow of information,"[438] says the petition.

PEMRA has a different view on the situation the spokesman said all concessions available in the ordinance remain intact and unaffected. "As a matter of fact, the authority of the chairman to act against violations has been delegated to a committee of the authority," it said. The government had only very recently enacted amendments to enable cross-media ownership as a manifestation of its resolve to further the cause of media freedom. The spokesperson also recalled that last week, the PEMRA had approved grant of TV license to owners of an English-language daily. "There is no cause for any apprehension on this account."[439]

Besides some minor amendments in PEMRA Ordinance, certain other sections were included, these, pertained to:

No material:

* That may aid terrorist activities
* That jeopardizes integrity of Pakistan
* That defames the administration
* That is deemed vulgar or obscene
* That promotes ethnicism
* That defames army

---

[438] "Amended PEMRA Ordinance challenged in Supreme Court" Daily Times 29th November 2007
[439] "New Laws against Electronic Media in Pakistan" 14th June 2007 in The Muslim Observer by; Mahvish Akhtar, Muslim Media News Service (MMNS)

* No broadcast of video footage of militants
* No programmes that incite violence
* No live coverage of incidents of violence[440]

***Some relevant clauses from PEMRA Ordinance (Amended)2007:***

**Section 2(j)** of the Ordinance states, "not broadcast video footage of suicide bombers, terrorists, bodies of victims of terrorism , statements and pronouncements of militants and extremist elements and any other acts which may, in any way, promote, aid or abet terrorist activities or terrorism."[441]

If we look at the circumstance then, this makes a lot of sense. Videos delivered at TV stations by unknown elements was run by some channels, not realizing that by so doing, two things could have happened, maybe did happen too: (a) unwittingly being a medium of further spreading the message of the terrorists and (b) if there was a code message within that video to fellow terrorists, it was being easily, loudly, clearly conveyed. By so doing, we need to do some soul searching here, are we not unwittingly, in order to gain larger viewership in a tough world of competition, abetting the terrorists? Showing bodies of people killed from any side can only lead to anger, reaction, justification of any wrong doing. I reproduce a piece titled, *"Showing of dead bodies on TV channels"* published on 27th April 2012 in ***The Pakistan Observer,*** [442] " It is almost a daily occurrence that gory scenes pertaining to victims of acts of terrorist or accidents are shown on television channels. Similarly, women and children are shown crying and beating their chests over dead bodies while scenes of badly injured people including children are also repeatedly shown.

"No doubt, it is duty of media to report what is happening around to its viewers but nowhere in the world things are reported the way we are watching on our TV screen. There are hundreds of television channels in different countries but seldom limbs and body parts are shown scattered all around as we do without realizing its effect on the overall society and especially the younger generation. The nation is already subdued and hard-pressed and such scenes add to the psychological woes of the people.

---

[440] INTERNEWS PAKISTAN Nov 4th 2007: http://www.internews.org.pk/mediaresource/monitor041107.php

[441] Annexure 'A'

[442] http://pakobserver.net/201204/27/detailnews.asp?id=152455

"Reporting of events is something else but screening of gory scenes is something quite different, which must be avoided as these generate more fear at the time of crisis. In this backdrop, PEMRA has done well by issuing show cause notices to 17 TV channels for airing unedited live footages of blood, gore, dead and mutilated bodies amid a private plane crash. Notices have also been issued for airing indecent, vulgar and unethical programmes, advertisements, shows, excessive foreign content and intruding on personal and family life of people. This shows PEMRA is mindful if its responsibilities but it is also a fact that action on the part of regulator is always misconstrued as unnecessary interference in media freedom. Therefore, we would urge owners and management of these channels especially Pakistan Broadcasters Association (PBA) to evolve a code of ethics, which must be adhered to by all on voluntary basis." [443]

**Section 2(k)** of the Amended Ordinance says, " ensure that no anchor person, moderator, or host propagates any opinion or acts in any manner prejudicial to the ideology of Pakistan or sovereignty, integrity or security of Pakistan."[444]

Anchor persons and Moderators are powerful opinion makers in society today. They have a huge viewership following and we see the viewership shifting with the anchor person to another TV channel if they make a change—at least so far as their programme is concerned. Ideology may be defined as a set of beliefs, values and ideals a group or a nation subscribes to, this set of principles or ideals has to be ingrained over a period of time in the social consciousness of the society. It may also be defined as, "An ideology is a belief or a set of beliefs, especially the political beliefs on which people, parties, or countries base their actions."[445]

**Rolf Schwarz,** in an excellent essay on Ideology, takes us through the geneses of the term and what the term came to mean for different people in different times. He says in the beginning of the essay, "Ideology" was a "science with a mission", it wanted to change the world, it wanted a democratic, rational, and scientific society, which liberated the mind of man from prejudice. Like so many of their contemporaries believing in and promoting enlightenment the "ideologues" regarded education as the key to social change. But the ideologues wanted more than just promoting

---

[443] Ibid.

[444] Refer Annexure A

[445] "Ideology", Collins Cobuilt

an all -embracing encyclopedic knowledge for everyone, they wanted more than just being teachers with different ideas, they wanted to actively bring about the new order of things."[446]

So the aforementioned Section directed the anchorperson or moderator of a programme not to opine or encourage an opinion against the Ideology of Pakistan. Neither against the integrity, sovereignty and security of Pakistan. We have discussed at length integrity, sovereignty and security of Pakistan as an exception to Freedom of Expression under Article 19 Constitution of Pakistan.

The anchor person being a strong opinion leader and steering a programme must ensure this. A balance, I would say must be the touchstone of our media .

***Mohammad Jamil,***[447] in an article for the ***Pakistan Observer***, titled, "Self-righteous in media exposed",[448] says, "The nation has to be on its guard from pseudo-intellectuals, analysts and panelists - Mir Jafars of media, because if the nation loses its guard, the enemies within can play havoc with our nation state."

**Sec2(l)** states, "not broadcast any programme inciting violence or hatred, or any action prejudicial to maintenance of law and order."[449]

In chapter 1, we studied that hate speech is a limitation world over against freedom of expression. I cannot spew hatred against an individual, a group of people; whether belonging to a profession, or, a religious or ethnic minority, or promote anything that is against the law and order of the country—in the guise of freedom of expression. On a SITE by **Aamir Mughal,**[450] an interesting piece posted starts off as stating, "Bete´ noire´ - Something especially hated or dreaded; a bugbear. It has become an obnoxious habit amongst several leading Pakistani Private TV Channels News Anchors/Correspondents to create an imaginary threat and take a cover behind that imaginary threat to fulfill their own agenda ........"[451]

---

[446] Titled "What is Ideology" ESSAYS: Rolf Schwarz LINK: http://www.rolfschwarz.com/Essays/ideology.shtml

[447] Lahore based writer

[448] Published 23rd June 2012

[449] Refer Annexure A

[450] Retired Officer of Intelligence Bureau, Government of Pakistan

[451] Titled "Partial Pakistan :Media Incites Hatred" published 25th May 2012 LINK: http://chagataikhan.blogspot.com/2012/05/partial-pakistani-media-incites-hatred.html

The question all media practitioners must ask is: what will be the cascading effect of any news/views or angle so shown? At the end of the day, media must be answerable to the society.

The second element within this section is, media must not promote, or be seen to promote any act that can clearly create a law and order situation in the country. This is promoting chaos that cannot be desirable or acceptable to any government.

**Section 2(m)**states, "not broadcast anything which defames or brings into ridicule the Head of the State, or members of the armed forces, or executive, legislative or judicial organs of the state."[452]

The purpose of this section was to reign in ridicule and defamation. Cartoons, skits, shows, with ridicule towards these institutions were high on list of TV programmes in 2007. Some still are, today. Whereas, justified criticisms of policies and wrong actions must be shown by our media, it must be remembered , this must not reach the degrees of insult and ridicule—however, by the same token, the Authority must not place a ban on honest coverage by the media either. In a piece published about curbs on journalists hamper election reporting, ***Human Rights Watch***[453] it says, 'Threats and censorship against the independent media, bias in state television, and a widespread ban on live broadcasting are limiting the public's right to information as Pakistan goes to the polls, Human Rights Watch said today. Recent curbs on the media prohibit coverage of election rallies, live call-ins, live talk shows, live coverage of protests, or any live broadcasts that could show the government in a negative light, severely restricting the right to free expression ahead of Pakistan's election on February 18, 2008."

However, there can be no justification of media to promote sensationalism and half-baked opinions. World over certain limitations exist as we read in chapter 1.

While we view the amendments, we must be mindful of the fact that according to the PERMRA Ordinance 2002, PEMRA is bound to accept the policy directions by the Federal Government which will be deemed binding upon PEMRA, who must ensure implementation of the same.

---

[452] Refer Annexure A

[453] Titled, "Pakistan: Media Restrictions undermine Elections" published 17th February 2008 LINK: http://www.hrw.org/news/2008/02/15/pakistan-media-restrictions-undermine-election

**Section 2(n)** states, "not broadcast any programme or discussion on a matter sub-judice."

This is also a part of Contempt of Court, Constitution of Pakistan which itself is part of the exception to Limitations on Freedom of Expression Article 19 Constitution of Pakistan, discussed at length earlier.

Nonetheless, very briefly let us look again at a matter sub-judice in light of media coverage. A matter that is already before a judge for adjudication, that matter is said to be sub-judice to the court. Legally, this is, already an existing law and part of our Constitution, therefore it cannot be seen as a "new" law imposed. Unfortunately, we have not seen the law being practiced by our media practitioners. Repeatedly, matters sub-judice to the court are converted into "media trials." The round-the-clock transmission demands ongoing discussions and "expert" views by those who may not be experts in the subject under discussion, though may be, in subjects of their specialization.

I share a piece published by ***Pak Tribune***, "ISLAMABAD: Pakistan Electronic Media Regulatory Authority has advised Satellite TV Channel not to air programme /talk shows, discussions and the interviews in which issues that are sub-judice before the Courts including the Apex Court are debated and commented upon, sometime in a manner, tantamount to a Media Trial. In a statement issued here on Wednesday, PEMRA spokesman said that this is not only objectionable but also against the "Term and the Condition of Licenses" issued to TV channels. He said that PEMRA took this notice after this was observed that the situation is created where various speakers are called and leading questions are asked by Anchors who then pass judgments. Anchors are moderators and not judges, he said. In certain cases anchors take up the topics in which they are neither qualified nor authorized, he added.

"The spokesman said that such practices are in contravention to PEMRA Code of Conduct for media broadcaster and the spirit of various directions of the Court issued from time to time. PEMRA, as a regulator, has always believed in 'Self -regulation' by Electronic Media but there are certain norms, limits and bounds beyond freedom become anarchy and licentiousness.

"Reiterating Authorities resolve, the spokesman saids that the independence, responsibility and maturity go hand in hand. Unbridled freedom, irresponsible comments and transgression of law and Code cannot and should not be allowed. He said that this step has been taken to urge media operators to understand their prime responsibility—to abide by law."[454]

**Section 2(o)** states, "Not broadcast anything which is known to be false or baseless or is mala-fide or for which there exists sufficient reasons to believe that the same may be false, baseless or mala-fide."[455]

Mala- fide may be defined as, "Undertaken in bad faith"[456] It is also defined as, "Bad faith. The opposite of *bona fide."*[457]

Mala-fide views, news will only happen if the channel is not impartial and if they know the news or views being aired is baseless or there exists reasonable ground to believe it is baseless—yet go ahead with it, besides,it is a violation of professional ethics. Unfortunately, in many cases, we have seen the law being ignored by many channels on different occasions.The reasons can be many, ranging from wanting a higher viewership, thereby indulging in speculative journalism, to lack of impartiality .

'The one function that TV news performs very well is that when there is no news we give it to you with the same emphasis as if there were." [458]

**Sec8(4)** : states that, "A licensee or permission holder shall ensure that nothing is transmitted or broadcast in violation of the provisions of the of the Ordinance or rules or regulations, and Code of Conduct and for this purpose shall install time delay equipment within its system to prevent any such violation."[459]

The rules therefore are binding upon our electronic media and noncompliance can result in punishments.

There exists also a **Code of Conduct For Media Broadcasters/Cable TV Operators** that is self-explanatory and is being included here to give the reader a well- rounded picture:

---

[454]PEMRA asks TV channels not to discuss sub-judice matters (2003) LINK: http://www.paktribune.com/news/print.php?id=190482

[455] Refer to Annexure A

[456] The Free Dictionary by FARLAX LINK: http://www.thefreedictionary.com/mala+fide

[457] BLACK'S Law Dictionary Centennial Edition(1891-1991) Pg 956

[458]David McClure Brinkley (July 10, 1920 – June 11, 2003) was an American newscaster for NBC and ABC in a career lasting from 1943 to 1997

[459] Refer Annexure A

## CODE OF CONDUCT FOR MEDIA

## BROADCASTERS/CABLE TV OPERATORS[460]

***Programmes:-***

(1) No programme shall be aired which:

(a) Passes derogatory remarks about any religion or sect or community or uses visuals or words contemptuous of religious sects and ethnic groups or which promotes communal and sectarian attitudes or disharmony;

(b) contains anything pornographic, obscene or indecent or is likely to deprave, corrupt or injure the public morality;

(c) contains an abusive comment that, when taken in context, tends to or is likely to expose an individual or a group or class of individuals to hatred or contempt on the basis of race or caste, national, ethnic or linguistic origin, color or religion or sect, sex, sexual orientation, age or mental or physical disability;

(d) contains anything defamatory or knowingly false;

(e) is likely to encourage and incite violence or contains anything against maintenance of law and order or which promotes antinational or anti-state attitudes;

(f) contains anything amounting to contempt of court;

(g) contains aspersions against the Judiciary and integrity of the Armed Forces of Pakistan;

(h) maligns or slanders any individual in person or certain groups, segments of social, public and moral life of the country;

(i) is against basic cultural values, morality and good manners;

(j) brings into contempt Pakistan or its people or tends to undermine its integrity or solidarity as an independent and sovereign country;

---

[460] PEMRA Website LINK: http://www.pemra.gov.pk/pemra/

(k) promotes, aids or abets any offence which is cognizable under the Pakistan Penal Code;

(l) denigrates men or women through the depiction in any manner of the figure, in such a way as to have the effect of being indecent or derogatory;

(m) denigrates children;

(n) contains anything which tends to glorify crime or criminals;

(o) contains material which may be detrimental to Pakistan's relations with friendly countries; or

(p) contains material which is against ideology of Pakistan or Islamic values;

(2) Particular care should be taken to ensure that programmes meant for children do not contain objectionable language or are disrespectful to their parents or elders;

(3) Programmes must not be directed against the sanctity of home, family and marital harmony;

(4) While reporting the proceedings of the Parliament or the Provincial Assemblies, such portion of the proceedings as the Chairman or the Speaker may have ordered to be expunged, shaii not be broadcast or distributed and every effort shall be made to release a fair account of the proceedings of the Parliament or the Provincial Assemblies.

***Advertisements:-***

(1) Advertisements aired or distributed by a broadcast or cable TV station shall be designed in such a manner that it conforms to the laws of the country and is not offensive to morality, decency and religious sects of the people of Pakistan.

(2) No Advertisement shall be permitted which:

(i) Promotes or supports sedition, anarchy or violence in country;

(ii) Is against any provisions of the Constitution of Pakistan or any other law for the time being in force;

(iii) Tends to incite people to crime, cause disorder or violence or breach of law or glorifies violence or obscenity in any way;

(iv) Glorifies adultery, lustful passions or alcoholic drinks or the non - Islamic Values;

(v) Distorts historical facts, traditions of Pakistan or the person or personality of a national leader or a state dignitary;

(vi) Fans racial, sectarian, parochial, regional or class hatred;

(vii) Promotes social inequality, militates against concepts of human dignity and dignity of labour;

(viii) Is directed against sanctity or home, family and marriage;

(ix) Is wholly or mainly of a religious or political nature;

(x) contains references that are likely to lead the public to infer that the product advertised or any of its ingredients has some special property or quality which is incapable of being established;

(xi) contains indecent, vulgar, or offensive themes or treatment; or

(xii) contains material which is repugnant to ideology of Pakistan or Islamic values;

(3) The goods or services advertised shall not suffer from any defects which are harmful to human health. Misleading claims about the goods shall not be made.

(4) No advertisement which is likely to be seen by children in large numbers should urge children directly to purchase goods of a particular brand or ask their parents to do so.

(5) All advertisements must be clearly distinguishable as such and be separate from the programmes and should not in any manner take the form of news or documentary.

More or less, the Code of Conduct, specifically of programmes is a rehash of the Ordinance(s) with an odd inclusion here or there thrown in.

***Issam Ahmed,*** writing for the ***Christian Science Monitor*** says, [461] that two Pakistani journalists, filing reports home from Washington are drawing their salaries "From US State Department funding through a non-profit intermediary highlighting the sophisticated nature of America's efforts to shape its image abroad." The same article states, "If an American journalist working as a foreign correspondent in Pakistan was paid in a similar manner, would it be morally or professionally acceptable for his news organization or audience?" asks Badar Alam, editor of Pakistan's prestigious English-language Herald magazine."[462]

"The amount currently allocated for the project is some $2 million over two years from the public diplomacy funds allocated by the State Department, according to State Department officials in Washington familiar with the project. That includes salaries for the two correspondents –both from two known TV channels."[463]

***Cambodian Times*** [464]commenting on the same says, "But the lack of transparency, particularly by the Pakistani news organizations, raises ethical issues for all parties involved," said Richard Wald, a journalism ethics professor at Columbia University in New York City.

"The essential question here is not who pays, but who knows who pays... In a correct world, if there were such a situation, people should make the connection clear - not simply to the editors and management of the Pakistani papers - but to the receivers of the information so they can judge it on their own," Professor Wald said."

The ethical issue here is NOT the lack of transparency, or who knows who pays, as stated by Professor Wald, but something deeper and more basic than what has been projected. The ethical issue is: when a media person draws salary from another country- with whom will the journalist's loyalty lie? Which country's interests will be guarded in the bargain? There has to be a conflict of interest. For example, drone attacks is an intrinsic part of US WOT[465]strategy, whereas Pakistan and her parliament views this as a violation of its sovereignty. Whom will this "paid" journalist support? There will be many other similar issues that will lead

---

[461] 2nd September 2011 "US funding of Pakistani Journalists raises questions of transparency"
[462] Ibid.
[463] Ibid.
[464] 14th July 2012 titled "America Funding Pak Journalists in a bid to counter ISI's anti-American propaganda?"
[465] War on Terrorism

to making a choice. Where is the role of gate keeping then? Answer: It is eroded.

Moving on to the next important point, what our TV channels lack, is a professional Editorial Policy. Usually, it is the proprietor of the channel who determines the editorial policy. In most cases, the proprietor is not someone from the field or aware of the ethics of journalism in broadcasting, They are pure and simple, businessmen, who are in the business to make a buck. As a result of the lack of an Editorial Policy, the role of broadcast media as gatekeepers has been eroded for lack of same. What should be shown, how to be shown—have become personal decisions of the proprietor or/and the channel. A strong media, built on grounds of accuracy is the need of the hour. Yet can this accuracy be achieved? "In most cases, barring the major cities of Lahore, Karachi, Pindi/Islamabad, and maybe a few others, TV channels do not have any reporters/correspondents. The channels hire people, they are unpaid workers of the channel, who volunteer to report on events for their area. Imagine the nuisance value and the niche the 'reporter' creates for himself. With no training, no knowledge of how things are to be reported, issues can be misreported, exaggerated, incorrect factually. A non-issue can be made into an issue, and an issue; a non-issue."[466]

Many incidents stand witness to our lop sided coverage. Suicide bombings and gruesome coverage is one example. Showing bits of bodies, destruction, has made the public immune to such happenings. For them, now, it is just "another suicide killing." Munawan Police Academy attack coverage sticks out like a sore thumb. Gunmen had stormed a Police Academy in October 2009, in Munawan. As I sat stunned in front of the TV screen, I saw more or less the same coverage on all TV channels. The security personnel trying to breach the wall to gain access to the building, as rescue operation was underway— all being shown and widely commented on by the TV reporters on ground. I am sure the same was being viewed by the terrorists inside too, making it easier for them to decide upon their counter plan.

This kind of coverage is in clear violation of clause(3) of Section(8) of the 2007 Amendment that stated: "Notwithstanding anything contained in this Ordinance the live coverage of incidents of violence and conflict shall not be broadcast."

---

[466] Dr Mehdi Hasan Dean of SMC Beaconhouse National University. Discussion on the subject by him on 4th July 2012

The list can go on, the attack on Sri Lanka's Cricket Team, the Earthquake in Pakistan, the floods. PEMRA had issued notice to many TV stations over airing the graphic footage of the crash of Bhoja Air plane. A piece in ***Dawn*** [467]says, "The body also sent out notices to a number of entertainment channels, saying 'vulgarity, obscenity and abusive' languages must not be aired on local television, terming it unethical and irresponsible. While the warning must be welcomed as a much-needed move, it remains unclear how PEMRA will gauge the levels of obscenity, vulgarity, dramatisation and so on."

Media has a duty to unite the nation, to boost their morale. Unfortunately, the lack of Editorial Policy by most stations have failed in this duty. On the contrary, TV programmes today, bring on depression and have further created a polarization in the society.

There is a recent trend of "exposing TV anchors" by other channel anchors— must be put an end to. It only leads to the disrespect of both— the anchors and the forum they represent.

I would like to discuss here two events that brought in question, the credibility of certain media persons.

Without sensationalizing the facts, *Duniya News* with two anchorpersons Mubashir Lucman and Mehr Bokhari interviewed Malik Riaz, of Bahria Town, who had accused Dr Arslan, son of Chief Justice Chaudhry Iftikhar of accepting kickbacks, bribes worth over Rs 340m.[468]

An off-air video footage of the interview was leaked on you tube. All hell broke loose. The anchorpersons were accused of running a planted interview. 'The footage shows conversations between Lucman, Bokhari and Riaz focused on the kind of questions they will be asking. Both anchors are also instructed against interrupting Riaz during the interview.

Bokhari is heard saying a question is planted towards the end of the video.

*"Say what you want... what question should we ask. It will appear as though it is planted... it is, but it shouldn't appear it is."*

---

[467] Media Watchdog, "04 25[th] 2012

[468] The NATION Newspaper titled, "Malik Riaz accuses Arsalan of accepting bribes worth over Rs 340m" dated 12[th] June 2012

The video begins with general conversation and is followed by Riaz questioning the anchors on why they are not asking why he is part of "deals." Lucman is then seen on the phone asking if the interview is going fine and defending himself by saying Riaz is being given a chance. Who is he speaking to? "Abdul Qadir Gilani", he says.[469]

Mubashir Lucman, explained his position in a you tube video released. In an article carried by *Pakistan Today,* I share an excerpt from it, "What some television anchors made out to look like crafted chatter off-the-screen is nothing compared to what actually transpires in their own shows. Any journalist who has spent a few years in the field will vouch for the fact that this is neither out-of-the-ordinary or unethical. Sadly, the biggest scoop of the day was made to look like the greatest scam of the year. Quotes were edited to give false impressions; a harmless phone call was made to appear as dictation by the federal government whilst a detailed text message by someone in the opposition was forgotten as a child's remark, for that suited them."[470]

The scandal above made it to the ***New York Times***. "What shocked ordinary Pakistanis was not the interview — Mr. Hussain had already made similar accusations in court — but rather evidence that it had been rigged. Leaked studio footage, shot just before the program went live and during breaks, showed the hosts, Meher Bokhari and Mubashir Luqman, chatting cozily with Mr. Hussain, discussing the questions and priming his answers. 'Why don't you start talking about it yourself, otherwise it will seem planted, which it is,' Ms. Bokhari is seen telling him in Urdu," writes ***Declan Walsh***.[471] The video of the link is available on the net. [472]

***Mazhar Abbas***[473] in his piece on **Media Watchdog**[474]writing on this episodes states, "However, what transpired in the behind-the-scenes video was shameful for the entire journalist community........*Dunya News* and the two anchors have managed to get a huge amount of publicity; unfortunately, this has all come from all the wrong reasons. It is sad that today, unethical journalism is getting more hits on social media

---

[469] Express Tribune titled: "VIDEO LEAK: Lucman, Bokhari run'planted show' with Malik Riaz on 14th June 2012" by Shehryar Popalzai

[470] "I Am Still Around" Mubashir Lucman in Pakistan Today 29th June 2012

[471] Titled "Coverage of Scandal Dents Credibility of Pakistani TV News" published 18th June 2012

[472]http://www.youtube.com/watch?v=x80EuIA4tpY

[473]Director current affairs Express News and has previously worked with ARY News. He is a former secretary-general of the Pakistan Federal Union of Journalists

[474] Blog for Express Tribune titled, "Meher-Mubashir: Time to re-visit Ethics" published 15th June 2012

forums than ethical journalism is. What we saw may go down in the history of journalism as a glittering case of non-professionalism and unethical journalism."

In another piece on the subject for ***Express Tribune***[475] he says, "Enforcement of the following code by all stakeholders can help the media regain its lost credibility and play a key role in rebuilding a democratic society in the long-run. 1) A journalist shall regard, as a grave professional offence, the acceptance of a bribe in any form (cash or gifts, tickets, plots, etc.) in consideration of either publication of an article or its suppression. 2) All associations of journalists, owners, editors and broadcasters should make it mandatory for all members to declare their assets every year. An accountability committee should be formed and those who don't do this should be barred from contesting union elections. 3) Owners and editors must issue standard operating procedures that no one from their respective organizations will go on official tours on government or a private party's expense. Editors or owners should not accompany the prime minister or president and instead should nominate reporters or anchors for such tours. 4) All unions must review their relationship with the government of the day particularly because of the tendency among governments to give members of press clubs plots. If we really think ourselves to be a mirror of society, we should behave and act like ordinary people. 5) News should not be suppressed or compromised based on commercial considerations. 6) Reporters should avoid expressing comment or conjecture as proven fact. 7) A journalist should always protect a confidential source of information. 8) A journalist shall ensure that any information he provides via his writings is fair, accurate and not subject to falsification or distortion. 9) A journalist should not distort or suppress the truth for commercial, institutional or other reasons. 10) The proprietor must not suppress a news report merely because of commercial considerations. 11) Journalists, editors or owners should never accept favours and bribes offered to influence their professional duties. 12) Journalists should aspire to be independent and this means that they should avoid being partisan. 13) To keep their record clean, all media bodies must invite independent audit companies for their annual audit and should then publish their financial reports for the information of the general public. We — journalists, editors and owners — have a moral responsibility to prove that we really are society's 'mirror.'"[476]

---

[475] "Time for Media to Hold itself Accountable" published 16th June 2012

[476] Ibid.

Unfortunate incident, no matter how one looks at it.

In another case of the release of Surjeet Singh, an Indian convicted of spying and jailed in Pakistan for two decades, our media again committed a faux pas. The name was a close one with another Indian convicted, Sarabjeet Singh. He was convicted of terrorism and also jailed in Pakistan. Many television channels started announcing his release on orders of President Zardari—India had long lobbied for his release. Jubilation was in the air. However, after 6 to 8 hours of the "breaking news" it was clarified that it was not Sarabjeet Singh but Surjeet Singh who was being released. ***Mazhar Abbas,***[477] in his article for ***Express Tribune***[478] wrote, "What one saw was that rather then get direct quotes from the officials of the ministries concerned, the media was more interested in getting reactions from various political parties and from Sarabjeet Singh's family." He continues to state, "We do not seem to be exhibiting the tendency of learning from our mistakes and instead we usually try and put the entire blame on officialdom, usually the government.

"It all started with three red tickers in various television channels, all titled 'Breaking news' and all quoting unnamed source. The first said that the president had commuted the death sentence of Sarabjeet Singh to life imprisonment. The second said that the president had ordered the release of Sarabjeet Singh and a third that the law ministry had sent a letter to the interior ministry to start the process of releasing the prisoner. There were some follow-up tickers and all of them were either about the background of the case or on reactions from Sarbajit's family."[479]

Another case refers to host of the show *Maya Khan* of SAMAA TV. In a morning show, Maya Khan with her crew was shown chasing couples deemed as "immoral" [480] who were shown dating in Karachi parks. She with her crew were fired after a great hue and cry went up by different sections of the society for violation of privacy in her show "Subah Savera Maya Ke Saath." In a mail to Mr Zafar Siddiqi, [481]by the Citizens' of the country, signed by over 5.000 petitioners online, it said and I share an excerpt:

---

[477] Director current affairs Express News and has previously worked with ARY News. He is a former secretary-general of the Pakistan Federal Union of Journalists

[478] "How the Media Messed Up Surjeet Singh's Release" published 5th July 2012

[479] Ibid.

[480] Maya Khan Gets Fired(Staff Report)PAKISTAN TODAY published 29th Jan 2012

[481] CEO SAMAA TV

**"Therefore we urge you to:**

Make public the written corrective directives and guidelines that have been put in place, proactively leading by example as a channel with conscience which is responsible and cares about its viewers and their sentiments.

2. Ensure a serious, genuine and unqualified apology from Ms. Maya Khan in which she accepts her deliberate misconduct and violation of the affected people, families, media consumers, viewers and the law.

3. Take this appalling show 'Subh Sawery Maya ke Saath' off air, as its very premise is based on the concept of moral policing and interference in people's personal lives.

Ensure that Ms. Maya Khan and all your other reporters, producers and hosts comply with the new directives in future, whether they are part of the news team or the entertainment team.

SAMAA TV has many credits to its name that we appreciate, and we as media consumers, genuinely want to see this channel realise its potential as a truly progressive channel. We assure you that we will support you in the mission to translate quality into greater viewership based on dignity, fairness, respect and equal rights, not tainted by substandard hosts and programming. You may want to have a look at the Code of Conduct Guidelines of The Society of Professional Journalists to consult while drafting their own guidelines."[482]

*On Sat, Jan 28, 2012 at 12:28 PM, Zafar Siddiqi wrote:*

Dear All

Your feedback is appreciated. As a responsible corporate citizen, SAMAA TV did what was required under the circumstances. We do not and have not in the past or intend to in the future to take our viewership or reporting requirements without the seriousness that they deserve.

You would appreciate that as an organization with a functioning management team, we had to conduct certain legal requirements over the

---

[482] Published by Teeth Maestro 28th January 2012

past week and internal review processes (which are operational in nature) before proceeding further.

As a result of which I can inform you:

**We asked Maya to apologise unconditionally which she did not.**

**The CEO asked her to do that on Friday which she refused.**

As a result of which the following will be put in place on Monday, Jan 30th.

**Maya and her team will receive termination notices.**

**Her show is being stopped from Monday morning.**

Our deeds and actions taken since this episode occurred are there for the record and hope this will settle issues as far as the station is concerned.

A lot has been written about the race for ratings. Well, we do absolve such behaviour irrespective of ratings that the show was getting.

With best regards and thank you for your understanding.

**Zafar Siddiqi**
Chairman CNBC Arabiya
Chairman CNBC Africa
President CNBC Pakistan[483]

What SAMAA TV did was was commendable. However, what happened in both scenarios of Maya and Lucman? They joined other channels. Two, an interesting point crossed my mind as I was writing, can one anchorperson or moderator be an expert and knowledgeable in diverse subjects ranging from politics, to law, to economics et al? Is it not then a case of "Jack of All trades, Master of None?" Can he/she ask focused questions if his/her knowledge of the subject matter is shallow?

---

[483] Insight Pakistan published 29th January 2012 LINK: http://www.insightpakistan.com/341/maya-khan-zafar-siddiqi-ceo-sacked-unconditional-apology-saamaa-tv-raid-karachi-park/

In the world of specialization we live in today, does this make sense? Does it lead to formation of an educated, well informed public opinion?

***Dawn Newspaper***,[484] in an article states "The sensationalism that accompanied the advent of TV journalism in Pakistan is fast becoming the bedrock of media professionals here.

"This feature is the natural outcome of a missing investigative spirit, the trivial nature of reporting and the absence of accountability. What were once regarded as journalistic ethics have been replaced by an insensitive media culture where information is spiced up and then fed to the audience..... In unstructured societies like Pakistan, where fixing responsibility and holding accountability is not part of media routines, there is considerable damage. News is measured less by how objective and credible it is and more in terms of the potential devastation it can wreak.

"Lack of organizational checks, not to mention encouragement, has seen news not only being dramatized but also created with ingredients being added to stimulate public interest. The result is that often unverified facts constitute a major part of the information telecast throughout the day, seven days a week. This has blurred the line between the do`s and don`ts of journalism in Pakistan."

### *Current problems in electronic media*

High level of inaccuracies is one. Untrained staff and focus on being the first to report and not necessarily the most accurate or truthful has created credibility issues. In target killings, or/and accidents, different channels often report wildly different numbers . Sensationalism is another issue. There is a strong tendency by the media to reflect and keep on reflecting, thereby sensationalizing issues, till something juicier comes along, on murders, kidnappings, rapes. Showing the relatives of the victims beating their chest, crying, wailing. This kind of news are sought and covered, not because of the national importance but because it is thought, it will attract better viewership. Poor coverage of important issues is another. Converting non-issues into issues unfortunately, happens. Earlier, I had mentioned what is in public interest and what the public may want to see can be mutually exclusive of each other. The "real" issues take a hit and are often relegated to the back burner because

---

[484] Sensationalism Not Journalism by Syed Irfan Ashraf

"issues" that may be either non-issues or minor issues are promoted as "the" issues. If talk shows are being aired, incessantly, they would more often deal with petty bickering, screaming matches between opponents invited, also leading to colorful exchange of abuses, rather than policy matters or a constructive discussion .Can the program anchor or producer cut off the voice from going on air live, in case of extreme acrimony? If yes, why is this not done? Our media suffers from a short attention span. What is a story today, is replaced by fresh meat tomorrow. Rarely do we see a consistent follow up to an issue, unless it is of a mammoth nature. In such cases we are subject to "Breaking News" every short while as a media circus rolls. The media is more focused on running the channel as a commercial venture rather than serving the people. And even when they do this, the quality of the output is dismal. The public remains uninformed and misinformed on many issues of importance. In case of an anchorperson goofing up, he walks to another channel, the previous owner makes up by covering the slot by hiring another. It's a media musical chair. A win-win situation for all involved. Who pays? The society!

If we look objectively at PEMRA Ordinance 2002 and Amendment of the Ordinance in 2007 , they have not addressed the issues at the basic level. The original Ordinance was more administrative in nature, the second borrowing heavily from the Constitution failed to address the questions pertinent to ***electronic*** medium of communication. Each medium of communication has its own needs, its own ways of dealing with issues owing to the nature of the medium. Although, if not earlier, in the Amendment 2007, these should have been included, keeping in view the issues arising. These issues that should have been addressed are encapsulated below :

## *The suggestions that PEMRA may like to look into are:*

1) Call for Editorial Policies by each media house for submission and approval by PEMRA and ensure these are displayed on channel websites.

2) The media policies must take into consideration the PEMRA Ordinance 2002 and Amendment 2007.

3) If an anchor goes against the guidelines and its channel Editorial Policy, he/she must be banned from joining another media

channel in any capacity for 3 years(As we see cricketers being banned from playing cricket if found guilty of a crime).

4) There must be an imposition of a hefty fine on the channel itself responsible for gross misconduct in following of the Editorial Policy by its staff and in case of an extremely serious nature of violation, a ban on the channel itself for a fortnight. OR, in worst circumstances, revocation of the license itself. This way, the channel will ultimately have to be responsible for any gross contraventions.

5) Guidelines should be given for appointing anchorpersons to avoid unsuitable persons as opinion makers. In case of a "fresh entrant" to the field, a training course must be given to the new appointee .

6) Anchors must be allowed to moderate only those programmes on subjects in which they have a strong background . Instead of awarding them a carte blanche on all issues.

7) In case of programme on specialized subject, the anchorperson does not have in-depth background in, the programme must be co-moderated by someone known as an expert in the field. For different issues, there should be different co-moderators.

8) Guidelines for training course of all staff must be given to the electronic media and checks and balances must be in place to ensure it is duly being carried out.

9) Or, should the Training Institute be under the auspices of PEMRA providing training in different fields ie reporting, photography, live coverage, anchors training etc or should this be relegated to the channels themselves?

10) 'Experts' of different fields must be invited on subject programmes as guests to ensure emergence of balanced and well-informed public opinion instead of allowing non experts who usually do so. For guidelines given of inviting 'experts' in a field as opposed to 'non-experts'(Refer to Definition of Experts later on in this chapter).Non-experts on a subject must not be allowed, that can only lead to murkiness and creation of confusion.

11) Should it be made mandatory for the channels to have a legal adviser to whom all materials of sensitive nature must be first cleared with as well as checking it against the channel's Editorial Policy, as done by BBC?

Failing the above, we witness musical chairs of anchor persons and the channel itself getting off without any repercussions. More importantly, lack of clear cut, well defined Editorial Policy by channels create a confused environment leading to a complete lack of accountability.

In an article related to the subject and my observations above, ***Murtaza Razvi,***[485] titled, "Balochistan and the media"[486] says, "It may be by turns disgusting and refreshing to see the ongoing debate in the electronic media over the political situation in Balochistan. It is disgusting because often the anchor person on a TV talk show displays more than palatable ignorance of the issues at stake; it is refreshing because never before dissident voices were given such an open forum from which to put across their points of view....It can be argued that the electronic news media in Pakistan has yet to come of age, especially when it comes to responsible reporting and holding a logical debate on current affairs."

When the attitude is 'Me First' with the news without verifying its contents, it leads to, disinformation, incorrect opinion formation and in some cases an impact on relationship between Pakistan and other nation(s). This especially must apply to picking of news from the social media.

### *A Comparative with BBC NEWS*

BBC (British Broadcasting Corporation) was the one channel that was shown in Pakistan from the very early days. On 25th July 2005, a new 'Editorial Guidelines' policy of BBC came into effect. "BBC staff are to be told that 'accuracy is more important than speed' in breaking news, as the corporation publishes the first major overhaul of its editorial guidelines ...."[487] It continues to state: 'The new guidelines mark the first time the BBC has made the commitment to accuracy explicit and are designed to reflect the 'changing media environment.'" The corporation

---

[485] The writer is a member of the staff at Dawn Newspaper

[486] Published 9th March 2012 in Dawn Newspaper

[487] Guardian UK published 23rd June 2005 titled : "BBC unveils new ethic code"

will also introduce a time delay on its live coverage of sensitive news events such as September 11 and the school massacre in Beslan. The time delay will last several seconds and will allow editors to cut any scenes they believe are too shocking for viewers. The BBC said it had made the decision following unease in some quarters over its coverage of Beslan last September, when several broadcasters were criticized for losing sight of the meaning of such tragedies in an effort to be first with the news. All the major news broadcasters reported live from the scene of the hostage crisis, in which more than 300 people died. *In some cases cameras were rolling as bloodied hostages, many of them children, fled the school.*

"Afterwards, senior news executives at Sky and ITN as well as the BBC admitted ferocious competition among news providers had led to mistakes. The revised guidelines will come into effect on July 25 and will replace the BBC's Producers' Guidelines to reflect Ofcom's new broadcasting code and the world's 'changing media environment.' It is the first updating of the BBC's codes on ethics, impartiality and taste and decency since the period of internal scrutiny that followed the Hutton report. Lord Hutton criticized the BBC's editorial system as 'defective' in his report on the death of scientist David Kelly."[488]

Most of us are aware of what came to be known as the *"Beslan School Hostage Crisis"* or the *"Beslan Massacre"*. To recap, in early September 2004 it lasted three days involving taking hostage of over 1.100 people this included 777 children and ended with the death of over 300 innocent people. On the third day, the school was bombed killing over 300 people. The Islamic Chechen terrorists had taken the school hostage.

The BBC, the biggest broadcaster in the world, with reported staff of 23.000 people, was founded on 18th October 1922. Yet, yet, yet, in the tragedy of Beslan, they showed bloodied hostages, bound to fan anger and hatred. Afterwards, senior news executives at Sky and ITN as well as the BBC admitted ferocious competition among news providers had led to mistakes.[489]

This has not been the only incident. Coverage of Iraq War was criticized by the corporation's own governors.[490] The board said "The

---

[488] Ibid.

[489] Ibid.

[490] MailOnline published 13th July 2004 titked."BBC Board slams Iraq War Coverage".

coverage had 'limitations' and failed to be skeptical enough over military sources."[491]

I would like to briefly comment here on the report of Lord Hutton,[492]the major points are being reproduced surrounding the death of weapons expert Dr David Kelly from BBC NEWS SITE itself:

- ☐ Dr Kelly took his own life and no third party was involved
- ☐ No-one involved could have contemplated that Dr Kelly would take his own life as a result of the pressures he felt
- ☐ Dr Kelly was not an easy man to help or to whom to give advice
- ☐ Cannot be certain of factors that drove Dr Kelly to suicide
- ☐ Dr Kelly probably killed himself because of extreme loss of self-esteem and would have seen himself as being publicly disgraced
- ☐ Dr Kelly would have felt his job was at risk and that his life's work could be undermined[493] On Andrew Gilligan's Report:
- ☐ Andrew Gilligan's report that Downing Street "probably knew" the 45-minute claim in its Iraq dossier was wrong was a grave allegation and attacked the integrity of the government and the Joint Intelligence Committee (JIC)
- ☐ The 45-minute claim in the Iraq dossier was based on a report received by the intelligence services that they believed to be reliable
- ☐ Whether or not that source was subsequently shown to be unreliable, the central allegation made by Andrew Gilligan in his BBC report was unfounded
- ☐ The allegation that the reason the claim was not in the original draft of the dossier was because it was only from one source and the intelligence service did not believe it to be true, was also unfounded

---

[491] Ibid.

[492] **James Brian Edward Hutton, Baron Hutton**, PC (born June 29, 1931), is a former Lord Chief Justice of Northern Ireland and British Lord of Appeal in Ordinary

[493] KEY POINTS: The Hutton's Report 28th January 2004 LINK: http://news.bbc.co.uk/2/hi/uk_news/politics/3437315.stm

- ☐ It is not possible to reach a definite conclusion as to what Dr Kelly said to Mr Gilligan

- ☐ Satisfied Dr Kelly did not say to Mr Gilligan that the government knew the 45-minute claim was wrong or that intelligence agencies did not believe it was necessarily true.[494] On the BBC Lord Hutton's Report's main points were:[495]

- ☐ Editorial system at BBC was defective in allowing Mr Gilligan's report to go to air without editors seeing a script

- ☐ BBC management failed to make an examination of Mr Gilligan's notes of the interview with Dr Kelly

- ☐ There was a defect in the BBC's management system relating to the way complaints were investigated

- ☐ BBC governors failed to investigate Mr Gilligan's actions properly

BBC Chairman Gavyn Davies resigned following publication of a judicial inquiry that sharply criticized the BBC's role in events that led to the death of British weapons scientist David Kelly.[496] It continued to state, "Davies told his fellow governors at a hastily convened meeting, that "I have been brought up to believe that you cannot choose your own referee, and that the referee's decision is final. There is an honorable tradition in British public life that those charged with authority at the top of an organization should accept responsibility for what happens in that organization. I am therefore writing to the Prime Minister today to tender my resignation as Chairman of the BBC, with immediate effect."[497]"I consider that the editorial system which the BBC permitted was defective in that Mr. Gilligan was allowed to broadcast his report ... without editors having seen a script of what he's going to say and having considered whether it should be approved," Hutton said. The judge also found that the BBC radio report was "unfounded."

"The BBC's board of governors, chaired by Gavyn Davies, should have conducted more detailed investigations into Gilligan's report,"

---

[494] Ibid.

[495] Ibid.

[496] MEDIA NETWORK titled "BBC Chairman resigns in wake of Hutton Report" published 28th January 2004

[497] Ibid.

Hutton said. "If they had done this, they probably would have discovered that the notes did not support the allegation...and the governors should then have questioned whether it was right for the BBC to maintain that it was in the public interest to broadcast the allegation in Mr Gilligan's report." he said.[498]

What Gavyn Davies did was incredibly honorable. It allows the public to repose confidence in BBC. Everyone can make a mistake. However, it is the acknowledgement of that mistake and effort to learn from it, is what makes the difference in the final analysis. Electronic media in Pakistan can learn a thing or two from this approach.

It was realized, that with changing times, rules and regulations ought to be changed to suit the new competitive environment. The power of TV cannot be underplayed owing to its reach into our homes. Reputations can be made or destroyed.

The BBC Editorial Guidelines, revised to reflect the requirements of the Ofcom Code and updated for the first time in five years, were launched in June 2005. The Editorial Guidelines given on the BBC News website[499] is a comprehensive document divided into many sections:

1- ***BBC's Editorial Values***

2- Using the Guidelines(Introduction, Roles & Responsibilities, Principles & Practices, Editorial Justification, Guidance, Other Sources of Advice).

3- Accuracy (Introduction, Principles, Mandatory Referrals, Gathering Materials, Finding Contributors, Note Taking, Avoiding Misleading Audiences, Managing Online Content, Checking Programmes, Correcting Mistakes).

4- Impartiality(Introduction, Principles, Mandatory Referrals, Breadth & Diversity of Opinions, Controversial Subjects, News, Current Affairs & Factual Output, Drama, Entertainment & Culture, Contentious Views & Possible Offence, Consensus, Campaigns & Security).

---

[498] Ibid.

[499] http://www.bbc.co.uk/editorialguidelines/guidelines/

5- Harm and Offences (Introduction, Principles, Mandatory Referrals, Audience Expectations, Content Information, The Watershed & scheduling for TV, Radio & Online, Live Output, Language, Violence, Intimidation & Humiliation, Nudity, Sex Portrayal, Alcohol, Smoking, Solvent Abuse & Illegal Drugs, Suicide, Attempted Suicide, Self-Harm & Eating Disorders, Imitative Behaviour, Tragic Events, Hypnotism, Exorcism, the Occult & the Paranormal, Flashing Images, Strobing & Images of very Brief Duration, Acquired Programmes).

6- Fairness, Contributors and Consent(Introduction, Principles, Mandatory Referrals, Contributors & Informed Consent, Anonymity, Contributors, Access Agreements & Editorial Independence, Deception, Intimidation & Humiliation, Right to Reply, Refusals to take part, Portrayal of Real People in Drama, Safety & Welfare of Contributors).

7- Privacy(Introduction, Principles, Mandatory Referrals, Privacy & Consent, Secret Recording, Webcams, CCTV Third Party Webcams and Other Materials from Outside Sources, Doorstepping, Tag-Along Raids, Reporting Death, Suffering & Distress, Personal Information).

8- Reporting, Crime and Social Behavior(Introduction, Principles, Mandatory Referrals, Reporting Crime, Dealing With Criminals & Perpetrators of Anti-Social Behaviour, Dealing with Witnesses & Victims of Crime, Investigations into Crime & Anti-Social Behaviour).

9- Children and Young People as Contributors(Introduction, Principles, Mandatory Referrals, Safeguarding the Welfare of under 18s, Informed Consent for Children & young people, The Impact of a Contribution).

10- Politics,Public Policy & Polls(Introduction, Principles, Mandatory Referrals, Reporting UK Political Parties, Political Interviews & Contributions, Parliamentary broadcasting, Political Broadcasts, Elections, Opinion Polls , Surveys & Votes).

11- War, Terror and Emergencies(Introduction, Principles, Mandatory Referrals, Accuracy & Impartiality, Identifying Victims, Demonstrations, Disturbances & Riots, Staged Events, Threats & Hoaxes, Hijacking, Kidnapping, Taking & Sieges, National Security &

Counter Terrorism, Hostile Environments , High Risk Activities & Events).

12- Religion(Introduction, Principles, Mandatory Referrals, Practices).

13- Re-use and Reversioning(Introduction, Principles, Mandatory Referrals, General, Accuracy Issues, Fairness, Consent & Privacy Issues, Harm & Offence Issues, Syndication & Distribution on Non-BBC Channels & Spaces, Request for BBC Materials from Third Parties).

14- Editorial Integrity and Independence from External Interests(Introduction, Principles, Mandatory Referrals, Product Placement, Product Prominence, Free & Reduced Cost Facilities, Product & Services, Online Links to Third Party Websites, Logos & Credits Online, BBC Commercial Channels, Services & Products, Game Shows, Advertising & the BBC Brand).

15- Conflicts of Interests(Introduction, Principles, Mandatory Referrals, News & Current Affairs, Other Output Areas, External Activities, Declaration of Personal Interests, Personal Benefits, On-Air Talent , Commercial Advertising Promotional Activity & Endorsements, Talent or Agent –owned Independent Production Companies).

16- External Relationships and Funding(Introduction, Principles, Mandatory Referrals, Funding from BBC Commercial Services, the Open-University & Co-Productions, Co-Funding, Ticket Sales, Makeovers, Location & Production Initiatives, Public Value Partnerships , Sponsored BBC On-Air Events, Sponsored Awards, BBC Off-Air Events, Joint Editorial Initiatives & Events, Sponsored Third-Party Events, The National Lottery, Charities).

17- Interacting with our Audiences(Introduction, Principles, Mandatory Referrals, Competition, Voting, Awards , Pre-Recorded of Repeated Programmes, Prizes, The Interactivity Technical advice, Telephone Services, Game Shows & Quizzes, Talent Shows & Pogrammes Offering Life Changing Opportunities, Phone-in Programmes User Generated Content Online, Mobile Content, Games & Interactive TV).

18- The Law(Introduction, Principles, Mandatory Referrals, Defamation, Privacy, Contempt, Victims of Sexual Offences, Other Reporting

Restrictions, Children & the Law, Copyright & Other Intellectual Property Rights, Data Protection acts).

19- Accountability(Principles, BBC Trust, Ofcom, Feedback & Complaints).

Each section is detailed in a document in itself which may be too long and detailed for discussion here, however, salient features will be discussed in the next few pages. "In a perfect world, the BBC's Editorial Guidelines would consist of one sentence: use your own best judgment. No set of rules or guidelines can ever replace the need for producers, editors and managers to use the wisdom that comes from experience, commonsense and a clear set of editorial values when confronted with difficult editorial challenges." So writes the BBC's Director-General Mark Thompson in his foreword to the latest edition of the BBC Editorial Guidelines.[500]

***Chapter 1*** termed as ***BBC's Editorial Values*** are discussed here that form a base of the overall rules and regulations:

### 1.2.1 Trust

Trust is the foundation of the BBC: we are independent, impartial and honest. We are committed to achieving the highest standards of due accuracy and impartiality and strive to avoid knowingly and materially misleading our audiences.

### 1.2.2 Truth and Accuracy

We seek to establish the truth of what has happened and are committed to achieving due accuracy in all our output. Accuracy is not simply a matter of getting facts right; when necessary, we will weigh relevant facts and information to get at the truth. Our output, as appropriate to its subject and nature, will be well sourced, based on sound evidence, thoroughly tested and presented in clear, precise language. We will strive to be honest and open about what we don't know and avoid unfounded speculation.

### 1.2.3 Impartiality

Impartiality lies at the core of the BBC's commitment to its audiences. We will apply due impartiality to all our subject matter and

[500] BBC Editorial Guidelines 2005 LINK: http://rthk.hk/mediadigest/20050815_76_120574.html

will reflect a breadth and diversity of opinion across our output as a whole, over an appropriate period, so that no significant strand of thought is knowingly un reflected or under-represented. We will be fair and open-minded when examining evidence and weighing material facts.

### 1.2.4 Editorial Integrity and Independence

The BBC is independent of outside interests and arrangements that could undermine our editorial integrity. Our audiences should be confident that our decisions are not influenced by outside interests, political or commercial pressures, or any personal interests.

### 1.2.5 Harm and Offence

We aim to reflect the world as it is, including all aspects of the human experience and the realities of the natural world. But we balance our right to broadcast innovative and challenging content with our responsibility to protect the vulnerable from harm and avoid unjustifiable offence. We will be sensitive to, and keep in touch with, generally accepted standards as well as our audiences' expectations of our content, particularly in relation to the protection of children.

### 1.2.6 Serving the Public Interest

We seek to report stories of significance to our audiences. We will be rigorous in establishing the truth of the story and well informed when explaining it. Our specialist expertise will bring authority and analysis to the complex world in which we live. We will ask searching questions of those who hold public office and others who are accountable, and provide a comprehensive forum for public debate.

### 1.2.7 Fairness

Our output will be based on fairness, openness, honesty and straight dealing. Contributors and audiences will be treated with respect.

### 1.2.8 Privacy

We will respect privacy and will not infringe it without good reason, wherever in the world we are operating. Private behavior, information, correspondence and conversation will not be brought into the public domain unless there is a public interest that outweighs the expectation of privacy.

### 1.2.9 Children

We will always seek to safeguard the welfare of children and young people who contribute to and feature in our content, wherever in the world we operate. We will preserve their right to speak out and participate, while ensuring their dignity and their physical and emotional welfare is protected during the making and broadcast of our output. Content which might be unsuitable for children will be scheduled appropriately.

### 1.2.10 Transparency

We will be transparent about the nature and provenance of the content we offer online. Where appropriate, we will identify who has created it and will use labeling to help online users make informed decisions about the suitability of content for themselves and their children.

### 1.2.11 Accountability

We are accountable to our audiences and will deal fairly and openly with them. Their continuing trust in the BBC is a crucial part of our relationship with them. We will be open in acknowledging mistakes when they are made and encourage a culture of willingness to learn from them.

### 1.3.1

The BBC's Editorial Values, and the Editorial Guidelines, are rooted in the Royal Charter and the Agreement.

The **Royal Charter** guarantees the editorial independence of the BBC and sets out its Public Purposes. These are defined as:

sustaining citizenship and civil society

promoting education and learning

stimulating creativity and cultural excellence

representing the UK, its nations, regions and communities

bringing the UK to the world and the world to the UK

in promoting its other purposes, helping to deliver to the public the benefit of emerging communications technologies and services and, in addition, taking a leading role in the switchover to digital television.

**1.3.2**

The **Agreement accompanying the BBC Charter** specifies that we should do all we can "*to ensure that controversial subjects are treated with due accuracy and impartiality*" in our news and other output dealing with matters of public policy or political or industrial controversy. It also states that our output is forbidden from expressing the opinion of the BBC on current affairs or matters of public policy, other than broadcasting or the provision of online services. The Accuracy, Impartiality and Politics, Public Policy and Polls sections of the Editorial Guidelines incorporate the BBC Trust's code as required under Paragraph 44 (5) of the Agreement, giving guidance as to the rules to be observed in connection with Paragraphs 44(1) to 44(4) of the Agreement.

**1.3.3**

In addition, the **Agreement** forbids any BBC service funded by the licence fee or grant-in-aid from carrying advertising or sponsored programmes. To protect editorial integrity and independence, the BBC has drawn up its own **guidelines on standards for advertising and sponsorship** for its commercial television and online services.

***Explanation:***

The lines of guidance stated here are extremely pragmatic and geared to address the needs of broadcasting. All its points rest on the base of "Editorial Policy". Accuracy deemed as most important. However, BBC News understood that reliable sources alone can result in accuracy. However, this remains a distant goal for broadcasters who rely on untrained, unemployed locals with mobile phones as a requirement, as their representative for coverage, as practiced in Pakistan by many.

Being impartial , is the corner stone for practicing journalism. Truth cannot be achieved with a pre-conceived mindset that is not impartial. Angles, spins happen when there is lack of impartiality. But how does the viewer discern what's most true, or what's least untrue?

However, there have been criticism of BBC over "misleading" coverage of methadone report as late as September 2011.[501] BBC was drawn in a huge discussion over the plus and minuses of treating heroin addicts. The charity DrugScope has written to the corporation complaining about its coverage of a report by a rightwing think tank, the Centre for Policy Studies, that warned the prescription of the heroin substitute methadone was "entrenching addiction". The report, *Breaking the Habit*, said "prescribing addicts with methadone had been an expensive failure and claimed there were 320,000 problem drug users on benefits, costing the taxpayer billions of pounds."[502] BBC was sucked into this polarized debate . The think tank was accused of quoting incorrect figures. DrugScope gave a complaint in writing that BBC gave too much coverage to the report. The complaint accused BBC of having failed "to check the accuracy of claims made, particularly about the cost of treatment and methadone prescribing."[503]

BBC recognizes the need of the medium to be independent of pressures of any nature ie political, economic, political or of any other shade or color. Interestingly, this basic rule is missing from PEMRA Ordinance. Unless and until, this freedom is maintained BBC cannot be expected to play a positive role in the society.

Clause 24 of the Select Committee on BBC Charter Review states, "We recognize that a broadcaster of news and current events programmes will experience some level of political pressure. John Humphrys, one of the presenters of BBC Radio 4's Today Programme, told us that politicians try to negotiate before an interview and suggest that particular topics should be off limits. But he told us "I do not find anything improper in that at all" (Q 174). In the same way, Gavyn Davies, Chairman of the BBC from 2001 to 2004, stated that "In normal times pressure, insofar as it existed was with regular meetings with MPs or with government ministers. It never bothered me in the slightest; I took that as part of the process of gathering informed opinion about the impartiality of the BBC's output." (Q 357)[504]

---

[501] **Guardian UK** "BBC attacked over coverage of 'misleading' methadone report" dated 25th June 2011

[502] Ibid.

[503] Ibid.

[504] www.parliament.UK: Chapter 3:Safeguarding the Independence of BBC

There will be pressures on media around the world. How well it stands up to these pressures will determine the impartiality and honor of that medium of communication.

Let us bear in mind, this was before the Revised Editorial Guidelines in 2005 by BBC. Balance is another trait BBC has inculcated in its Editorial Policy. The policy to protect the vulnerable and the weak.

An excellent policy guideline is providing specialized experts to discuss a subject. And then to offer a forum for discussion on an issue. I am so glad to see this guideline, Who is an expert ? The answer is comprehensively given, one does not need to re-invent the wheel! ***Christine L.F Diesche**, PhD. and **Janet Caldwell** of **Oklahoma State University*** in their paper titled, "***Where are the Experts? Psychologists in Media***", write and I quote, "Before as assessment of the types of experts who appeared on television was made, a definition of 'expert' was constructed. According to Webster's New World Dictionary (1982) an 'expert' (noun) is someone is 'very skillful, having much training and knowledge in some special field' (p. 493). Similarly, Webster's Ninth New Collegiate Dictionary (1987) defines an expert as 'one with the special skill or knowledge representing mastery of a particular subject' (p. 437). By the first definition, a person would need to complete some type of schooling and/or apprenticeship (i.e., training) and also demonstrate knowledge of the field to become an expert. According to this definition, experts might include such people as electricians, college professors, hair stylists, and psychologists. By the second definition, a person would need to acquire mastery of a subject, which means the person possesses or displays great skill, knowledge, or technique in some work, profession, or science (Webster's Ninth New Collegiate Dictionary, 1987: Webster's New World Dictionary, 1982). While this second definition does not specify 'training' as a prerequisite for mastery, it does imply that the person is well-versed in the subject area of 'expertness'.

"Thus, in addition to someone who has received formalized training in a specific area of knowledge, someone with extensive life experience in a particular area might be considered an expert (e.g., a do-it-yourself home repair person) as might someone who engaged in a process of self-study (informal training) to learn about a particular subject (e.g., a self-taught classical pianist).

"Based on the above definitions of 'expert', one important point must be made: Just as a single case study is not accepted as representative of a population being studied, having had one life experience does not make someone an expert. A personal experience (e.g., having lived in Iowa) is the beginning of a foundation of knowledge that leads to expertness, but the experience in and of itself does not necessarily make the person an expert (one who can address the subject area with thoroughness that is representative of the subject area as a whole). Thus, for the purposes of this research those people who appear on television to discuss personal experiences cannot be considered experts unless they also possess or display extensive skill, knowledge, or technique in their particular subject area."[505]

It does not, according to the above, include as experts, people giving half- baked views to fill 24/7 slots whether or not they fall within the definition of "expert" of a subject. By the very virtue of putting in this clause BBC understands and supports the value of an expert opinion which is different and distinct from half-baked opinions of people with little or no knowledge on the subject matter.

Next is fairness and clean dealings. Not only with the audience but also its contributors. Another brilliant clause, "Private behavior, information, correspondence and conversation will not be brought into the public domain unless there is a public interest that outweighs the expectation of privacy." As a reporter, or a media person , he may come across information that maybe has nothing to do with the subject under question. Exposure can lead to violation of privacy to which every person has a right to. This, however, is a judgment call. Unless and until it is felt that the particular information will be in greater public interest, it will not outweigh right to privacy. This makes a lot of basic sense to me.

An extremely important element that must form part of the programme formatting is scheduling programmes according to both contents and timings to ensure the welfare and well- being of the children and the vulnerable. Programmes must be made keeping in mind the possible cascading effect on these segments of the society. So programmes which may not be advisable for kids are not to be aired at times that offer them likely exposure.

---

[505]Paper presented at the 101st annual convention of the American Psychological Association, Toronto, Ontario, Canada, August 1993

Another educated move is offering labeling content online. This makes it extremely easy for readers/viewers to determine whether or not they want to access the material, especially in case of suitability of material offered for children.

BBC makes itself as accountable as it makes others. It accepts the margin of being wrong itself, but then feels it will take cognizance of the mistakes and learn from them. This is a VERY correct and fair approach. Everyone should be accountable. No one is above mistakes or law. The important thing here is, to accept the mistake instead of making excuses and shying away from accepting responsibility for it. This is the honorable and right course of action to take. Half of the issue is resolved if a mistake is accepted. The latter half, when corrective measures are taken.

According to the Charter giving BBC broadcasting rights, it clearly entails impartiality in issues that are controversial. This will include coverage of facts, giving both sides to a picture, impartiality by the anchorperson/moderator, having an "expert" for views on the subject matter to project an impartial view helping in formation of public opinion.

If you visit the BBC website, each point discussed above is comprehensively covered by breaking it down in a "chapter" offering a detailed guideline of its editorial policy. Let us focus on the main feature, the ground-laying operative principles:

### *Some of BBC's ground-laying, operative principles*

#### Accuracy:

Emphasis on gathering first- hand information as first priority. BBC to its credit believes in cross checking, not relying on one source only. If one source is to be relied on, the name-on-record-source is preferred. This makes the story clean and above board. If recording is inhibiting for source, detailed notes must be made. Any material shared needs close scrutiny to ensure it is accurate , especially if there is a doubt that it is furnished by a vested interest lobby. Special care must be exercised when researching on internet. A check must be made to ensure its genuine. Any material from a Third Party must only be relied upon if it can be substantiated by a BBC correspondent or if it is attributed to a reputable news agency. Credentials of contributors must be checked and vetted out. Audiences must not be misled, all sources must be disclosed as well as credentials of significant contributors. If any source information has to be with—held, all steps must be taken to protect their identity, but, audience must not be misled to the nature of the status of the source.

**Impartiality:**

Open mindedness in evaluating all evidence available is a must. "Breadth and diversity of opinion may require not just a political and cultural range, but, on occasions, reflection of the variations between urban and rural, older and younger, poorer and wealthier, the innovative and the status quo, etc. It may involve exploration of perspectives in different communities, interest groups and geographic areas." [506] In dealing with a "controversial subject" described at length, BBC requires a wide range of views, with due weightage and prominence when controversy is active. A clear line is laid down here ie opinion must be distinguished firmly from facts. In any coverage regarding public policy, culture, controversial subjects; "services should normally aim to reflect a broad range of the available perspectives over time." Subjects like elections, referendums need special handling to sensitivities.

**Harm & Offence:**

Strong language is clearly defined, and BBC understands the impact of the same on people from different ethnic , religious groups and those belonging to different age groups etc. Interestingly, though BBC states strong language to *include;* sexual swearwords, terms of racist or ethnic abuse, terms of sexual and sexist abuse or abuse referring to sexuality, pejorative terms relating to illness or disabilities, casual or derogatory use of holy names or religious words and especially in combination with other strong language. PEMRA does not lay out the meaning and parameters in which to interpret words like "obscene or indecent or is likely to deprave, corrupt or injure the public morality" —words like these are always subjective in nature and open to different interpretations. BBC states further, "Our audiences, particularly children, can be frightened or distressed by the portrayal of both real and fictional violence. We should make very careful judgments when we plan to include violence in our output; there is increasing public concern about violence in society in general and as portrayed in the media, both in factual and fictional content. Consideration should be given to the editorial justification for any depiction of violence, and violent content should normally be clearly

---

[506] http://www.bbc.co.uk/editorialguidelines/page/guidelines-impartiality-breadth-diversity-opinion/

signposted. When real life violence, or its aftermath, is shown on television or reported on radio and online we need to strike a balance between the demands of accuracy and the dangers of desensitization or unjustified distress. There are very few circumstances in which it is justified to broadcast the moment of death. BBC does not believe in humiliating an individual, a group , race or an institution. It believes it giving respect." The guideline states, "Some content can be cruel but unduly intimidatory, humiliating, intrusive, aggressive or derogatory remarks aimed at real people (as opposed to fictional characters or historic figures) must not be celebrated for the purposes of entertainment. Care should be taken that such comments and the tone in which they are delivered are proportionate to their target." Bravo!

**Reporting Crime & Anti-Social Behavior:**

"Any proposal to interview a criminal active in, or wanted in, the UK must be referred to Director Editorial Policy and Standards. Interviews should only proceed if they are clearly editorially justified, for example by eliciting important information or insight." If any interview is taken, it must not be done in a way to cause potential distress to the relatives. Interviews with active criminals and/or convicted criminals must not glamourize the wrong act, celebrate flouting of a judicial process or give the details of a crime in such details that it makes it easy to be copied . Interviewing witnesses to a crime, BBC takes extra precautions so no contempt of court is committed. The BBC Editorial Policy further states, "Witnesses should not normally be interviewed about their evidence once proceedings are under way and until the verdict has been reached. Any proposal to do so must be referred to Programme Legal Advice and Editorial Policy. Witnesses sometimes claim to have been coached by a journalist. To protect ourselves against any unfair accusation and, with the knowledge of the interviewee, we should record and keep the whole interview, including any pauses, interruptions, prompting, repeat questions, or re-takes."

Do our channels have legal advisers to refer to in case of a programme of a sensitive nature to avoid gaffes that may also lead to legal implications?

**War, Terror & Emergencies:**

Accuracy and impartiality must be maintained at all cost. In case of war reporting or national/international emergencies, disasters etc, information quoted must be from the most reliable source if numbers of casualties (in case of war or accidents) differ. Sources must be stated to bring authenticity to the news. "When reporting demonstrations, disturbances and similar events, we should treat estimates of involvement with due skepticism, report wide disparities and name the sources of the figures. We aim to offer a comprehensive and impartial view of events. When it is difficult for reporters located on one side of a confrontation to form a clear overall view, their material should be put into a wider context for broadcast."

## Conflicts of Interest:

"News and current affairs output may at any time deal with any issue, cause, organization or individual and there must be no doubt over the integrity and objectivity of editorial teams. For this reason, there are specific constraints on those working in BBC News and Current Affairs, Global News and news output in the Nations. Staff, correspondents and free-lances primarily known as BBC news presenters or reporters are affected by these constraints." It further states, "*The onus is on the journalist, content producer or on-air talent to let the BBC know if they (or, in certain circumstances, their family or close personal contacts) have any outside interests which could be perceived as a conflict of interest.*"An extremely professional and honorable approach indeed. Any interest of a personal nature regarding an issue, is bound to have an impact on the nature of the coverage.

## Law:

BBC realizes that to bring news it might at some point be in conflict with a law. BBC in such a situation will see its impact on BBC, its impact on viewers, its effect on BBC future coverage of the region. Broadcasters need to have a good back up to what they claim to avoid defamation suit. "Contempt can take many forms but the most serious for the BBC is publication of prejudicial material when legal proceedings are said to be 'active'." On privacy, the policy states, " If there is a reasonable expectation of privacy, the court will seek to balance the individual's right to privacy against the media's right to freedom of expression. When broadcasting a story which contains private information, each piece of private information will need to be considered separately. If private information is conveyed by pictures, these will be subjected to special scrutiny."

## Accountability:

BBC holds itself accountable and answerable to public scrutiny. BBC expresses its willingness to accept mistakes and learn from them. BBC's online presence provides proper reporting to public about complaints received and actions taken.

## *In a Nutshell:*

I have tried to convey the essence of BBC policy as concisely as possible –what stands out throughout the Editorial Guidelines is an understanding of the medium and a successful effort to provide "custom made" set of rules that does not hide behind big sounding words, but creates guidelines that trickle down to the roots, covering every aspect that electronic media faces or is likely to face. It cuts through the flak to reach each and every area of its operation to provide crystal clear direction to its employees. What more can an Editorial Policy do?

## *Coverage of Issues by BBC:*

In spite of this, BBC has been criticized on different grounds. I would like to discuss two cases here:

BBC's "Frozen Planet" series is admittedly the most breathtaking series in the subject of natural history(2011). Whether it is the photography or the crew's stupendous efforts to complement the powerful commentary of Sir David Attenborough, the series are awesome to say the least. It was the final part of the series that came under fire by ***Chritopher Booker***[507] he says, "The BBC is committed by its charter to report with 'accuracy and impartiality'. Yet on climate change, it has adopted a clear 'party line', which has run through almost every aspect of its broadcasting........Sir David used the awesome shots of the frozen polar wastes to hammer home his belief that the world is facing disaster from man-made global warming. No one can doubt the passion of his belief. But in putting across his apocalyptic message so forcefully, too many important questions on this hugely important subject were last night neither asked nor answered."[508] Booker goes on to outline how the BBC has not maintained an impartial stance on the issue of global warming.

---

[507] 8th December 2011 MailOnline , titled: "The BBC and an inconvenient change about climate change"
[508] Ibid

The second incident where BBC has been criticized is for the Queen's Diamond Jubilee river pageant. The reason for attracting the ire was "Camera angles and sound quality were also said to have been not up to scratch," while a mistaken description of the Queen as 'HRH' - rather than 'Her Majesty.'[509] Comedian Stephen Fry - host of the BBC panel show QI - led a chorus of disgruntlement on Twitter, branding the coverage as "mind-numbingly tedious."[510]

But the BBC defended its coverage. A spokesman said: "We're very proud of the quality and breadth of the BBC's coverage of this extraordinary event."[511]

In spite of the criticism leveled against BBC , it has done much better generally in discharging its duties than its contemporaries elsewhere. One example of job done better is an internal review BBC conducted in 2004 focused on Palestinian-Israeli conflict. The contents of the ***Balen Report*** directed by Malcolm Balen, was not released for public knowledge. BBC spent £250,000 for a very successful averting of legal efforts to get the report published. It was eventually released publically in its coverage of the "Arab Spring" commissioned by BBC Trust. [512]

BBC has understood the need of the electronic medium and devised policies aimed to serve the nature of this medium best—besides following them. Otherwise, rules without implementation are not worth the piece of paper they are written on.

## *Concluding Comments*

Whereas PEMRA has given some outlines and a Code of Conduct to broadcast media, the Editorial Policy that is the touchstone of broadcasting houses, should have been submitted to PEMRA by all channels— a detailed line of coverage policy guideline covering all aspect of coverage. If it has, the same is not carried by the websites of the broadcasting houses websites I visited. If there is an Editorial Policy, it

[509] The Telegraph UK 3rd June 2012 titled "BBC under fire over 'lamentable' Jubilee coverage"
[510] Ibid.
[511] Ibid.
[512] Op-Ed: BBC Exposes its Middle East Bias? By Simon Plosker on 2nd July 2012 *"HONEST REPORTING"* (Defending Israel from Media Bias)

must be on the SITE of every channel. "Local channels do not have an editorial policy," says ***Dr Mehdi Hasan***.[513]

Like BBC News, who has made a clear map flagged by its Editorial Policy, likewise TV channels in Pakistan too, need to chart out their editorial policies for clear cut guideline to avoid blunders, as a channel or by any of its staff member.

If we compare the PEMRA Ordinances 2002 and Amendments 2007, along with the Code of Conduct with the BBC rules and regulation, we can see a difference. One is lack of shared Editorial Policy by channels, second is, guidelines need to be developed that filter down into working operational guidelines for all and discussed at some length above. We do not need to re-invent the wheel. Simply use the best one available!

Media, to work effectively, must charter a navigation map to determine the course of direction for itself and its employees.

[513] Telephone conversation on 7th July 2012

# Chapter VIII

## Social Media

A mention of social media becomes important as the use of computer and networking between people over internet is increasing. This chapter briefly touches upon this vehicle of communication that cannot go unaddressed. Social media is a collection of online platforms and tools that people use to share content, profiles, opinions, insights, experiences, perspectives and media itself, facilitating conversations and interactions online between groups of people.

***Bryan Eisenberg***, author of "*Waiting for your Cat to Bark*" defines social media as, "We are still trying to come to terms with the definition of social media. To start I think we should look at what it is not. The biggest problem I have with the term 'social media' is that it isn't media in the traditional sense. Twitter, Facebook, LinkedIn, and all the others I don't have the word count to mention aren't media; they are platforms for interaction and networking. All the traditional media — print, broadcast, search, and so on — provide platforms for delivery of ads near and around relevant content. Social media are platforms for interaction and relationships, not content and ads."[514]

***About.com*** defines it as, " Social media includes the various online technology tools that enable people to communicate easily via the internet to share information and resources. Social media can include text, audio, video, images, podcasts, and other multimedia communications."[515]

---

[514] Heidi Cohen: 30 Social Media Definitions: http://heidicohen.com/social-media-definition/

[515] Social Media Definition: http://jobsearch.about.com/od/networking/g/socialmedia.htm

Social Media has changed the face of politics. ***Bambi Turner,*** in her piece[516] says, "Many argue that without the Internet, Obama never would have won his party's nomination, much less the presidency. When he entered the race in February 2007, the then-46-year-old Illinois senator had spent very little time in Washington and was considered a long-shot candidate by many.

" However, the Obama campaign's deft use of technology allowed this relatively young and unknown candidate to connect with millions of voters via social media, including Facebook, Twitter and his own campaign Web site. Perhaps even more significant, the Internet helped the Obama campaign break down many of the financial barriers which are commonly associated with an upstart presidential campaign. For example, people spent more than 14.5 million hours watching official videos that Obama staff placed on YouTube. To run these videos on television for the same amount of time would cost an estimated $47 million [source: Cain Miller]. Internet technology also revolutionized campaign fundraising by making it easy for anyone to donate small amounts, which added up to one of the best-financed campaigns in history. By the time of the election in 2008, Barack Obama's campaign raised more than $600 million [source: Stirland]." [517]

## ***Problems with Social Media***

The biggest issue, I have seen on Twitter, my favorite forum, is that false information can spread like fire racing through a dry forest. Many users of both Twitter and Face book can be careless about first verifying a news before putting it on board. Once on board, other users are at a liberty to "share" it (as in the case of face book) or "retweet" (as in case of Twitter).

According to ***Peter Jackson,*** BBC News,[518]riots in England spread, as did disinformation about them fuelled by social networking sites like Twitter. He says in his piece, "As the rioting moved to other parts of London and England, inaccurate - at times inflammatory - information began appearing on social media sites."[519] People tend to comment, spread

[516] "How has internet changed politics?" on Curiosity.com LINK: http://curiosity.discovery.com/question/how-has-internet-changed-politics

[517] Ibid.

[518] "England Riots Dangers behind false rumors" published 12th August 2011 BBC News

[519] Ibid.

information, sending messages "off the hip" without research and any verification.

When on net, people are less sensitive when they are making comments on others. Many times, they do not know each other personally, it is easy therefore, to be discourteous giving rise to a culture of intolerance. No doubt, internet brings information that is way beyond what the mainstream media offers. Having said that, certain standards of journalism and verification of news is associated with mainstream media. Unfortunately, in certain cases unscrupulous people, including some bloggers, with or without fake IDs, can spread venom, disinformation and arguments based on pure disinformation without any fear of any consequences whatsoever.

Another concern is, with social media; stalking becomes easier. All it takes is "adding" them or "following" them. "Trolls" have become a reality. They select their victims to throw insults at. They may be operating independently or supporters of a political party. Since the interaction is not face-to-face these trolls do not feel the need to adhere to the rules of engagement. "One Web site breaks trolls into categories: the hater, the moral crusader, the debunker, the defender. But trolls might not retain those qualities in real life. It's just that the Internet's anonymity makes it impossible for them to resist spewing vitriol from the protective cave of cyberspace. Psychologists call it the 'disinhibition effect,' in which 'the frequency of self-interested unethical behavior increases among anonymous people... the combination of anonymity and an audience brings out the absolute worst in people."[520] The piece further states, "Only a psychotic person, incapable of empathy, or someone perpetually engulfed by rage, would say such things in public. But people feel alone when they're typing on a computer, even if they're in a public 'place,' -- a chat room, on Facebook or within the comments section of an article. MIT professor Sherry Turkle calls this 'being alone together'; the Internet causes 'emotional dislocation', so we forget about the together part."

The positive side to these forums is increased social activism. Those who do not have a say in the mainstream media can have their voice heard. However, in case of Face Book, pictures posted are exposed and may be misused. I personally know of cases where, in case of young girls, the pictures were taken, photo shopped and used on porn sites. One needs

[520] Lisa Selin Davis for AlterNet on 31st July 2012 titled, "Why Online Comments are so Toxic".

to exercise extreme caution in whom we are taking on- board as a virtual friend.

Excessive networking can lead to lack of social interaction in reality, the net itself becomes their reality. In a research conducted in Germany, " more than 700,000 people spend around 35 hours per week on the Internet, which is accepted as a symptom of 'Internet addiction'. It was underlined in that research that these people have difficulty in making friends, and they see the Internet as a method for socialization."[521] Social media offers both advantages and disadvantages.

***Increasing Power of Social Media***

That it is a powerful medium of communication, of this there is no doubt. The world first learnt of Osama Bin Laden's compound being attacked via the Twitter. Without really realizing what he was reporting , ***Sohaib Akhtar*** through his Twitter ID ***@ReallyVirtual***, actually live-tweeted the raid that led to the killing of bin Laden. Sohaib is an IT Consultant, based in Islamabad. He talked about helicopters hovering around 1AM in Abbotabad—a rarity, no doubt that's why it caught his attention. It was not till later, when news broke of bin Laden's killing, that he must have realized, he had reported a top secret operation. After the news broke, he tweeted, "Uh oh, now I'm the guy who live blogged the Osama raid without knowing it."

The second big news that broke via Twitter was the resignation of Ambassador of Pakistan to USA; Hussain Haqqani as a result of what has come to be known as *Memogate Scandal*. In news published by **Asia Society,** [522] " Pakistan's Ambassador to the United States Husain Haqqani announced from his Twitter account (@husainhaqqani) this morning that he asked Prime Minster Yousaf Raza Gillani to accept his resignation. The resignation has been accepted." The same piece states, "Following the tweet of his resignation as Ambassador, a position he had held since 2008, Haqqani followed with the message:

---

[521] Social Media and Social Problems published 30th October 2011 LINK: http://www.sundayszaman.com/sunday/newsDetail_getNewsById.action?newsId=261353

[522] Memogate: Pakistan's Ambassador to the US resigns, Twitter Reacts published on Asia Society on 22nd November 2011 by Annie Ali Khan

*I have much to contribute to building a new Pakistan free of bigotry & intolerance. Will focus energies on that."*[523]

The importance and impact of social media was discussed in an interesting TV programme aired with host ***Kashif Abbasi*** titled "*Off the Record*" dated March 29th2012,Thursday, [524] on ***ARYNEWS.*** The show link available gives it the headline, "*$50 million from America to Pakistan media.*" Kashif Abbasi stated that $50 million was allocated for Pakistan media by the US. Americans are holding discussions with various channels to negotiate how the Pakistan media can help be more positive towards USA and how the channels will be duly compensated for the efforts. The discussion revolved around whether the funds were to be given out to the media to be more pro-American and thereby change the perception of the masses towards US to a more positive tone. His guests were Talat Hussain(Senior Journalist), Ansar Abbasi(Analyst) and Rauf Klasra (Analyst).The programme showed a video clip of Hilary Clinton saying, " We are in an information war, and we are losing that war..." Reference to the programme is being shared here because of a comment on social media made in the programme by Ansar Abbasi, at the onset. His comments were words to the effect that one can see certain elements there showing strong "enmity", where it comes to anything that is related to Pakistan, Islam, or the Armed Forces.[525] The people there, he said, " speak with a desire to diminish the stature of the institutions."

Such like views can and will impact, at least a certain segment of public opinion. Social media make social movements possible. Online petitions are a new tactic of bringing pressure on to concerned authorities. "'We are moving from a gatekeeper paradigm to a networking paradigm in journalism. The newsroom will remain the focal point for broadcast and accountability, but this concept of networked journalism will continue to grow," predicted Amadou Mahtar Ba, director of the African Media Initiative."[526]

The same piece shares another opinion, "In fact, half the world's population does not have computers or Internet access," said Mark

---

[523] Ibid.

[524] LINK: http://www.pakistanherald.com/program/50-million-from-America-to-Pakistani-media-March-29-2012-Kashif-Abbasi-10166

[525] Ibid.

[526] Eudevdays.eu : 'NEW MEDIA ARE POWERFUL .BUT WHAT ABOUT ACCOUNTABILITY AND ACCESS? LINK: http://www.eudevdays.eu/2011forum/news/articles/new-media-are-powerful-what-about-accountability-and-access

Wilson, executive director of Panos London. "While we know that social media has a phenomenal capacity for organization and the dissemination of information we need some perspective," he cautioned. "Democracy 3.0 sounds fantastic, but poor and marginalized communities are outside of this world."[527]

An article was carried by ***Foreign Affairs,*** excerpt of which I share here, "On January 17, 2001, during the impeachment trial of Philippines President Joseph Estrada, loyalists in the Philippines Congress voted to set aside key evidence against him. Less than two hours after the decision was announced, thousands of Filipinos, angry that their corrupt president might be let off the hook, converged on Epifanio de los Santos Avenue, a major crossroads in Manila. The protest was arranged, in part, by forwarded text messages reading, "Go 2 EDSA. Wear blk." The crowd quickly swelled, and in the next few days, over a million people arrived, choking traffic in downtown Manila. The public's ability to coordinate such a massive and rapid response -- close to seven million text messages were sent that week -- so alarmed the country's legislators that they reversed course and allowed the evidence to be presented. Estrada's fate was sealed; by January 20, he was gone. The event marked the first time that social media had helped force out a national leader. Estrada himself blamed 'the text-messaging generation' for his downfall."

We have seen, the effect of social media had led to revolutions. Political revolutions in Libya, Egypt, Tunisia— that have changed the face of the nation's politics forever. ***Aidan White,*** [528] in his article, commenting on social media, states, " This new generation of journalists comes equipped with technical know-how and social networking skills but many of them remain ignorant about why journalism is important for democracy."[529] There is a threat in Pakistan, he feels, where both the state and non-state actors apply political pressure.

"Since the rise of the Internet in the early 1990s, the world's networked population has grown from the low millions to the low billions. Over the same period, social media has become a fact of life for civil society worldwide, involving many actors – ordinary citizens, activists, nongovernmental organizations, telecommunications firms, software providers, governments. This raises an obvious question for the US

---

[527] Ibid.

[528] The writer is former general secretary of the International Federation of Journalists and currently director of the Ethical Journalism Network.

[529] Published in Express Tribune 23rd July 2012 , titled, "Journalism & Social Media"

government: How does the ubiquity of social media affect US interests, and how should US policy respond to it?

"As the communications landscape gets denser, more complex, and more participatory, the networked population is gaining greater access to information, more opportunities to engage in public speech, and an enhanced ability to undertake collective action. In the political arena, as the protests in Manila demonstrated, these increased freedoms can help loosely coordinated publics' demand change..."[530]

***The Big Question: Can Social Media be held accountable?***

Ironic though this may sound, blocking a SITE(ie Face Book, Twitter etc) has been the only tactic used by authorities to check social media. Social networking SITES have often been blocked by different governments at various times for certain periods. By many countries.

According to AFP, "Access to social networking site Facebook was cut in the Libyan capital on Friday and access to the Internet was intermittent amid deadly anti-regime protests, computer users reported. From early evening it was impossible to access the popular Facebook site, and connections to other sites were either very slow or not possible, they said. The state of Internet connections in the rest of the country was not known.

"Al Jazeera also mentions Facebook explicitly, but only says that specific opposition group pages have been blocked. At the same time, it notes that its website Aljazeera.net throws up an error when accessed from Libya."[531]

In an interview with ***Yasmin Alem*** posted 15th February 2012 in ***The Iranian Primer***, "With less than three weeks to parliamentary elections, the Iranian authorities are choking internet access in Iran. Social networking sites and international news sites have either been blocked or the connection is so slow that they are difficult to access.

"Email providers such as Yahoo, Gmail and MSN have been cut off sporadically, as have many sites with secure coding (https) that protects users from third-parties accessing their information. All of these disruptions have increased since the beginning of February."

---

[530] By Clay Shirky January/February 2011

[531] ZDNet: Libya Blocks access to Face Book ,Al Jazeera , others. By Emil protalinski

There have been many occasions that governments by different countries have imposed restrictions—owing to want of any regulation in place.

### *Concluding Comments*

It is a choice we have today—can we self -regulate and be responsible in our networking OR face regulations? The choice may be ours today. It may not be a choice anymore tomorrow.

Saudi Arabia is already considering a law against insulting Islam. [532] 'The potential regulations come five months after a Saudi blogger and columnist Hamza Kashgari, 23, was arrested for tweeting comments deemed as insulting the Prophet Mohammad. Kashgari said there were things he liked and disliked about him.

"Within the next two months the Shura Council will reveal the outcome of study on the regulations to combat the criticism of the basic tenets of Islamic sharia," unnamed sources with knowledge of the matter told al-Watan, adding that there could be "severe punishments" for violators."[533]

Twitter has suspended the account of a British newspaper's Los Angeles correspondent following, "his acerbic reporting of NBC's coverage of the Olympics". The news, states further, "The social media network hummed with the indignation of thousands of its users after the Twitter feed of Guy Adams of the Independent disappeared. The paper's deputy editor, Archie Bland, confirmed the suspension, calling it 'heavy-handed'. NBC said it had complained to Twitter after Adams published the email address of one of its senior bosses. "We filed a complaint with Twitter because a user tweeted the personal information of one of our executives." According to Twitter, this is a violation of their privacy policy. Twitter alone levies discipline. "Rachael Horwitz, a spokeswoman for the San Francisco-based firm, confirmed that it does not 'actively monitor' users' accounts, and added that it was company policy not to comment on individual users. NBC acted after Adams published a tweet that included the email address of Gary Zenkel, the president of NBC Olympics, encouraging people to complain to him about the TV network's delayed broadcast of the opening ceremony of the Games. Twitter's terms and

[532] Reuters: "Saudi Arab considers law against insulting Islam" 15th July 2012
[533] Ibid.

conditions state that users must not post private email addresses, unless they are already available on the internet. Adams said the email was not a private one but a corporate account, and that Zenkel's address is identical in form to thousands of other NBC employees."[534]

In another very recent case, "The Manchester United defender Rio Ferdinand has been charged with improper conduct over comments he posted on Twitter, the Football Association has announced."[535]

"The allegation is that the player acted in a way which was improper and/or bought the game into disrepute by making comments which included a reference to ethnic origin and/or colour and/or race," the FA said in its statement."[536]

If we fail in being socially responsible on the social media—we may face regulations of various natures. Of course we can always raise a hue and cry that our freedom of expression has been violated. As I repeatedly state, and cannot emphasize enough, with freedom of expression comes responsibility. The more the freedom, the more the responsibility.

---

[534] The Guardian UK titled, "Twitter suspends British journalist critical of NBC;s Olympic coverage" by Ed Pilkington published 30th July 2012

[535] The Guardian UK titled, "Manchester United's Rio Ferdinand charged by FA over Twitter comments" published 30th July 2012

[536] Ibid.

# Chapter IX

## *Social Responsibility of Media*

With the development of time, media too, has developed. Not only technically, but also in terms of the "number of gates" of communication.

The role of "gate keeping of media" is of extreme importance in the world of global village we live in today. However, this role is gradually and surely being eroded in a world of ferocious competition.

The importance of the role of press in the conceptualization of ideas and the subsequent duty of the press as a "gate keeper" cannot be understated. In post-war America, the theory of "Social Responsibility" was developed post-war America underwent many changes on economic, political and social fronts. "Peterson sought to reconcile the growing centralization of ownership and decreasing competition in the printed press, the rise of an inherently centralized and expensive electronic media, as well as social science research and real world events which raised concerns regarding the stability of democratic systems and the civic capacity of democratic citizens"(Berelson, 1952; Schumpeter, 1942). In essence, the social responsibility theory conceded the inevitability of both a centralized, privately owned media and of a less-than-engaged public, and transferred much of the civic responsibility of the latter to a new class of information elites. The Theory of Social Responsibly of Media is universally accepted by nations around the world, today.

The responsibility of the media at the end of the day is towards the society. Media must determine the impact of the news it seeks to share with the public. The cascading effect of the news/views shared can have a positive or a negative impact on the public exposed to the media. The degree to which public opinion is actually shaped by the outcome of this struggle has been explored by a generation of scholars. Employing a wide variety of increasingly sophisticated empirical methods, mainstream political communications researchers have found powerful and convincing evidence that the media, acting as gatekeepers, exercise significant influence on public opinion.

What we face today, is not one "traditional" media gate through which information can be transmitted. The media environment today offers many "media gates" that includes not only the traditional press(newspapers and magazines) , but also TV, the biggest blockbuster medium of communication, in countries with low literacy rates, TV, and to some degree radio, offer a window to the world that everyone, can look through. TV offers many options of channels, more often than not, guided by the goal of earning profit. The growing impact of computers ie mails, social forums like Face Book and Twitter cannot be undermined. Newspapers have online editions therefore, geographical boundaries in transmission of news and views has lost their importance. Language plays a huge role here in attracting audiences. New York Times (Blog Section) launched this section in Chinese language a few months ago. A brilliant move in breaking down the communication barrier owing to language. This point of interaction constitutes the gate through which information passes to the public. Blogs, are a forum of growing information. Often, angles that are inadvertently or deliberately overlooked by the mainstream media are covered by the social media. An example is the "Memogate" scandal. Overlooked initially by the mainstream media, it was brought to prominence by the social media. Social media, blogs etc unfettered by traditional rules of engagement, can be instrumental in bringing attention to issues that may be presented in a distorted manner—or in a forthcoming way based on truth—though truth too, remains a subjective word. It really depends on who wields the pen—or in this case; the keyboard. The new media environment has done away with the traditional media lines, in the world of communication we knew before. The audience no longer remains "disengaged" as envisaged by Peterson way back in 1956. Researchers must mould their research according to this new media environment, or, their research will fail to convey the bigger picture.

The division of media organizations into separate news, entertainment, and sports divisions, while still in place, have become more porous. Journalists, management executives, public officials, and entertainers develop celebrity identities that transcend any specific genre and allow them to move freely between these different genres. The distinction between "fact" and opinion or analysis is much less clearly identified by simple rules such as where it appears, who is saying it, or how it is labeled. Public affairs "time slots" have become overwhelmed by the range of options open to citizens: traditional news can be gotten any time of the day through cable or the world wide web, or equally ignored at any time of the day. This makes it important for regulations, rules to be followed by the custodians of the "gate keepers."[537]

We can divide rules for broadcast media and print media in Pakistan. However, the main crux should be Editorial Policy of any medium of communication. In Pakistan this is decided by the owner of the medium. The entire approach lacks professionalism. The Editorial Policy must be based on impartiality, fairness, accuracy editorial integrity. Ingredients largely missing in the world of Pakistan Media.

However, before we go in a detailed discussion of the concept of social responsibility of media—success or failure, let us first examine the *theories of press.*

There are four theories of Press/Media:

Authoritarian Theory

Libertarian Theory

Social Responsibility Theory

Soviet Media Theory

In their book, "Four Theories of the Press", Fred Siebert, Theodore Peterson and Wilbur Schramm give the concepts of the "normative theories of the press". The word, "Normative Theory" found introduction in USA in times when the cold war between US and Russia peaked. For the reason of its origin, these theories are also known as the western theories of the press. A Normative Theory presents the most ideal method whereby press can be "controlled" and it's workings operated by various segments ie the government, leader, public, authority. These four theories have their origin in different sources. These theories(unfortunately) focus less on the equation between the press and the public and more on the relationship between the government and the press. They look into the

[537] Peterson 1956

question of the ownership of media and on who operates its control button.

## *Authoritarian Theory:*

As the term itself explains, the Authoritarian are there, in form of governing elites, in form of certain authorities, in form of powerful individuals who influence and control the media. Licenses are awarded by these authorities to the media, certain conditions of compliance to rules is required failing which license can be cancelled. Authoritarianism to some degree is deemed necessary to check the otherwise unbridled power of the media, it allows a leverage to the Authority to have some control over the media. In case of the media violating the principles or laws laid down by the license giving authority, there can be punishments in form of fines, or outright revocation of the license. This check is aimed to protect the public from harmful news as deemed by the Authority. Towards this end, *censorship* is a tool often used. Censorship is used to protect the rulers usually to prevent a "media trial" on sensitive issues that can create a pressure on the authorities—without taking in cognizance(at times) of the facts and legalities of issues involved.

Censorship may be defined as controlling the information that is to be made available to the public at large. Censorship has more often than not, been practiced by dictatorships. It is not necessary that censorship has to come from external forces. It can be in the form of self -regulation as well. Determination by the media itself, to analyze the impact of a news on the society. This is a judgment call. Media must rise above "Me First" tendency here in breaking a news, which may well be less than accurate as we have studied in the last chapter.

Different countries around the world have different acceptable rules culturally, morally, in terms of norms and religion. Therefore the kinds of censorship according may differ. The most acceptable kind of censorship is in terms of pornographic material. It looks towards controlling human behavior to acceptable behavior norms. Censors can be on different fronts ie moral censor, political censor, military censor, corporate censor being the main ones.

Moral censorship will mean to be suppressing materials that may be considered offensive by the public. This is not only the most known form of censorship but can raise questions on the common acceptance by public itself as to what is morally incorrect. It can also be different at different times in the same society. During the times of General Zia-ul-Haq as President, women appearing on PTV screen were supposed to cover their heads with a duppata(head scarf). This was deemed mandatory. Today not only we do not see this as a mandatory requirement, we see girls, women in western dresses too.

Political censorship means when any political party or the government refrains from sharing any information which it does not want to be aware of for reasons of criticism or the news being sensitive in people nature. An interesting tactic these days in vogue by the authorities is to either give out disinformation on another issue or provoke attention elsewhere to distract attention.

Another example of Authoritarian Theory is the King. Whatever the King does may not be challenged by anyone. "*The French king Louis XIV was concentrated in his person parliamentary, law making and judicial power. He was the authority of Supreme Court as well as he can condemn a men to death penalty without any rights appeal.*"[538]

Dictatorship is another example. Press in World War II were controlled by the world's two known dictators; Mussolini and Hitler. No one dared question what information was given by them.

More recently, some countries blocked ***wikileaks*** from their websites. Basically because it defied censorship and released information that has changed the face of international relations. Wikileaks site was launched in 2006 under the Sunshine Press Organizations. Julian Assange, is the founder, editor-in-chief and director, being an Australian Internal Activist. Interestingly, Australia was one of the countries that blocked wikileaks. It has put wikileaks on its banned list in May 2009. According to **ZDNet**[539] this was done because the pages linked to websites on Denmark's blacklist. ACMA later confirmed wikileaks is off the blacklist.

Interestingly, Pervez Musharraf took over power from Nawaz Sharif, the PML-N head and the then Prime Minister in 1999. Since its inception in 1947 and many governments that have come and gone in Pakistan- not one, thought of making electronic media independent. It took a "dictator"

---

[538] LINK: http://communicationtheory.org/authoritarian-theory/

[539] "WikilEaks removed from ACMAblacklist" Nov 29th 2010, by Josh Taylor

Musharraf who allowed private television channels, followed by radio stations. A phenomenon that has changed forever the face of communication in Pakistan.

## *Libertarian Theory:*

This theory originates from the 16th century in Europe. The libertarians oppose the authoritarians. They believe in no censorship, no control of any kind. Any authority and any control whatsoever. It believes in greater share to individualism and less share to the government. The supporters of the theory state that a "free media" allows people to have a fair picture of the issues—but is this true? If media is not controlled by a "visible" Authority does it equate with media without any vested interests? It is the ownership that determines the independence of media. Should then media be in the hands of a few individuals ? Does that ensure media independence? Or does it create a monopoly over traditional media? Who will check the standing and caliber of those owning the media? Whether they understand about the tenets of ethical journalism, and what is shared with the public IS for their good? Are these "Media Kings" impartial and neutral? Media houses are more often than not, accused of bias and for good reason. Critics like ***Chomsky and Herman***, relying on their analysis of the US media, assert that privately owned US media largely function through a class-based monopoly of ideas, whereby "money and power are able to filter out the news fit to print, marginalize dissent, and allow the government and dominant interests to get their messages across to the public." (Herman and Chomsky 1994: 2)

It gives more values for individuals to express their thoughts in the media, they say. But does it? Are views diametrically opposed to those of a "Media King" tolerated on his channel or op-ed pages? Or their channels? Think again! "Experts" who dish out half -baked ideas, whether or not they have an iota of idea on the subject , yet, the "real experts" will sit in the sidelines. Ignored!

The theory places great reliance on media's willingness to meet their responsibilities – a theory only?

This theory ignores the need for some degree of control. Self-regulation alone, does not lead to responsible journalism. Unless and until the factor of accountability to some authority exists, privately owned media, propelled by profits, with lesser focus on being responsible, will flounder.

### *Soviet Media Theory:*

The Soviet Union, after revolution was resurrected on the base of Marxist-Leninist Principles. So the Soviet originates a theory from Marxist, Leninist and Stalinist thoughts, with a mixture of Georg Wilhelm Friedrich Hegel ideology called "**Soviet Media Theory**" also known as "**The Communist Media Theory**". The same theory was developed and followed by Adolf Hitler's Nazi in Germany and Benito Mussolini in Italy. The government undertakes control of the media— providing information, education , entertainment et al. It is geared towards developing a certain class of workers. Under this theory, the entire media is under the control of the leader of the nation.

The authoritarian and soviet media theory differ at the very base. In the former, no public feedback exists, the communication may be deemed to be a one-way communication, in the latter it is a two way communication, allowing a feedback. There is no provision of allowance of a private media—since there is no "blockade" by an authority, it serves people better, its supporters state.

The restrictions by this theory, they argue are in national interest, not based on a matter of individual taste—the latter pointing out to Media King's vested interest in a Libertarian Theory. This too is a fallacy. Media controlled as we saw under Mussolini and Hitler, provided a completely one-sided view— "*their view*". People had to subscribe to a certain mindset that suited the leader. Individuality, and, independence of thought were shunned.

The role of the media under this theory ceased to be that of a watchdog, rather a support organ to the leader of the nation. Since media is controlled by the leader, it must deliver the message directed to deliver. What if you end up with a leader who is undesirable and a detriment to the nation? The media cannot work as a watchdog, it's role is a different one under this theory, so who points out the leader's errors? Where is the check and balance ? Or will it be the case of the Emperor with new clothes?

Let us now turn our attention to the *Social Responsibility Theory.*

### *Social Responsibility Theory:*

Most of the countries in the 20th century , whether from developed nations or developing countries subscribe to this theory. This theory is associated with "the Commission of the Freedom of Press" in United States at 1949. In the book "Four theories of Press" (Siebert, Peterson and Schramm) it's been stated that "pure libertarianism is antiquated, out dated and obsolete." That paved way for replacement of Libertarian theory with the Social responsibility theory. This theory lies between the Libertarian and Authoritarian theories. It allows a free press. However, it believes that the media has to accept any input from public or professional self -regulation, or both.

The ***SASKATCHEWAN RN ASSOCIATION*** defines professional self- regulation as: "Professional self-regulation is the regulation of a profession by its members. The primary purpose of professional self - regulation is protection of the public from harm. Professional self-regulation is characterized by professional conduct and competence, fairness, transparency, accountability and public participation. In professional self-regulation, the regulatory body is accountable for ensuring members are competent and act in the public interest in providing the services that society has entrusted to them. Individual members are personally accountable for their practice through adherence to codes and standards and maintaining competence and conduct."[540]

In ***The Media Self-Regulation Guidebook,***[541] Miklos Haraszti says, "Codes of ethics provide guidance on editorial standards, while complaint mechanism offer a kind of 'quality assurance."

According to another explanation on self-regulation, by the ***Media Institute of Southern Africa,***[542] "Under self-regulation the media voluntarily commit to uphold a code of ethics that they themselves draft. They establish a complaints mechanism, often called a media council or complaints commission, to which the public can complain about perceived breaches of the code. The independent council adjudicates on the complaints and decides upon appropriate remedies. The courts play no role in enforcing the code of practice. Compliance with the code is

---

[540] "Professional Self-regulation" LINK:
http://www.srna.org/images/stories/pdfs/nurse_resources/pos_state/self_reg.pdf

[541] By Organization for Security and Co-operation in Europe(OSCE )in 2008

[542] LINK:
http://www.sz.misa.org/index.php?option=com_content&view=article&id=96&Itemid=93

voluntary and the media does so out of a desire to secure the credibility of their profession and the trust of the public."

Professional self-regulation offers no space for Media Kings with little or no professional background, to determine how the newspaper, radio station or/and TV channel is to be "self-regulated". They must clearly have an Editorial Policy Guideline, done by a professional for their employees to follow.

The Social Responsibility Theory places great onus on media itself to create check and balances. Freedom of speech, yes, but counter balanced with responsibility. This theory moves beyond "Objective Reporting" (based on facts) and into Interpretative Reporting which is investigative reporting.

However, with this freedom comes a high degree of responsibility. It must subscribe to a standard of truth, accuracy and sharing of correct information.

Censorship is described in the ENCYCLOPEDIA OF THE SOCIAL SCIENCES as:

".. the policy of restricting the public expression of ideas, opinions, conceptions and impulses which have or are believed to have the capacity to undermine the governing authority or the social and moral order which that authority considers itself bound to protect."[543]

Media today, is a dynamic organ, vibrant, with an opinion on everything under the sun, from politics, to economics, to culture, to reporting on every-day issues, entertainment....the list is long and unending. However, at the end of the day, media, is answerable to the society.

In a report by a Commission led by the then-President of University of Chicago, ***Robert Hutchinson,*** the commission deliberated for four years, before putting up its recommendations in 1947.[544]

The five guidelines for a responsible press given by the Commission were:

---

[543] Harold D. Lasswell, Censorship, Encyclopedia OF THE SOCIAL SCIENCES (New York, 1930) I1, 290.

[544] Research Paper, "Indian Media: Social Responsibility and the Challenges Ahead"

1) *a truthful, comprehensive, and intelligent account of the day's events in a context which gives them meaning;*

(2) *a forum for the exchange of comment and criticism;*

(3) *the projection of a representative picture of the constituent groups in the society;*

(4) *the presentation and clarification of the goals and values of the society;*

(5) *full access to the day's intelligence.*

The report further states, "I feel the ***media*** should be accountable and responsible to the various stakeholders in the following ways:

- *" First and foremost to their audiences, to whom they owe correct news reportage, analysis and editorializing.*

- *To government, to which they owe constructive criticism, a relay of popular opinion and adequate feedback from the populace.*

- *To their proprietor, to whom they owe the survival of the* ***media*** *organization as a business venture as well as a veritable source of education, enlightenment and entertainment.*

- *To themselves, to whom they owe fulfillment in their calling, satisfaction and an entire success story. When any of these "judges"' of journalistic responsibility is shunted, accountability is dented and automatically, responsibility is affected adversely." (Owens-Ibie, 1994)*

Media cannot be discussed without its relationship to society. Its impact on the psyche of the nation is deep. What is conveyed, how it is conveyed, who is conveying it—is of utmost importance. Who is conveying it will determine angle of news, the leading of the reader/viewer to a conclusion the conveyer wants the reader/viewer to reach. But is that what media is about?

One of the foremost Communication scholars ***Denis McQuail*** summarized the basic principles of Social Responsibility Theory as the following:

- Media should accept and fulfill certain obligations to society.
- These obligations are mainly to be met by setting high or professional standards of informativeness, truth, accuracy, objectivity and balance.
- In accepting and applying these obligations, media should be self-regulating within the framework of law and established institutions.
- The media should avoid offensive content triggering crime, violence, or civil disorder or harm to minority groups.
- The media as a whole should be pluralist and reflect the diversity of their society, giving access to various points of view and rights of reply.
- Society and the public have a right to expect high standards of performance, and intervention can be justified to secure the, or a, public good.
- Journalists and media professionals should be accountable to society as well as to employers and the market.[545]

The role of media is to educate, share information, be futuristic and in the process be healthy, vibrant and compatible with the social structure. It must not be a borrowed, cheap rehash of a foreign culture. Destruction of the cultural fabric, setting forth trends that are opposed to the ethos of their own culture is the worst disservice media can render to the society. Should press be completely unfettered? Should there be a degree of regulation?

***N. Bhaskar Rao*** *states,* "An unfettered press without ethical concerns can be a threat to a free society and to its very independence."[546]

The definition of "media ethics" in the newsroom must translate itself into the broader picture of social responsibility.

---

[545] "Media And Social Responsibility: A Critical Perspective with Special Reference to Television: By Dr B.K Ravi Associate Professor ,Department of Communication, Bangalore University India. Vol 1 2012(Academic Research International)

[546] Media Ethic Getting Complex : The Tribune December 2005

"The power and near monopoly position of the media imposes on them an obligation to be socially responsible, to see that all sides are fairly presented and that the public has enough information to decide; and that if the media do not take on themselves such responsibility it may be necessary for some other agency of the public to enforce it."[547]

"In both the Hutchins Commission report and the theory put forth by Siebert et al., the concept of public interest, albeit inexplicitly, lies at the heart of the definition of social responsibility. This highlights the crucial role of the communications sector in shaping societal processes: the formation of public opinion and civil society movements, social and political development patterns, including more tangible processes such as the unfurling of elections campaigns and their outcome.'"[548]

How responsibly has the media discharged its duties?

There have been many occasions when the media failed in this duty to be socially responsible. And many examples where they *were* socially responsible. In Journalism, media must withhold information, if it feels, sharing the same may cause damage to the society. This includes withholding someone's name if it can place a life in danger, names of minor children , crime victims' names and so on. It may include withholding a story altogether.

Before we go any further , I would like to share, some of the Code of Ethics put forward by organizations to have a more responsible media. Some codes, particularly of the European countries includes restrictions on the discriminatory comments based on race, religion etc. The purpose is to create unity amongst diverse ethnic, multi-religious groups, not create a wedge and further splintering. Matters sub-judice to the court are clearly avoided internationally, a respected canon of journalism. An acceptable and workable code of ethics will face *a conflict of interest* and *ethical dilemmas* .These can be overcome with the help of clear cut Editorial Policies by media houses.

The ***Society of Professional Journalists (SPJ)*** is the oldest organization representing journalists in USA. It was established in 1909 as a ***DePauw University***.

---

[547](Siebert et al., 1956)

[548]Habermas and discourse ethics (c. 1983)

The Preamble to its Code of Ethics states:

*...public enlightenment is the forerunner of justice and the foundation of democracy. The duty of the journalist is to further those ends by seeking truth and providing a fair and comprehensive account of events and issues. Conscientious journalists from all media and specialties strive to serve the public with thoroughness and honesty. Professional integrity is the cornerstone of a journalist's credibility.*

I would like to share here the Code of Ethics by the **Society of Professional Journalists,**[549] the site states, *"The SPJ Code of Ethics is voluntarily embraced by thousands of writers, editors and other news professionals. The present version of the code was adopted by the 1996 SPJ National Convention, after months of study and debate among the Society's members.*

*Sigma Delta Chi's first Code of Ethics was borrowed from the American Society of Newspaper Editors in 1926. In 1973, Sigma Delta Chi wrote its own code, which was revised in 1984, 1987 and 1996."*

***SPJ Code of Ethics:***

***Seek Truth and Report It:*** Journalists should be honest, fair and courageous in gathering, reporting and interpreting information.

Journalists should:— Test the accuracy of information from all sources and exercise care to avoid inadvertent error. Deliberate distortion is never permissible.

— Diligently seek out subjects of news stories to give them the opportunity to respond to allegations of wrongdoing.

— Identify sources whenever feasible. The public is entitled to as much information as possible on sources' reliability.

— Always question sources' motives before promising anonymity. Clarify conditions attached to any promise made in exchange for information. Keep promises.

— Make certain that headlines, news teases and promotional material, photos, video, audio, graphics, sound bites and quotations do not

[549] From their website: http://www.spj.org/ethicscode.asp

misrepresent. They should not oversimplify or highlight incidents out of context.

— Never distort the content of news photos or video. Image enhancement for technical clarity is always permissible. Label montages and photo illustrations.

— Avoid misleading re-enactments or staged news events. If re-enactment is necessary to tell a story, label it.

— Avoid undercover or other surreptitious methods of gathering information except when traditional open methods will not yield information vital to the public. Use of such methods should be explained as part of the story — Never plagiarize.

— Tell the story of the diversity and magnitude of the human experience boldly, even when it is unpopular to do so.

— Examine their own cultural values and avoid imposing those values on others.

— Avoid stereotyping by race, gender, age, religion, ethnicity, geography, sexual orientation, disability, physical appearance or social status.

— Support the open exchange of views, even views they find repugnant.

— Give voice to the voiceless; official and unofficial sources of information can be equally valid.

— Distinguish between advocacy and news reporting. Analysis and commentary should be labeled and not misrepresent fact or context.

— Distinguish news from advertising and shun hybrids that blur the lines between the two.

— Recognize a special obligation to ensure that the public's business is conducted in the open and that government records are open to inspection.

***Minimize Harm***: Ethical journalists treat sources, subjects and colleagues as human beings deserving of respect.

Journalists should:— Show compassion for those who may be affected adversely by news coverage. Use special sensitivity when dealing with children and inexperienced sources or subjects.

— Be sensitive when seeking or using interviews or photographs of those affected by tragedy or grief.

— Recognize that gathering and reporting information may cause harm or discomfort. Pursuit of the news is not a license for arrogance.

— Recognize that private people have a greater right to control information about themselves than do public officials and others who seek power, influence or attention. Only an overriding public need can justify intrusion into anyone's privacy.

— Show good taste. Avoid pandering to lurid curiosity.

— Be cautious about identifying juvenile suspects or victims of sex crimes.

— Be judicious about naming criminal suspects before the formal filing of charges.

— Balance a criminal suspect's fair trial rights with the public's right to be informed.

***Act Independently***: Journalists should be free of obligation to any interest other than the public's right to know.

Journalists should:—Avoid conflicts of interest, real or perceived.

— Remain free of associations and activities that may compromise integrity or damage credibility.

— Refuse gifts, favors, fees, free travel and special treatment, and shun secondary employment, political involvement, public office and service in community organizations if they compromise journalistic integrity.

— Disclose unavoidable conflicts.

— Be vigilant and courageous about holding those with power accountable.

— Deny favored treatment to advertisers and special interests and resist their pressure to influence news coverage.

— Be wary of sources offering information for favors or money; avoid bidding for news.

***Be Accountable***: Journalists are accountable to their readers, listeners, viewers and each other.

Journalists should:— Clarify and explain news coverage and invite dialogue with the public over journalistic conduct.

— Encourage the public to voice grievances against the news media.

— Admit mistakes and correct them promptly.

— Expose unethical practices of journalists and the news media.

— Abide by the same high standards to which they hold others.

SPJ places great emphasis on seeking of truth. Seeking the truth led to the uncovering of the "Watergate Scandal". And many other events we know of. Who is saying a thing makes a whole lot of difference. The reason is, a person giving information may have ulterior motives and vested interests—in a rush to be "Me First" it is unethical to publish information without seeking the other point of view. A chance must always be given to the person/institution about whom the news is being carried to give his or her point of view.

Interesting, one finds much over-lapping between the BBC Editorial Policy and the SPJ Code of Ethics in terms of values. Both aspire to standards of journalism that mature journalists should aspire to.

***Shuchman and Wilkes*** cite two examples where they feel that in almost all examples of journalists', "failures to be accurate, to identify vested interests to follow up on stories, and to cover important health issues," the negative consequences are ultimately borne by patients. [550]

1) In the spring of 1995, news wire services reported that 6 million persons in the United States who were receiving calcium channel blockers

[550] Social Responsibility in the Media Melisande Middleton Center for International Media Ethics CIME Oxford University PCMLP March 2009

for hypertension might be increasing their risk for a heart attack by 60%. Persons who were being treated for hypertension became frightened; in some cases, they stopped taking prescribed medication. Physicians' offices were flooded with calls. (Shuchman and Wilkes, 1997) Many criticized that the media coverage was out of proportion with the findings, leading to anxiety and in some cases severe health risks for concerned audiences.

2) The second example emphasizes how, conversely, sowing hope among audiences through the media can wreak just as much havoc as in cases when it triggers anxiety –namely by inaccurately portraying the effectiveness of new treatments: An unusual and invasive treatment for Alzheimer disease was widely publicized after a small, unblinded pilot study; fluoxetine hydrochloride (Prozac, Dista Products and Eli Lilly and Company, Indianapolis, Indiana) was hailed as a certain cure for depression when it was introduced; and melatonin recently received excessively positive media treatment as a "cure" for aging. (Shuchman and Wilkes, 1997)

The study concludes that in cases like this both journalists and scientists must share the blame for the consequences of having spread false information. Ultimately, the accuracy of health news reporting depends on the reporter's responsibility to take special care in communicating effectively with his or her sources in the medical profession, especially when portraying complex scientific concepts, which can be easily distorted by the journalist and misinterpreted by layperson audiences."[551]

That media plays a deep role in formation of opinions, we cannot deny. I would like to quote ***Joseph Pulitzer***, who said, "I am deeply interested in the progress and elevation of journalism, having spent my life in that profession, regarding it as a noble profession and one of unequaled importance for its influence upon the minds and morals of the people."

Should showing of dead bodies be allowed in media? Can this not result in deep distress to the family and friends of the deceased? We have seen bodies and body parts being shown during the Lal Masjid Operation and later when two of our private carrier planes were downed during the last few years. Is this responsible journalism?

---

[551] Ibid.

The M.A Semester II , School of Journalism & Mass Communication, Beaconhouse National University, did a group project, for semester ending early June 2012. The topic was "International and National Media Coverage on closure of NATO Supply Routes from Nov 2011 to May 2011." There were seven groups in all. They covered US-Pakistan relations over time, in both local and international media coverage of newspapers, blogs and television.

I share here with the readers extracts from one of the submission.[552] 'The entire foreign media coverage implies an insidious and widespread bias contravening the standards of journalism rather than the news element. Analysis of the writers, and anchors prevail throughout the duration of the write-up or interview especially in coverage of foreign electronic media channels where the hosts angle up the anti-Pakistan approach to a very heightened extent...."

They continue to state, "The overall analysis of the local media in a nutshell would generally be that it is undoubtedly emotional ,aggressive against the government, rather than policymakers' lack of homework, sensationalizes the issue......"

*The students opine, "If the government of Pakistan orders an 'academic and impartial review' of the information landscape concerning campaigns in the media, the ownership media policy can be better reviewed."*

Well said, indeed. Our youngsters are taking us to task over lack of Editorial Policy!!The second point on which emphasis is placed by the Code of Conduct of SPJ is minimizing harm. Any reporting has cascading effects on the society. It is a judgment call: should the news, even if it's a scoop be carried if it damages the very fabric of the society?

Pandering to cheap needs of a segment of the society is not clean journalism—exploiting sex crimes, abnormal behaviors can lead to more of the same by furnishing ways and conveying ideas to others. Can we show compassion to those who have suffered and those who are suffering or are we so enchanted by thoughts of higher ratings and wider readership, that those we should protect and who are most vulnerable, we expose the most? An association with anything but the Oath taken as a journalist can taint him and destroy his credibility forever.

---

[552] Shared with approval of students

Is media based on propaganda? Are journalists bought? ***James Dunnigan*** in his piece, "*Journalists for Sale, Cheap*" published February 2005 [553] writes, "The U.S. Department of Defense is investigating allegations that American Information Warfare operations included paying journalists to write pro-American stories for web sites that are read by many in Moslem countries. This sort of thing is always controversial in the United States, but during the Cold War the communists bought foreign journalists on a large scale. It wasn't hard to do, as in most parts of the world, reporters regularly take money from people who want a more favorable story. Actually, this practice goes back to the beginning of modern journalism two centuries ago. The concept of independent reporting is largely an American one. However, in the United States, favorable media coverage is still bought. It's just that cash is rarely used. Publicists and spin masters trade favors and influence to get the stories they want."

Fair? Ethical?

No. And No.

There is a NEED for a truthful media. Not a sold one. Independence of media, free from favors of any kind, whether monetary, or in kind, or in form of commercials must be avoided at all costs. It must be free and be perceived as such. How can otherwise it be deemed to be unbiased and unfettered from external pressures?

The last point emphasized is accountability of media. No one is above the law. Neither is the media. Media must be held accountable for any misdeeds it is responsible for. If a wrong is committed, this must be accepted freely, and effort made not to repeat the wrong . Union Minister Kapil Sibal states, " Media should be made accountable as reputations were being tarnished by TV channels."[554] The errors committed by media may be deliberate or inadvertent but they cannot be held above the law.

Media must be "politically accountable" too. Can the media "take sides" as a policy ? In one's primary capacity as a reporter of news one must be objective, impartial and as accurate as possible. There is no room for the injection of opinion. Someone reading a news item in a

---

[553] Martin Frost's former web site LINK: http://www.martinfrost.ws/htmlfiles/journos_bribe.html

[554] "Sibal wants media to be accountable too" Indian Express 8th July 2011

newspaper or listening to it on radio or television should have no idea what the reporter thinks about the story. "It is the reporter's job to tell the story, not to let people have his opinion on it. Tell the tale properly and let people form their own opinion; never try to tell them what to think. It is patronizing and highly unprofessional."[555]The piece goes on to state, "A free press is an indispensable bulwark of an open, democratic society. Without it, democracy will not survive..... Given the amount of sloppy, incompetent and tendentious reporting that exists, far from being triumphant about our role we should be acutely aware of the damage that can be done. As has been well said, a microphone in inexperienced or biased hands can be more deadly than a machine gun. The chilling example of Rwanda when Radio Mille Collines played an overt role in the genocide reminds us that there is an end result, sometimes catastrophic, to careless and inflammatory reporting. Some of the journalists involved were later prosecuted and convicted"[556] What is said here, applies equally to us, in Pakistan! In repeated discussions on TV channels, media has also involved judiciary into controversy by discussing matters sub-judice to the court.

It is further stated in the same piece, "A truly good and professionally written newspaper is a blessing to any country in which it exists, helping to inculcate attitudes of rationality, moderation, respect and compromise. It is something we must all aim for. Dare one say it, it could even play a constructive role in the evolution of the society and the building of the nation."

The paper is so beautifully written that I cannot but quote extensively from it, "As publishers, editors and journalists, we have to establish our bona fides. People cannot take us on trust. They have to decide, on the basis of our work, that we are conscientious, fair, well researched and competent. Everyone gets it wrong sometimes but that should not be a regular occurrence. There is room for error but never for malice or recklessness.

"It is our right to speak out forthrightly on issues of the day but before doing so we should reflect, take counsel, seek such wisdom as we might find within ourselves. We have an unparalleled opportunity to influence opinion, a virtual pulpit from which to address our readers. If

---

[555] "Should the Media be Accountable & responsible." By STABROEK STAFF Posted 1st November 2009 on Stabroek News; Sunday Stabroek

[556] Ibid.

we do it casually or carelessly or without properly informing ourselves we have only ourselves to blame for wasting the opportunity....Let us deal here with the question of our responsibility for the opinions we express in our editorial columns and the positions we take on issues of the day. Make no mistake, these opinions can have consequences and as responsible media persons we bear responsibility for them."[557]

I would like to refer here to the lecture of ***Isiah Berlin,***[558] at Oxford. In his speech he reminded the audience of the German poet *Heine*, who had categorically warned the French not to undermine the strength and power of ideas and not to downplay the importance of philosophical concepts that are developed in a Professor's study. This has the power to destroy a civilization. It is not for nothing that there is a saying, 'The pen is mightier than the sword." Let us substitute "pen" here for media, as the communication gates now are many as I briefly expressed in the opening of this chapter. Media, used carelessly, to suit vested interests, can and will lead to the destruction of a society.

Again reverting to the piece heavily quoted above, it goes on to say, "This challenging profession of journalism, I put it to you, entails other weighty responsibilities. We have a responsibility to promote peace not war, both regionally and globally, to oppose unjust claims to the territory of a state, to spread environmental awareness, not to be petty chauvinists, to be men and women of the world, to know who we are and what we're doing, to agonize about our countries, to try to understand our ...identity, to help build the nation, to be peacemakers not fomenters of disputes. Ours is a difficult and demanding task if we come to grips with its true dimensions."[559]

*Former Editor of The Punjabi Tribune,* ***Mr S. S Bhullar,*** pointed out, " That in the recent elections many vernacular media had sold out front page news space to publish news-stories of political parties on payment that drastically affects the credibility of the newspapers. It is unfortunate," he lamented, " that the Fourth Estate which was respected for its accuracy and truthfulness has now been reduced to a commodity,

---

[557] Ibid.

[558] Isiah Berlin:a British social and political theorist, philosopher and historian of ideas of Russian-Jewish origin, thought by many to be the dominant scholar of his generation, He excelled as an essayist, conversationalist and raconteur

[559] "Should the Media be Accountable & responsible." By STABROEK STAFF Posted 1st November 2009 on Stabroek News; Sunday Stabroek

and the emphasis is on publishing sensational and negative news only at a cost of the more positive and developmental stories that abound around us."[560]

In another story carried by ***The Hindu,*** Prime Minister's Media Advisor ***Sanjaya Baru*** advocated "the need for media institutions formulating a code of conduct to keep a vigil on institutions of governance. He further said that active, honest and free media can play a pivotal role in good governance. "This will also be applicable to the media," Dr. Baru said, adding that media should be accountable to readers and viewers. He regretted that despite the appeal from the Securities and Exchange Board of India, media, especially the business newspapers, failed to evolve a code of conduct to govern its journalists."[561]

In yet another incident, the US military was alleged by "The Los Angeles Times" to have covertly paid Iraqi newspapers through a Washington-based defense contractor, Lincoln Group, to print pro-American stories.

Prompted by the published report in this context, Senator John Warner, chairman of the Senate Armed Services Committee, had asked the Pentagon to respond to the allegations.

In India too, the menace of media corruption has deep roots. ***Rahul Singh***, a former editor of "The Reader's Digest" and "The Indian Express," had quite recently pointed out in one of his articles that in India, "bribing, or influencing, journalists by business houses or by the government is nothing new. Indian chief ministers have 'discretionary quotas' of plots of land - sold at much below the market rate - which they hand out liberally to their favorites, or those they want to influence, which includes judges and journalists."[562]

***Let us now turn our attention to Pakistan***

First, we must see, what our local organization ***PFUJ****(Pakistan Federal Union of Journalists)*has done in terms of setting up a code of

---

[560] "Media should be accountable to remain credible" 14th March 2007 India PR WIRE LINK: http://www.indiaprwire.com/pressrelease/advertising/200703142230.htm

[561] Online Edition of THE HINDU published 3rd September 2007 under title, "Mass Media should be accountable" :Sanjay Baru

[562] All States ,except Pakistan audit secret funds-Part II Sabir Shah for The News published July 8th 2011

conduct for practitioners of the field. PFUJ has a long history of struggle against tyranny in Pakistan. Their Constitution was approved in 1950 in Karachi. On its website is a **Code of Conduct** [563] that practitioners of the field are supposed to follow. This is being reproduced on these pages for further discussion.

### *Code of Conduct by PFUJ:*

Like other trade unions, formed for mutual protection and economic betterment the Pakistan Federal Union of Journalists desires and encourages its members to maintain good quality of workmanship and high standard of conduct.

A member of the Union has two claims on his loyalty, one by his Union and one by his employer. These need not clash so long as the employer complies with the agreed Union conditions and makes no demand for forms of service incompatible with the honor of the profession or with the principles of trade unionism. Members of the fraternity becoming members of PFUJ pay a nominal amount.

1- A member should do nothing that would bring discredit on himself, his Union, his newspaper, or his profession. He should study the rules of his Union, and should not, by commission or omission, act against the interests of the Union.

2- Whether publication or suppression, the acceptance of a bribe by a journalist is one of the gravest professional offences.

3- Every journalist should treat subordinates as considerately as he would desire to be treated by his superiors.

4- Freedom in the honest collection and publication of news facts and the rights of fair comment and criticism, are principles , which every journalist should defend.

5- Unless the employer consents to a variation, a member who wishes to terminate his employment must give notice according to agreement.

6- No member should seek promotion or seek to obtain the position of another journalist by unfair methods. A member should not directly

[563] LINK: http://pfuj.pk/code-2/

or indirectly, attempt to obtain for himself or anyone else, any commission, regular or occasional held by a freelance member of the Union.

7- It is unprofessional conduct to exploit the labor of another journalist by plagiarism, or by using his copy for linage purposes without permission.

8- Staff men who do linage work should be prepared to give up such work to conform with any pooling scheme approved by the FEC or any Union plan to provide a freelance member with a means of earning a living.

9- A member holding a staff appointment shall serve first the paper that employs him. In his own time a member is free to engage in other creative work, but he should not undertake any extra work in his rest time or holidays, if by so doing he is depriving an out of work member of a chance to obtain employment. Any misuse of rest days won by the Union on the sound argument that periods of recuperation are needed after strenuous hours of labor is damaging to trade unions aims for a shorter working week.

10- While a spirit of willingness to help other members should be encouraged at all times, members are under a special obligation of honor to help an unemployed member to obtain work.

11- A journalist should fully realize his personal responsibility for everything he sends to his paper or agency. He should keep Union and professional secrets and respect all necessary confidences regarding sources and information and private documents. He should not falsify information or documents, or distort and misrepresent facts.

12- In obtaining news or pictures, reporters and Press photographers should do nothing that will cause pain or humiliation to innocent, bereaved, or otherwise distressed persons. News pictures and documents should be acquired by honest methods only.

13- Every journalist should keep in mind the danger in the laws of libel, contempt of court and copyright. In reports of law court proceeding it is necessary to observe and practice the rule of fair play to parties.

Though the Code of Conduct may have been perfectly in line two or three decades ago, and most of it is still relevant, it may like to look at the Code of Ethics of the Society of Professional Journalists and borrow from the tenets encapsulated within, to give a firmer and well defined guideline to a journalist for his day-to-day working,

PFUJ Code of Conduct lays out admirable values like not being susceptible to bribes, being honorable, should not violate any laws, observe fair play to parties, not to take picture to cause pain and humiliation to the innocent , so on and so forth. But in case this is not followed, totally or partially, what is the repercussion to the journalist? PFUJ may temporarily suspend the membership of the member, or cancel it in severe cases, says Mazhar Abbas when put the question. But is this really enough?

Newspapers by and large have maintained a better sense of following the Code of Conduct than has the electronic media. Many newspaper establishments have dabbled into the electronic media, becoming powerful houses of communication. "The publishers of newspapers tried to benefit from the possibilities of running non-government (not necessarily independent) TV channels," says the renowned journalist ***I. A. Rehman***.[564] He says, "The hottest subject in our exalted chambers of gossip is neither the executive-judiciary confrontation nor new causes of tension between Pakistan and the US; it is the sudden spurt in cash flows to some television channels."[565]

***Times of Pakistan***[566] states talking of the Malik Riaz and Dr Arslan case but it can be interpreted in a wider perspective, "The issue is very serious and damaging to the country. These people have immense power and influence through media. If they become biased, playing wrong with ideology, and security of the country, situation becomes alarming creating disharmony and frustration among the masses. There is a big question mark today not only on the reliability of anchors who are supposed to enlighten the nation about social and political issues, but also upon the media which is supposed to be unbiased and free from vested interest.

"It is need of the hour to take strict action against these black sheep in the media, and TV channels who are involved in planted discussions

---

[564] Article: Focus on Media published by Dawn Newspaper in August 2012

[565] Ibid.

[566] "Media Persons Await Accountability" published 14th July 2012

and interviews against the national interest. There must be a quick, unbiased and fair probe against them and the culprits should be taken to the task as per the laws.

"The Pakistani media must establish its reliability by protecting national interests, the opinions of the analysts should be unbiased and free of partiality. Their analysis must lead to constructive recommendations for the policymakers to safeguard national interests. **There must be a revised code of ethics for media** ....."

I could not agree with the last line more!

Holding media trials on sensitive issues, churning out one "expert" opinion after the other, holding one talk show, one article, one editorial after the other on matters sub-judice to the court— is a destruction of reputations, the morale of the society and against all norms of journalism.

In his article, ***Shaheen Sehbai*** [567] says, "Accountability to determine integrity should not just include professional and financial conduct of journalists but it should also try to understand the reasons why objective journalism and traditional professional journalists are fast becoming an extinct breed and almost all opinion writing, analysis and interpretation work has been taken over by 'lateral entrants' --- people who had no journalistic training, who never went through the mill, who acquired writing skills doing something else and when they failed in their professions, took refuge in journalism. These 'lateral entrants' mostly comprise ambitious generals, politicians, bureaucrats, technocrats and opportunists, all masquerading as journalists, opinion makers and columnists of the highest order. Most of them have no reporting or editing skills and some appear to even have been planted by vested interests."

I would like to add here, the best of talent, the best of pieces will be thrown out like a piece of junk if it is not in line with the "thought process" serving certain interests, of the newspaper/TV. The door will be closed on your face.

However, PFUJ needs to cater to the changed world of journalism today. It may like to review the following questions:

---

[567] Who will Bell the Bad, Fat Cats? Siasat.pk LINK: http://www.siasat.pk/forum/showthread.php?118062-Who-will-Bell-the-Bad-Fat-Cats

1) What must be PFUJ's policy if any journalist is found guilty of serious misconduct? Will it recommend a bar for 3 years or in worst conditions for life to work in the profession?

2) Should PFUJ scrutinize accounts and other holdings of its members and that of his/her immediate family on a regular basis?

3) What training must a new entrant undergo before being made responsible for duty?

4) Should the PFUJ prepare the course for a training programme for all employees. This then, must be an ongoing process.

5) Should there be a training institute or, this training be left to the employers?

6) What checks and balances PFUJ will put in place to ensure the training of the new entrant is being done as directed in case it is the employer undertaking the training?

'The world of journalism in Pakistan has had, over the years, some extremely fine and world class writers who have always wielded their pens, now their keyboards, in the name of all that is right and good and they, irrespective of outraged mud-slinging, will continue, often against incredible odds, to uphold the journalistic profession with sincere integrity and true grit. They have, each and every one of them, worked tremendously hard and for far longer hours than most people realize, to get where they are and to serve the public to whom they are, ultimately, responsible and their honest dedication should not be brought into question as the result of the disgusting greediness and downright betrayal of a handful of irresponsible idiots with cash registers in their craniums where brains are supposed to be."[568]

Media practitioners must realize with freedom comes responsibility. The more the freedom, the more the responsibility. I cannot say this enough ! However, self-regulation suggested by many has not worked. Media is not an island removed from this society. It is a part of the society itself. Therefore the corruption and malpractices that have seeped into our society have also seeped into the media. Just like there are courts and other forums to check wrong doings in society, there must be effective, vibrant forums for media to ensure positive, honest journalism. Forums

---

[568] "The good and the bad" Zahrah Nisar 9th July 2012 The Nation

that have the mandate to carry out implementation, toothless forums are just a drain on the exchequer, with nothing to show for their existence.

***Sir Stephen Sedley,*** born 9th October 1939 styled The Rt. Honorable Lord Justice Sedley, was a judge of the Court of Appeal of England and Wales from 1999 to 2011.

The Levinson Inquiry,[569] was an ongoing public inquiry into the culture, practices and ethics of the British press following the News International phone hacking scandal. The Levinson inquiry invited submissions from public and Core participants. Sir Stephen Sedley presented his own submission to Levinson Inquiry. In the report Sir Stephen Sedley presented his model of statutory regulation of the media. I share from his report, some clauses we , in Pakistan may look into, from what Sir Sedley has termed, "A Modest Proposal."[570]

### *A Modest Proposal:*

Regulation is not licensing despite editorial efforts to conflate the two. There is no tenable cause for prior censorship. Newspapers and broadcasters should continue to have responsibility, preferably with competent legal advice, for deciding what to publish. But if they decide to publish and be damned, then some form of meaningful condemnation ought to be available. Given the extent of justified and necessary regulation in key parts of our society, there is nothing egregious in the notion that this should be done by an independent statutory regulator . It is the media who is in this respect out of step with society.

What I would commend for consideration , in outline, is the setting up of a statutory printed media regulator, governed by rules authorized by Parliament and designed to ensure a fair inquisitional rather than an adversarial procedure . Such a procedure will place the responsibility for the initiation and conduct of an inquiry on the regulator rather than the complainant , but will afford the respondent a right to full notice and disclosure and a right to be heard at every stage. Judicial review should be available where a failure of due process is credibly alleged.

1) The regulator needs as its primary tool an uncapped power to impose fines. Uncapped is, of course, not unsolicited. The fine must be

[569]The Levinson Inquiry (Official website)

[570]**Sir Stephen Sedley proposes statutory media Proposal to The Levinson Inquiry**

tailored to the gravity of offence and means of the offender. Regulatory penalties should be accordingly be open to appeal or review if they go beyond (or for that matter fall below) a fair range. Fines of course will go to public funds ;the regulator's budget cannot depend on them in any way.

2) A regulator will need powers to dispose summarily of complaints which are merely querulous or vindictive, as well as those which , however understandable, are seeking to penalize fair comment or responsible journalism. There is no reason why a publisher should be expected to spend time and resources on a complaint that is going nowhere.

3) The tenability of a civil claim will become clear in course of the regulatory investigation, making litigation an unlikely sequel. Equally however, there may be cases where a court action has to precede a reference to the regulator. In that event, regulation should follow the law. Likewise, if the regulator's investigation establishes it is an unjustifiable invasion of privacy or libelous untruth, it ought not to be open to the regulator to dismiss the complaint.

4) More problematical will be the cases in which a publication of a possibly untrue statement is defended as responsible journalism, but it is arguable that a specialist and impartial regulator is at least as well placed as a court to decide such a question. A principle of priority will accordingly be needed to prevent the same issue from being decided twice, and possibly inconsistently , in co-ordinate forums.

5) Perhaps the most difficult question is: who should be subject to regulation? The daily printed media is an obvious candidate., but how about periodicals, weeklies, monthly, quarterly magazines how about books—how about the internet?

6) Nobody yet knows how to control the internet. Even though, some of it is libelous and a good deal of it cannot be true. But the problem, although it requires international cooperation, is not insoluble, and the present want for a solution cannot be an excuse for doing nothing—meanwhile about the mainstream media.

7) As to non-mainstream media, a range of solutions is possible. One is to set a criteria by which the regulator is to list the media which it will supervise. The problem with this is not only what is drawn up with create controversy and look arbitrary, but that media that is not listed will instantly become vehicles for what the mainstream media finds too risky to publish.

8) The press should remain free to refuse to publish a required correction or retraction, following any adverse adjudication, if it does so, any regulatory fine should rise steeply.

## *Conclusion*

The foregoing is a long way from a complete scheme. It is designed simply to suggest that there is now a powerful case for independent statutory regulations of the mainstream media; that regulation can sort a number of problems for which neither regulation nor self-regulation is proving adequate; and that it can be done fairly and effectively without either licensing the press or giving the regulator monopoly of the truth.[571]

## *Concluding Comments*

The issue as I see it is unwillingness to follow laws. An unwillingness to look towards public good over private interests. We have our share of good journalists and good media institutions. Unfortunately, they are overshadowed by the rouge within the system. Since media is larger than life in today's world, a wrong deed does not get ignored. It gets magnified.

We need an independent press, without pre-censorship, but we need rules that makes a socially irresponsible journalist pay. Literally.

Without the media realizing its first and last responsibility lies to the society, it defeats the purpose of its very creation.

I cannot end the chapter with quoting the thirty-fifth President of USA, **John F. Kennedy,** " There is a terrific disadvantage in not having the abrasive quality of the press applied to you daily. Even though we never like it, and even though we wish they didn't write it, and even though we disapprove, there isn't any doubt that we could not do the job at all in a free society without a very, very active press."[572]

The question that I leave the reader with is : where does the buck stop?

---

[571] Ibid.

[572] http://www.netplaces.com/john-f-kennedy/the-personal-side-of-john-f-kennedy/kennedys-view-on-a-free-press.htm

# *Annexure 'A'*

**Text of PEMRA(Amend)Ordinance[573]**

**Ordinance No LXV of 2007**

**AN**

**ORDINANCE**

Further to amend The Pakistan Media Regulatory Authority Ordinance, 2002.

WHEREAS it is expedient further to amend the Pakistan Electronic Media Regulatory Authority Ordinance , 2002(XIII of 2002)for the purposes hereinafter appearing; AND WHEREAS the National Assembly is not in session and circumstances exist which render it necessary to take immediate action; NOW, THEREFORE, in exercise of the powers conferred by clause

(1) of Article 89 of the Constitution of the Islamic Republic of Pakistan, President is pleased to make and promulgate the following Ordinance:

(1) Short title and commencement:- (1)This Ordinance may be called the Pakistan Electronic Media Authority(Third Amendment) Ordinance, 2007.

(2) It shall come into force at once.

[573] Published in The Nation 4th November 2007

(2) Amendment of section 20 , Ordinance XIII of 2002- In the Pakistan Electronic Media Regulatory Authority Ordinance 2002 (XIII of 2002), hereunder referred to as the said Ordinance in section 20-

(a) In clause 'd' after the word "rules" the words "and regulations" shall be inserted;

(b) In clause 'h' at the end the word, "and" shall be omitted, and,

(c) In clause 'i' for the full stop at the end, a semi-colon shall be substituted, and thereafter the following new clauses shall be added, namely:-

(j) not broadcast video footage of suicide bombers, terrorists, bodies of victims of terrorism , statements and pronouncements of militants and extremist elements and any other acts which may, in any way, promote, aid or abet terrorist activities or terrorism;

(k) ensure that no anchor person, moderator, or host propagates any opinion or acts in any manner prejudicial to the ideology of Pakistan or sovereignty, integrity or security of Pakistan.

(l) not broadcast any programme inciting violence or hatred, or any action prejudicial to maintenance of law and order.

(m) not broadcast anything which defames or brings into ridicule the Head of the State, or members of the armed forces, or executive, legislative or judicial organs of the state.

(n) not broadcast any programme or discussion on a matter sub-judice; and

(o) not broadcast anything which is known to be false or baseless or is mala-fide or for which there exists sufficient reasons to believe that the same may be false, baseless or mala-fide.

(3) Amendment of section 25, Ordinance XIII of 2002:- In the said Ordinance in section 25, in clause 'd' after the word, "organization" , the words, "including any foreign, non-governmental organization" shall be added.

(4) Amendment of section 27, Ordinance XIII of 2002:- In the said Ordinance, in section 27, after the word "operator" the words "or owner" shall be inserted.

(5) Insertion of section 27,-Ordinance XIII of 2002-(1) In the said Ordinance, after section 27, following new section shall be inserted, namely;

"27A: Prohibition of foreign broadcasts:- A person who is issued a broadcast media license or a landing rights permission under the Ordinance shall not enter into an agreement with any foreign broadcaster to sell its airtime or otherwise provide its airtime to another foreign broadcaster without prior written permission of the Authority".

(6) Amendment of Section 29, Ordinance XIII of 2002:-In the said Ordinance, in section 29, in sub-section (6),for the word "one" the word "ten" shall be substituted.

(7) Amendment section 30, Ordinance of XIII of 2002:-In the said Ordinance in section 30:

(a) in sub-section (1) , for clause(b) , the following shall be substituted, namely;

"(b) the licensee has contravened any position of this Ordinance or rules, or regulations made thereunder, or an order passed under section 27", and,

(b) after sub-section (3),the following new sub-section shall be inserted, namely:-

"(4) Notwithstanding anything contained in sub-section (5) of section 29 or any other provisions of this Ordinance, where the Authority takes action under sub-section(3) without notice by reason of necessity in the public interest, the Authority or the Chairman, as the case may be, may seize broadcast or distribution equipment or seal the premises of the licensee:

Provided that in a situation of emergency the Authority or the Chairman may direct closure of any broadcast or distribution network for such period as it may determine".

(8) Amendment of Section 31, Ordinance XIII of 2002□1) In the said Ordinance, in section 31, after sub-section(2), the following new sub-sections shall be added, namely;

"(3) Notwithstanding anything contained in this Ordinance the live coverage of incidents of violence and conflict shall not be broadcast.

(4) A licensee or permission holder shall ensure that nothing is transmitted or broadcast that is in violation of the provisions of this Ordinance, rules, regulations and Code of Conduct and for this purpose shall install time delay equipments within its system to prevent any such violation".

(9) Amendment f section 33 Ordinance XIII of 2002:- In the said Ordinance in section 33(a) for sections (1) and (2) the following shall be substituted, namely;

"(1) Any broadcast media, licensee or its representative who violates or abets any violation of any provision of this Ordinance shall be punishable with imprisonment for a term which may extend to three years or with a fine that may extend to ten million rupees or both;

(2) Any distribution service licensee or its representative who violates or abets violation of any provision of the Ordinance shall be punishable with imprisonment of a term which may extend to one year or with a fine which may extend to five million or both."

(10) Substitution of section 34 Ordinance XVIII of 2002 :- In the said Ordinance, for section 34 following shall be substituted, namely;

"34: Offences to be cognizable and compoundable: The offences under the section 34 shall be cognizable and compoundable."

(11) Omission of section 34-A, Ordinance XIII of 2002:-In the said Ordinance A shall be omitted.

**GENERAL(PERVEZ MUSHARRAF)**

**PRESIDENT**

---